SCOTTISH HISTORY SOCIETY

FOURTH SERIES

VOLUME 14

Scottish Industrial History

A Miscellany

Scottish Industrial History

A Miscellany

★

★

EDINBURGH

printed for the Scottish History Society *by*

T. AND A. CONSTABLE LTD

1978

ISBN 0 906245 001
Printed in Great Britain

CONTENTS

INTRODUCTORY ESSAY

by Professor R. H. Campbell[1]

★

MOST ACCOUNTS of the industrial history of Scotland concentrate on the leading textile and heavy industries of the last two hundred years and centre geographically on the life of west-central Scotland. Documentary deficiencies lead to further concentration on the activities of large and successful firms. Lack of an analysis of the defects of Scottish industry, of failure as well as of success, of decline as well as of growth, and in places and industries other than the great staples of the central belt, is characteristic of the historiography of Scottish industry, even in the increased work on Scottish industrial history of recent years.

The miscellany is a timely corrective to this failure. Its diverse documents show industrial ventures operating in remote parts of the country and not only in west-central Scotland; an interest in mineral deposits now largely forgotten; commercial links stretching directly even to London from a minor woollen enterprise in the Borders; activities, such as the railways, which, while ruinous to individuals even in years of general industrial prosperity in Scotland, were beneficial to society in the long run. The documents do more than provide evidence of industrial activities which contrast sharply with many accounts, for all Scottish industry, leading sectors or not, had to tackle similar problems. The experience of even the unconventional is instructive because the study of Scottish industrial history requires less attention to an examination of aspects of the well-known outline of industrial growth and more to an investiga-

[1] I much appreciate help given to me in writing this introduction from the four contributors to the miscellany and from colleagues in the University of Stirling.

tion of the nature of the transformation, of why Scotland changed in a century and a half from an agrarian economy to an acknowledged industrial leader, and also why Scotland failed to maintain the lead.

*

Industrial enterprises were not uncommon in Scotland before the birth of the modern industrial structure in the later eighteenth century, but the influence of many was limited, and restricted by isolation to local, frequently closely knit communities. Subordination to agricultural or commercial enterprises with which they were closely integrated restricted the influence even of wider industrial progress, as with industrial projects of enterprising landowners, whose activities have to be viewed as one aspect of plans to exploit the full resources of their estates, and as with early industrial concerns brought into being in Glasgow to supply the needs of the city's growing overseas trade. Such isolated and subordinate ventures, however successful individually, did not represent the industrial society which Scotland was to become. Increased specialisation was a necessary prelude for industrial transformation and with it the isolated nature of many enterprises gave way to an integrated industrial economy which affected all Scottish society. Population grew and its distribution was altered. The balance between agriculture and industry changed. As industry came to depend on world markets, and the standard of living on the imports paid for by the exports, Scottish economic life was part of a world-wide mechanism of trade and industry. In these conditions the typical Scot was not a rural but an urban worker, often of non-Scottish birth or descent, his life moulded by industry in a pattern shared with those in industrial areas elsewhere in Britain.

The foundations for industrial growth were formed over many years; its acceleration was more rapid, but precise dating is a matter of controversy. 'For those who like to be precise in such matters' the date of the lighting of the first blast furnace at Carron has been suggested as the beginning of the industrial revolution in Scotland,[1] but even those who do not seek such precision do not make a

[1] T. S. Ashton, *The Industrial Revolution* (Oxford, 1948), 65. Ashton gives the date as 1 January 1760. It was 26 December 1759.

common choice. The choice may fall earlier in the eighteenth century,[1] with a case based on an expansion of trade, most dramatically of Glasgow's tobacco trade, of which the 'heroic age'[2] had begun by 1741, or as late as the earlier nineteenth century, with a case based on the growth of fixed capital formation on the scale required by some modern expositors of the stages of economic growth and reached only in the railway age or later.[3] An intermediate date is the last years of the eighteenth century, from the later 1780s, with a case based on the emergence of the cotton industry, its 19 spinning mills of 1787 increasing to 91 in 1795, and distributed throughout Scotland in those years before the supplanting of water by steam power led to increased concentration around Glasgow. The case for the cotton industry as the leading sector in promoting industrial growth lies more in the nature than in the scale of its contribution to industrialisation.[4] Since its links with the older linen industry were many, its growth followed the stimulus to linen production in the mid-eighteenth century, but the cotton industry's spinning mills marked the most striking introduction of new forms of industrial organisation and new patterns of industrial location which led ultimately to the urbanisation of the population of modern Scotland.

By the middle of the nineteenth century the change to the new pattern of living was evident. Rural depopulation was a harsh fact: three Scottish counties recorded their peak population in 1831, one in 1841, four in 1851, five in 1861. In 1851 only a little over a quarter of Scotland's working population was engaged in the primary industries of agriculture, fishing and forestry; a slightly larger proportion was in the textile and allied trades, over-

[1] H. Hamilton, 'Economic Growth in Scotland, 1720-1770', *Scottish Journal of Political Economy*, vi (1959), 85-96.

[2] J. M. Price, 'The Rise of Glasgow in the Chesapeake Tobacco Trade', *William and Mary Quarterly*, third series, xi (1954), reprinted in P. L. Payne (ed.), *Studies in Scottish Business History* (London, 1967), 300. See also H. Hamilton, *An Economic History of Scotland in the Eighteenth Century* (Oxford, 1963), 256.

[3] P. Deane and W. A. Cole, *British Economic Growth, 1688-1959* (Cambridge, second ed., 1969), 260-1, 266. P. Deane and H. J. Habakkuk, 'The Take-Off in Britain', in W. W. Rostow, *The Economics of Take-Off into Sustained Growth* (London, 1963), 74-75.

[4] Deane and Habakkuk, *op. cit.*: 76. S. D. Chapman, *The Cotton Industry in the Industrial Revolution* (London, 1972), 68

shadowed only by those in the service trades, including building. By the middle of the nineteenth century further change in the industrial structure was imminent. The cotton industry passed its zenith in the boom of 1825 and from the same time the iron industry began a phase of growth comparable to that of cotton less than half a century earlier. Twenty-seven blast furnaces in 1830 increased to 143 in 1850. After the financial crisis of 1857 and the cotton famine of the 1860s, the cotton industry declined until its final virtual extinction between the wars, with only a residual, specialised textile legacy remaining – jute in Dundee, thread in Paisley – employing in 1951 only 8 per cent of the labour force. By contrast, the heavy industries prospered from the mid-nineteenth century. The proportion of the labour force employed in mining, quarrying and the metal trades doubled to 17·8 per cent in the half-century to 1901 and rose to 20·7 per cent in 1951, about one-third of all those employed in manufacturing industry.

★

The textile industries of wool and linen shared the hazards in the path of industrial growth in the early eighteenth century. As befitted a largely pastoral agrarian economy, the woollen industry was of long standing throughout Scotland. Before the union of parliaments in 1707 several legislative enactments aimed at building up fine cloth manufacture, hoping to rival established English success, and to be markedly different from the more traditional manufacture of coarse woollens. The ventures failed even before the freeing of trade after 1707 finally made them impracticable. Before 1707 even the export trade in coarse woollens, which had expanded in the seventeenth century, was in decline. The barriers to be overcome were too great. The Scottish wool crop was of poor quality and most of the finer grades had to be imported, while low levels of skill ensured poor manufacture. In these circumstances complete commercial integration after the Union of 1707 threatened the livelihood of growers and manufacturers alike. The Board of Trustees for Fisheries and Manufactures, instituted to administer some of the funds granted to Scotland as compensation for higher taxation after the Union, and charged with the management of

Scottish economic life, by precept, by the provision of superior knowledge, and by finance, gave only 'niggardly and in some ways ill-directed' aid, so the mere survival of the woollen industry in the competition after 1707 was an achievement in itself.[1] The Border counties did more than survive. Wool was exported to the West Riding and by the second half of the century Border spinners and even some weavers were working on commission for English manufacturers, and in the nineteenth century the Borders established their reputation in the quality production of tweeds.[2]

The linen industry competed more successfully than the woollen industry with English production, and before 1707 exported to England and overseas, so successfully to England that a threat to stop the trade helped to push the Scots into the acceptance of parliamentary union. After the Union many pundits advocated encouragement to the linen in preference to the woollen industry and it became a favoured supplicant for the limited resources at the disposal of the Board of Trustees. The problems faced by the linen industry were similar to those faced by the woollen industry. The raw material was poor, flax badly grown, and the different operations in preparation for spinning incompetently performed; at the other end of the process of production the cloth was often bleached badly or not at all. Though output increased sharply from 2·2 to 24·2 million yards between 1728 and 1800, and its growth is recognised by historians with a surprising degree of unanimity as the most striking industrial success of the earlier eighteenth century, success had limitations. In spite of rising prices and encouragement from the Board of Trustees the output of flax in Scotland remained stagnant and, even with the aid of imports, its supply was so restricted in some areas, and so expensive, that the manufacture of linen was retarded. Wages of spinners increased, and when agricultural improvements offered more rewarding employment in an alternative occupation, the supply of labour was disrupted. Though the finishing of cloth was improved, and by 1754 the practice of sending Scottish brown linen to Holland for bleaching disappeared, a large proportion of production went to markets where high quality

[1] C. Gulvin, 'The Treaty of Union and the Scottish Woollen Industry, 1707-1760', *Scottish Historical Review*, l (1971), 131 and 137.

[2] C. Gulvin, *The Tweedmakers* (Newton Abbot, 1973).

was not required and which were protected. On one estimate overseas markets absorbed about one-third of Scottish production in mid-century,[1] and the plantations took the bulk, aided by an export bounty. By contrast, competition with continental producers in their home market was ineffectual, except under special conditions, as when the German linen industry was disrupted by war between 1759 and 1761. In spite of some success, the problems which beset the linen industry were different only in degree from those which beset the woollen industry.

While the woollen industry survived after the Union, and the linen industry grew, the large-scale exploitation of the geological resources of central Scotland for industrial purposes still lay in the future. Dramatic confirmation comes from the choice of location for the ironworks of the earlier eighteenth century: first, in 1727, at Invergarry and later, in 1753 and 1755 respectively, at Taynuilt and Inverleckan, now Furnace, in Argyllshire. In every way apart from location these works were English: ore and labour came from the south and finished products went to English markets. Scotland offered the advantage of adequate supplies of charcoal as fuel for smelting, and the iron works were attempts to combat local shortages of fuel which plagued locations in the south.

When these earlier industrial activities were often struggling for survival, the foundations of greater and more lasting success, though often in other fields, were appearing. A key foundation lay in the expansion of markets from the eighteenth century.

The most evident sign of a growing internal market provided no solution by itself. Population grew from Webster's estimate of 1,265,380 in 1755 to the 1,608,420 of the first census of 1801, to 2,888,742 in 1851 and to 4,472,103 in 1901.[2] But the experience of parts of Scotland shows that rising population by itself provides no guarantee of industrial growth. Increased subsistence had to provide additional means of support if the rise in population was not to end in a catastrophe of over-population and could come either directly through an increase in agricultural production, or indirectly through the exchange of industrial products. The latter was the way

[1] A. J. Durie, 'The Markets for Scottish Linen 1730–1775', *Scottish Historical Review*, lii (1973), 30–49.

[2] *Scottish Population Statistics*, ed. J. G. Kyd (Scottish History Society, 1952).

of economic salvation for most of Scotland, and as a result the increase of Scottish population was distributed towards the new industrialising and urban areas. Of their demand for agricultural produce there can be no doubt. It helped provide the incentive for agricultural improvements which in turn sustained industrial growth, but the buoyancy of the direct demand of the industrial population in Scotland for the products of Scottish industry is less obvious, both because of the nature of Scottish industrial production and because Scottish incomes were possibly lower than those of the United Kingdom as a whole. Available evidence is fragmentary and from a later period[1] but is of critical importance. Lower incomes in Scotland – unless they reflected lower productivity – suggest that as powerful as the stimulus of rising domestic incomes to industrial expansion may have been the contribution of relatively low incomes to the maintenance of Scotland's external competitiveness through their effect on industrial costs.

By the eighteenth century the external market was also expanding, and in new directions. For generations Scotland's foreign trade, other than with England, had been with the continent of Europe, the only significant overseas trade in the west being with Ireland. Since the more rapidly growing markets were not those of the continent but of the New World, the direction, and with it the pattern, of trade was changing even before the political changes of 1707.[2] The Union provided free and more protected trade: freedom in access to markets in England and in her colonies, protection in the trade being confined to those under the political umbrella of English commercial law. The linen industry was a beneficiary, so too the cattle trade, but the most dramatic effect of the restrictions lay in opportunities given to corner some branches of trade. The activities of Glasgow's tobacco merchants of the third quarter of the eighteenth century illustrate both opportunity and possible limitation. The opportunity lay in importing tobacco, which was re-exported to the continent of Europe; the possible limitation lay in any failure to develop a fully complementary industrial economy.

[1] A. D. Campbell, 'Income', in A. K. Cairncross (ed.), *The Scottish Economy* (Cambridge, 1954), 46–64; H. M. Begg, C. M. Lythe and R. Sorley, *Expenditure in Scotland, 1961–1971* (Edinburgh, 1975), chapter 4.

[2] T. C. Smout, *Scottish Trade on the Eve of Union: 1660–1707* (Edinburgh, 1963).

The limitation is a matter of some dispute,[1] because of differences of opinion on the direct effects of the trade on the demand for Scottish industrial products. The Glasgow merchants offered access to a variety of markets, but they were not always supplied with goods manufactured in Scotland, and their demand was not that on which the more extensive expansion of Scottish industry was based in the later eighteenth century. On the indirect effects of the growth of the tobacco trade on industry there is no serious disagreement. Capital and entrepreneurs filtered from foreign trade to a wide variety of Scottish enterprises, sometimes immediately to industry, more frequently by way of agricultural improvements.

The external market grew wider still in the later nineteenth century with the adoption of freer, if not of free trade, on an international scale, especially when it was supported by improved communications and financial facilities and by a range of institutional developments which underpinned the complex network of world trade. Communications improved by other countries following Britain's lead in the construction of railways; by improvements in shipbuilding, the change in construction from wood to iron, and then to steel, and the change in propulsion from sail, through steam engines and turbines to the diesel engine; by the development of specialised shipping, refrigeration in the 1880s and the beginning of the construction of tankers in the years before 1914; by the construction of ship canals, above all the Suez Canal in 1869, giving easy access to vitally important markets in India and the East. British overseas investment rose from £1,000 million to £4,000 million between 1875 and 1914, supported by the growth of financial institutions. Though it is impossible to judge its quantitative significance Scotland made its own contribution to the exploitation of real estate in America and in Australasia.[2]

Complementary internal improvements in communications, by canals then by railways, paved the way for the effective exploitation

[1] T. M. Devine, 'The Colonial Trades and Industrial Investment in Scotland, c. 1700-1815', *Economic History Review:* xxix (1976), 1-13.

[2] W. G. Kerr, 'Scottish Investment and Enterprise in Texas', and R. E. Tyson, 'Scottish Investment in American Railways: the Case of the City of Glasgow Bank', in P. L. Payne (ed.), *Studies in Scottish Business History* (London, 1967); D. S. Macmillan, *The Debtor's War* (Melbourne, 1960).

of the expanding internal and external market. The possibility of linking the estuaries of Forth and Clyde was long attractive, but construction of a canal, started in 1768, was slow and intermittent: Glasgow was reached from the Forth in 1777, but the complete link to Bowling only in 1790. At the same time the Clyde was artificially deepened. The Monkland Canal, conceived at the same time as the Forth and Clyde, stretched into the geologically rich, but landlocked parishes of north Lanarkshire; the Union Canal, completed only in 1822, linked the Forth and Clyde direct to Edinburgh. Together they provided a canal network giving access from the central belt and north Lanarkshire to Glasgow and Edinburgh, to the Clyde and Forth, to Europe and America. Initially railways complemented the canals and competed with them. The Monkland and Kirkintilloch Railway gave access from Old Monkland to the Forth and Clyde Canal; both the Glasgow and Garnkirk Railway, the first to use steam locomotion from its start in 1831, and the Edinburgh and Glasgow Railway, opened in 1842, competed directly with the Monkland and the Forth and Clyde Canals respectively. The initial use of railways was to exploit the natural resources of the central belt, but with the opening of the Edinburgh and Glasgow, and particularly of the North British, the first railway across the Border in 1846, the railways provided a move towards economic integration with England comparable with the political changes of 1707.

The freeing of trade which followed the Union and the later growth of the international economy facilitated the flow of both imports and exports. Of their relative influence on Scottish industry one aspect is clear. The growth industries of the later eighteenth and nineteenth centuries were dependent on export markets. The adoption of free trade by Britain, more extensively and more permanently than by others, was of no direct help to them. Even its adoption by others was of limited help, because many products of the staple industries were easily sold in markets overseas, especially when entry was facilitated by British investment. Free trade helped industrial growth more generally and more directly through the provision of cheap and adequate raw materials such as cotton, and of cheap food. Thereby primary producers became more ready recipients of British exports and, perhaps above all, cheap food increased real wages and helped engender the surplus above subsistence on which internal demand for industrial goods was based.

Dependence on external demand required that Scottish industry be cost competitive. In the aftermath of Union mere survival required that the costs of Scottish industries, such as the woollen industry, be competitive with those of English and other producers trying to sell in Scotland. In the linen industry, with home markets more secure, costs had to compare favourably with domestic producers in markets the Scots were trying to enter or with those of rivals in third markets. The same comparisons applied more forcefully to the cotton industry and to the finished products of the heavy industrial complex, as they relied extensively on markets out of Scotland. The growth of linen exports in the eighteenth century, and of cotton piece-goods and heavy industrial products in the nineteenth century, demonstrate that Scottish costs were competitive, but progress was not uninterrupted. By the second quarter of the nineteenth century the Scottish cotton industry was experiencing competition from domestic producers in European markets, and so came to rely more on markets in less well developed regions. Effective competition from rivals in either the woollen industry in the eighteenth century or in the cotton industry in the nineteenth century did not have a detrimental effect on Scottish industry in the aggregate, because in the eighteenth century the linen and not the woollen industry was in the ascendant, and in the second quarter of the nineteenth century the heavy industries were in the ascendant. The industrial history of the late nineteenth century and especially of the twentieth century was sharply different. Then the changing pattern of comparative costs affected the heavy industries adversely and no new industry was growing to absorb idle resources. Escape from the problem of the double-edged effect of the opportunities and problems of the world-wide market was not possible for the Scots, though its exact form differed with changes in the industrial structure. So long as one industry was able to maintain a comparative cost advantage even when others failed, the total collapse of the economy did not occur. When that could not be done any longer in the twentieth century, then total collapse did come.

Under such conditions the increasing adoption of protection in the later nineteenth century affected the prosperity of Scottish industry more than the earlier adoption of free trade, because it arose when Scottish industry was becoming less competitive for a variety of reasons, and so any further closure of markets, either through being dislodged by more effective competition from other producers or through the barriers of protection, forced increased reliance on markets, frequently traditional markets in the Empire or other less well developed areas, which were not so affected. In these circumstances the benefits of the maintenance of free trade by Britain still applied, and any adoption of protection, always giving rise to the possibilities of retaliation by others, was something which could only be harmful to much Scottish industry. In sum, the effects of commercial policy in increasing the demand for Scottish products must be treated with some care. Any mercantilist or neo-mercantilist measures were harmful, and so the release from them, first, on a limited scale from the Union until the later eighteenth century, and then more generally in the following century, were beneficial, but as important in expanding the market were the beneficial effects of cost competitiveness, and it depended on the nature of the internal response, on supply as well as on demand.

★

Some interpretations suggest that social attitudes common before the eighteenth century inhibited any possibility of internal response: that theological demands for the right to individual judgement hindered the growth of social stability necessary for economic growth, or, more powerfully still, that the idea of progress could not be accepted because of tradition-bound pre-occupation with the theology of earlier centuries. That Scotland had first to break free from disruptive theological obsessions is a strong argument, but theological obsession was not the only cause of economic backwardness, and may not have been entirely disruptive. Any alleged inhibiting influence in the seventeenth century was largely irrelevant, because of the absence of many other factors essential to economic progress. More positively, religious attitudes may have produced incentives and disciplines which equipped the Scot for entrepreneurial action, and his theology, while not otherworldly, condemned so many other activities that he was left with few in which to exercise his talent other than economic enterprise.[1]

The eighteenth century made its contribution to the social fabric of industrial success by the application of qualities of mind, partly derived from the theological obsession of earlier years, to wholly secular affairs, and in ways which avoided social tensions which retarded economic enterprise. Scotland did not suffer from revolutionary social fervour because the leaders of the secularisation of Scottish thought, while intellectually revolutionary, were politically and socially conservative, especially as far as property rights were concerned. For them the political changes of 1688 and 1707 sufficed and they had no desire to perpetuate any religious dissension of the previous century in secular guise. Such social stability was strengthened when accompanied by an acceptance of political, social and economic change by powerful influences in society, especially by Scotland's traditionally powerful landowners. They accommodated, even welcomed, economic change until it was too late to stop it, and by their agricultural activities facilitated economic growth on a wider front.[2]

Favourable social attitudes encouraged the indigenous responses of increased agricultural production and of industrial development, necessary to avoid the Malthusian crisis which came in those regions where there was no internal response as population increased. Both responses were linked to the widening markets, especially internationally: any agricultural deficiencies required increased imports and industrial successes led to increased exports, while the resultant balance of trade ultimately determined the liquidity of the financial network which aided both agricultural and industrial growth in Scotland.

The financial needs of industry are not easily determined. Some

[1] T. C. Smout, *A History of the Scottish People: 1560-1830* (London, 1969), 94-100; H. R. Trevor-Roper, 'The Scottish Enlightenment', *Studies on Voltaire and the Eighteenth Century*, cviii (1967), 1635-58; A. C. Chitnis, *The Scottish Enlightenment* (London, 1976), 247-54.

[2] T. C. Smout, 'Scottish Landowners and Economic Growth 1650-1850', *Scottish Journal of Political Economy*, xi (1964), 226.

recent quantitative work, based especially on insurance valuations,[1] may give the impression that capital requirements, even of the growth industries of their day – cotton and iron – were small in the earliest development of modern industry, from which it is easy to assume – too readily perhaps – that they were met easily. Increased capital requirement is a feature of the nineteenth century, coming most conspicuously with the advent of the railways, and so coming when Scottish industry was firmly established. Yet it would be as misleading to underestimate as to overestimate the capital needs of industry. All estimates are subject to massive qualifications, and calculation of aggregate capital investment, or in isolation from the effects of its availability on individual firms, detracts from its contribution to the growth of key firms. More important still, the way in which some ventures were unable to proceed during years of financial stringency, particularly those (the Forth and Clyde Canal is an example) which were providing social capital necessary for more extensive industrial development, provides evidence that any contraction of the supply of capital was detrimental even if its aggregate amount was limited.

That a continued increase in the supply of capital was essential is evident at those times in the eighteenth century when economic expansion in Scotland led to such an expansion of credit that it became necessary to meet demands for bullion in Scotland by importing from London, movements which had limits, and movements which led to a higher rate of interest in Edinburgh than in London.[2] Any strain on the balance of trade was exacerbated from the mid-eighteenth century, when the needs of the rising population changed Scotland from being a net exporter to being a net importer of grain, in spite of the improvements in Scottish agriculture which can be detected earlier in the century. Both the need for additional reserves to meet the expansion of credit and the need for foodstuffs

[1] S. D. Chapman, 'Fixed Capital Formation in the British Cotton Manufacturing Industry', in J. P. P. Higgins and S. Pollard (eds.), *Aspects of Capital Formation in Great Britain, 1750-1850* (London, 1971), 102-3; S. G. E. Lythe and J. Butt, *An Economic History of Scotland, 1100-1939* (Glasgow, 1975), 172-4; J. Butt, 'Capital and Enterprise in The Scottish Iron Industry, 1780-1840', in J. Butt and J. T. Ward (eds.), *Scottish Themes* (Edinburgh, 1976), 72-73.

[2] H. Hamilton, 'Scotland's Balance of Payments Problem in 1762', *Economic History Review:* v (1953), 344-57.

strained the balance of payments, and when both operated adversely at the same time a difficult financial and economic situation emerged and halted expansion. In these conditions good harvests in the short run, and increased agricultural efficiency in the long run, eased any such periods of stringency, and so the long run improvement of agriculture was an essential prerequisite for any sustained period of industrial growth. Widespread improvement came with the Napleonic Wars and the early nineteenth century, when the pressure of rising urban demand on agricultural prices gave conditions sufficiently profitable to ensure that the agricultural improvements, applied in earlier years in a small and limited way, became more general. With such agricultural improvements, coinciding with the period of rapid industrialisation, old restraints on continued Scottish industrial expansion were removed. Thereafter the contribution of agriculture to industrial growth, and to the general prosperity of Scotland, diminished as the industrial society was supported increasingly by imports from overseas, helped especially by free trade and better transport as world supplies were tapped. As Scotland was transformed into an industrial society, prosperity rested on cheap food. Whatever the adverse effects may have been on Scottish agriculture, ultimately disastrous in the less well endowed areas, the increasingly urban and industrial population stood to gain, never more so than in the depressed conditions of the inter-war years.

The structure of Scottish banking: its characteristics of joint-stock banking, branches, cash-credits, paper money, provided an advanced institutional structure for Scottish industry, but its contribution to industrial growth is qualified by the restraints placed on the availability of capital by any weaknesses in Scotland's balance of trade and especially in the eighteenth century by any inability of Scottish agriculture to dispense with imports.[1] Further qualification arises from attempts to give greater provision to the contribution of the banks by trying to measure it. Measurement of the capital requirements of industry leads to a cautious view of their extent in the eighteenth century; similarly with attempts to measure bank deposits. But the two calculations cannot be compared without further qualification, because they do not refer to the same factors.

[1] S. G. Checkland, *Scottish Banking, a History, 1695-1973* (Glasgow, 1975), 215.

The banks did not lend exclusively for fixed capital formation in industry, and the capital needs of the industrialists were not met exclusively by banks. Unfortunately an analysis of how the banks lent between different sectors of the economy cannot be calculated from the records, but such quantitative evidence as is available indicates the importance of bank lending to agriculture and to trade, lending which would, of course, help industry indirectly by the release of funds to it. Complementary qualitative evidence from the records of business firms shows that much capital investment in industry was financed from sources other than the banks, particularly from the personal resources of the industrialists or from the profits which they ploughed back into their concerns.

It may then be possible to conclude that Scottish banks, for all their contributions to the evolution of banking practice, did not play a major role, beneficial or otherwise, in the evolution of Scottish industry, were it not for the critical comments of individual business enterprises, as are to be found in the miscellany, and as may be deduced from the objections which were raised against the Scottish banks and which gave rise to such protests within the banking system as the formation of the Commercial, Western and City of Glasgow Banks. The complaints are, of course, mostly those of borrowers who did not obtain what they considered adequate funds, and whether that was a limitation on major expansion or a pinprick is not easy to determine, and the complaints are more vigorous, and lead to the formation of new banking institutions in the nineteenth century, when the capital intensity of industrial production had increased. It may be fair to conclude that the supply of finance was not a major determinant of the growth of industry in the long-run, but that does not exclude the possibility that it could be critically important in the short-run, and to individual firms. No firm could survive in the long-run if in chronic financial difficulties, but few were without experiencing some difficulties in the short-run.

*

It is possible to determine two strands in the industrial structure built on these foundations: first an attempt to enter and appropriate ever-widening markets by competitive pricing, by engaging in what may be described in the language of today as the unskilled production of low-priced goods: the cotton piece-goods, the coal and the pig iron, which supplied world markets, especially in the nineteenth century; and, second, the specialisation by firms, and sometimes areas, in producing high-quality and often high-priced goods: tweeds and other woollen goods, ships, locomotives and a wide range of engineering products, products of skilled labour and techniques, which gave their manufacturers some protection against competition even when prices, and costs, were less competitive.

Growth was a discontinuous process. Expansion encountered bottlenecks which a specialist producer sometimes side-stepped by limiting production to methods or qualities unaffected by them, but large-scale production, especially of low-cost goods or semi-manufactures, required their elimination by technical change. Bottlenecks were various: in the provision of power, both generally and in dealing with such special requirements as the drainage of coalmines; and in production, notably in improving the supply of raw materials at reasonable cost. The major technical changes which eliminated them are well known: in textile production, the series of improvements from the later eighteenth century in spinning, weaving, printing and bleaching; in the iron and steel industries, improvements in production were the use of coke in iron smelting at the blast furnaces in the middle of the eighteenth century, and in iron refining at the forge towards the century's end; in the chemical industry the old method of bleaching fabric by exposure or by boiling in ashes and in sour milk was replaced by the use of sulphuric acid, by chlorine, and from 1798 by the use of bleaching powder. Fundamental to changes in production were those in power, especially the invention of Watt's separate condenser in the steam engine in 1769. However limited its earliest application, its long-term consequences for Scottish industry were radical and comprehensive, especially when the engine evolved from a single reciprocating stroke, no more than a steam pump, to rotary motion and its application to a wide range of mechanical uses.[1]

[1] E. Robinson and A. E. Musson, *James Watt and the Steam Revolution* (London, 1969); J. R. Harris, 'The Employment of Steam Power in the Eighteenth Century', *History*, lii (1967), 133-148; A. E. Musson and E. Robinson, *Science and Technology in the Industrial Revolution* (Manchester, 1969), chap. xii; B. F. Duckham, *A History of the Scottish Coal Industry, 1700-1815* (Newton Abbot, 1970), 363-5.

Many Scots contributed to the new technology. Apart from the classic example of Watt, a major contribution was made in the chemical industry.[1] Francis Home pointed out the possibilities of vitriol, or sulphuric acid, in bleaching; John Roebuck, an Englishman, most of whose education and industrial ventures, generally unprofitable to himself, were in Scotland, pioneered its industrial manufacture, leading to sulphuric acid becoming 'the first modern industrial chemical';[2] Charles Tennant discovered how to produce bleaching powder, much safer to use than sulphuric acid. The Scottish contribution was not confined to bleaching. James Hutton and the 9th Earl of Dundonald demonstrated the possibilities of chemical extraction from coal. Among several activities, though not in Scotland, James Keir made soda from common salt by using sulphuric acid. George Macintosh introduced cudbear dyeing to Glasgow and his son, Charles, the waterproofing process which led to the family name becoming a household word.

The Scottish contribution to technical changes was not always dominant, and, where it was, aid from other quarters was sometimes required. The steam engine provides an illustration. The mechanism was not new, though the critical invention of the separate condenser emerged from Watt in the context of exchanges with John Anderson and Joseph Black in the University of Glasgow. The initial partnership to exploit the invention was formed in Scotland but failed, and success came to Watt only in partnership with Matthew Boulton in Birmingham and with cylinders bored by the precise methods of John Wilkinson at Broseley and not by the imprecise methods of Carron Company. In spite of the contribution of Watt in Glasgow the Scottish contribution to the development and application of the steam engine was limited. Even when success was unequivocally Scottish, any long-term retention of technological discovery – to one firm or country – was not easy. Activity closely akin to industrial espionage was known even in the eighteenth century and the evidence of Kalameter's diary may be supported

[1] A. and N. L. Clow, *The Chemical Revolution* (London, 1952).

[2] D. W. F. Hardie, 'The Macintoshes and the Origins of the Chemical Industry', *Chemistry and Industry* (June 1952), 607. Liebig believed that '. . . we may fairly judge the commercial prosperity of a country from the amount of sulphuric acid it consumes'. See D. W. F. Hardie and J. Davidson Pratt, *A History of the Modern British Chemical Industry* (Oxford, 1966), 18.

by those of others.[1] The Swedes were especially concerned over the growth of the iron industry and the threat it implied to traditional markets. Knowledge of the new methods was not readily obtained. For long Carron Company was the industrial concern in Scotland which most attracted such investigators, but it guarded its activities so closely, even when there was little need for secrecy, that one Swede could not 'under any circumstances get to see these works, which are also for this reason now enclosed by a wall'.[2] Not all visitors were as easily turned aside and inspection of the more successful aspects of Scottish industry continued into the nineteenth century.[3] As unsuccessful as efforts to retain secrets were the efforts, backed by legislation, to prevent men and machines from leaving the country. Though the legislation still stood to be investigated by Select Committees in the 1820s, its ineffectiveness was recognised. Circumvention was always possible '. . . if you pay a sum of money equal to 25 per cent on the account of your machinery, you can have the conveyance of it guaranteed to any part'.[4]

Technical change altered the combinations of the factors of production employed, and, though the initial objective of many of the changes was to deploy capital to reduce labour costs, the expansion of output to meet the increased demand of expanding markets required increased supplies of both capital and labour.

The limited nature of the early capital requirements of industry has already been mentioned. Later the increased demand for capital, especially with the advent of the railways, was met, both because more was available to invest and because institutions channelled funds in appropriate directions. By the mid-nineteenth century the agricultural improvements, which were a notable feature of the early years of the century, and the increasing flow of industrial

[1] M. W. Flinn, 'The Travel Diaries of Swedish Engineers of the Eighteenth Century as Sources of Technological History', *Transactions of the Newcomen Society*, xxxi (1958), 95-106.

[2] E. T. Svedenstierna, *Tour of Great Britain 1802-3*, trans. E. L. Dellow (Newton Abbot, 1973), 137.

[3] See the report after the successful use of the hot blast in Scotland by M. Dufrénoy, Engineer of Mines, 'Report to the Board of Directors of Bridges, Public Roads and Mines, upon the use of Heated Air in the Iron Works of Scotland and England (Paris, 1834)', trans. S. V. Merrick, *Journal of the Franklin Institute*, xv (NS), 212.

[4] *Select Committee on Exportation of Tools and Machinery*. British Parliamentary Papers, 1825, V, 27. Evidence of Timothy Bramah.

products overseas removed the strains placed on internal liquidity by the need to import, and surplus funds were available, mostly from agricultural sources and areas, for investment in industry.[1] Frequently no transfer was required, since the main sources for investment in many firms were their own accumulated profits, or the resources of families which owned them, but where necessary transfer was aided by the continued growth of those characteristics of the banking system which had been pioneered in the eighteenth century, notably the extension of branches, by over 50 per cent between 1850 and 1865, and the growth in the nineteenth century of joint stock enterprise and of the capital market, essential if the full marketability of shares was to be exploited. Public utilities, notably the railways, gained initially from joint stock enterprise. Partly because of legal difficulties, manufacturing concerns were floated as joint stock companies only later in the nineteenth century, and sometimes not to raise capital for expansion but to enable a family to surrender a leading financial stake in, but not control of, a company.

It is less easy to overestimate the contribution of improvements in the supply of labour than of capital. Its supply was transformed in the nineteenth century when rising population in Ireland and in the Highlands of Scotland coincided with increased demand from Scottish industry, particularly the heavy industries. Coalmines and ironworks used the unskilled labour; shipyards and engineering workshops used the semi-manufactures they produced, but needed skilled labour for their own output. The skills were geared to the needs of the heavy industries, and with their success a labour force, less mobile occupationally and geographically, emerged. But that was a problem for the future.[2]

Of the increased quantity of labour there is no doubt; of its costs the evidence is less certain. Yet cost was critical, because many Scottish industries were labour intensive. In the 1890s labour costs were estimated to be about 60 per cent of total costs; about 50 per cent in finished steel; and from 33 to 66 per cent in shipbuilding.[3]

[1] Checkland, *Scottish Banking*, 234.

[2] See below, p. xxxvii.

[3] *Report to the Board of Trade on the Relation of Wages in Certain Industries to the Cost of Production*. British Parliamentary Papers, 1890-1, LXXVIII, 23. The official figures agree with estimates made from the records of a number of Scottish firms.

The level of wage rates contributed to the level of wage costs and so to Scotland's cost competitiveness. Information on Scottish wage rates is not readily available, and when it is, rates are not easily comparable. Some evidence which suggests more buoyant, or even higher, wages in agriculture in parts of Scotland in the later nineteenth century may reflect higher productivity and high net emigration as labour moved to industrial openings elsewhere.[1] Other evidence that rates other than in agriculture were not low in Scotland is sometimes chosen from unrepresentative examples or based on comparisons with areas with few industrial opportunities. Somewhat different evidence may be derived from comparisons of computed average annual earnings based on the wage rates returned in the wages census of 1886, which shows that in most cases those for Scotland were below those for the United Kingdom as a whole, and, though present evidence is slight, it is not easy to explain the difference wholly by different levels of productivity. The few higher rates were exceptional, usually only minimally so, and in specialised regions. One was important. In coalmining and pig iron smelting the Scottish average was slightly above that for the U.K. But in general it is not unreasonable to hold that the increased quantity of labour which became available in the middle of the nineteenth century ensured expansion and yet kept wage rates and earnings below those in some other industrial, and so potentially competitive, regions.[2]

Whatever their benefits, increased supplies of labour and capital provided no more assured basis for Scottish industrial prosperity than advanced technical change. Even the application of the most up-to-date technology, in whatever combination of factors of production minimised costs, did not guarantee a perpetual lead. Only some favourable influences confined as far as possible to Scotland could do so. Two such influences were the possession of

[1] George Houston, 'Farm Wages in Central Scotland from 1814 to 1870', *Journal of the Royal Statistical Society*, Series A (General), 118, Part II (1955), 224-8. A full-scale study, and a major contribution to the entire problem is in E. H. Hunt, *Regional Wage Variations in Britain 1850-1914* (Oxford, 1973).

[2] The detailed evidence is in a series of parliamentary papers: *Returns of rates of wages in the Principal Textile Trades of the U.K.*, C.5807, 1889, LXX; *Returns . . . Mines and Quarries*, C.6455, 1891, LXXVIII; *Returns . . . Police . . . Roads, etc. and Gas and Water Works*, C.6715, 1892, LXVIII; *General Report on the Wages of the Manual Labour Classes in the U.K. in 1886 and 1891*, C.6889, 1883-4, LXXXIII, Part II.

adequate endowments of those natural resources on which the necessary technical change relied and the existence of social, particularly educational characteristics which ensured a perpetuation of a technological lead over competitors.

The contribution of the possession of natural resources to the effective application of the new technologies of power and production is clear in the growth of the textile and the heavy industries. The use of water for industrial power makes its specialised modern contribution in the provision of hydro-electricity, but its first contribution to the pattern of industrial expansion was to determine the location of the new cotton spinning mills of the later eighteenth century. One of the earliest – improbably in Rothesay – had an elaborate network of dams, still visible, and so it was with the well-known concerns: New Lanark beside the Clyde; Deanston on the Teith; Catrine on the Ayr. Similar needs for ample water led to marked concentration of calico-printing and dyeing in the Vale of Leven. The location of the early cotton mills, from Spinningdale in Sutherland to Newton Stewart in Wigtownshire, gave way to concentration when the steam engine, using Scotland's ample, but – unlike water – permanently exhaustible supplies of coal, began to provide supplementary power, and by the early nineteenth century construction was more concentrated, particularly in Glasgow, but even such areas relatively remote from the main coalfields as Dundee and Arbroath were emancipated from the restrictions which local lack of water-supplies had placed on earlier textile production.[1]

Technical change in textile manufacture removed the bottle-neck of the supply of raw materials at reasonable cost, but not using Scotland's own resources. Long-standing defects in the raw materials used in the textile industries were removed when the cotton industry enjoyed the enormous stimulus of increased supplies of its raw material from the American plantations at diminished cost and when the woollen industry substituted imported wool for the domestic clip in the nineteenth century. But dependence on an imported raw material has drawbacks: it has to be paid for and interruption to its supply, as to that of cotton at the time of the American Civil War, when the Scottish cotton industry was

[1] W. H. K. Turner, *The Textile Industry of Arbroath since the early 18th Century*, Abertay Historical Society Publications: No. 2 (1954), 11.

already in difficulties, can prove damaging. Competition from overseas producers was never far removed under such conditions.

By contrast the iron industry did not suffer initially from any need to import and the repercussions of its expansion were therefore even more widespread, as it involved corresponding expansion in Scotland of coal production and of some subsequent processes of manufacturing iron. Natural resources were available to complement the new technology. As demand grew, and as better transport enabled the richer collieries to tap still wider markets, so the inadequacy of natural methods of drainage, on which the industry had relied, became still more inadequate. Mechanical methods to lift water from pits were used instead of natural drainage by gravity flow, and from the end of the eighteenth century they were supplemented, and later supplanted, by steam power vertical cylinder beam engines. As technical change, especially Watt's patent, improved the availability of power, several changes provided the necessary technical break-through in the production of iron, and again they used resources Scotland possessed in full measure: smelting with coke instead of with charcoal, the process pioneered in the early eighteenth century, but adopted first in Scotland by Carron Company in 1760; refining by coke, adopted generally with a fair measure of success in the 1780s after some earlier and less successful efforts. And particularly important for Scotland, the use of hot air instead of cold air in the blast at the furnaces – J. B. Neilson's hot blast, patented in 1828 – which enabled the rich blackband iron ore resources of Scotland to be exploited, and the area's splint coal to be used uncoked in the process. Technology and geology were then combined with signal success in the second quarter of the nineteenth century. Since the coal and iron ore could be mined easily and transported in adequate quantities because of the earlier improvements in the provision of power, the industrial transformation of Scotland was achieved.

So there came the major expansion of iron production and of related industries, particularly in west-central Scotland, from around 1830. The existing ironworks expanded and a whole crop of new works appeared in the decade. They produced low-cost, semi-manufactured, pig iron, and so differed from the earlier successful example of Carron, which was little affected. The iron produced was technically more suitable for the casting of a variety of goods in foundries, and from this phase in particular may be dated the appearance of a large number of foundries, and the growth of the light castings industry of central Scotland. Other forms of the further processing of iron, especially into malleable or wrought iron, were much less successful;[1] indeed, often they were not even tried, and a large part of the Scottish output left Scotland without being processed further: about one-third of the total production was shipped coastwise to England and about as much went directly overseas. By about 1850 the iron industry of Scotland was therefore mainly converting the rich indigenous geological resources of the country into pig iron and not manufacturing it further.[2]

It is possible to suggest that the strength of the industrial development of Scotland rested on a fortunate combination of circumstances, particularly the appearance of a number of technological changes for which Scotland had appropriate natural resources: water; coal; iron ore. The mid-eighteenth to the mid-nineteenth century was the period of most impressive Scottish industrial prosperity because it was the period when the Scots gained passively from an expanding world market and a technology of power and of production for which they had the supreme good fortune to have the appropriate resources and had plentiful and cheap labour, the most essential factor of production needed to exploit them.

The good fortune was not unalloyed. Whatever the immediate benefits of the exploitation of the ample endowments of natural resources in encouraging the growth of industry, the perpetuation of such benefits rested on the ability of Scots to supplement natural advantages with those acquired by entrepreneurial action and initiative, but, paradoxically, the initial ample natural endowments fostered at least two entrepreneurial deficiencies in the heavy industries. The first, a direct result of the plentiful supply of cheap

[1] W. Vamplew, 'The Railways and the Iron Industry: A Study of their Relationship in Scotland', in M. C. Reed (ed.), *Railways in the Victorian Economy* (Newton Abbot, 1969), 46-47.

[2] For an important study of another case of the relationship between technical change and natural resources in Scotland see, J. Butt, 'Legends of the Coal-Oil Industry (1847-64)', *Explorations in Entrepreneurial History*, ii (1964), 16-30; 'Technical Change and the Growth of the British Shale-Oil Industry (1680-1870)', *Economic History Review*, xvii (1965), 511-521; 'The Scottish Oil Mania of 1864-6', *Scottish Journal of Political Economy*, xii (1965), 195-209.

coal, lies in the way the Scottish iron and later the steel industries failed for many years to adopt even the most elementary methods of fuel economy, as in the notorious practice, which persisted long after the earliest days of the iron industry, of failing to utilise the waste gases from the blast furnaces, and the reluctance to adopt even the most rudimentary forms of conserving heat by hot-metal practice, far less by complete integration, even when the organisational changes of the inter-war years provided new opportunities of doing so. The second example is in the failure to develop fully the further processing of some of the semi-manufactures produced by the heavy industries, by a failure to move as far as possible to the more secure marketing position of the specialist producer of skilled goods. So malleable iron production in Scotland lagged, and some of the successful Scottish ironmasters never produced cheap steel when that became possible in the later nineteenth century.

The failures were not conscious failures. To have expected both technological and entrepreneurial action other than what took place is to expect action in the long run interests of society as has been revealed by the passage of time. In the short run cheap natural resources, and a ready supply of cheap labour, ensured that the immediate objective of earning, though not necessarily maximising, profits was realised, but in the long run any decline in these twin advantages was likely to be disastrous for an economy so geared to their availability. In these circumstances the perpetuation of industrial prosperity rested even more on the existence or emergence of a society capable of maintaining a technological lead even without such supports. Some have suggested that such a lead was possible in Scotland and may be a more accurate explanation of the country's industrial success.[1]

In modern parlance a scientific approach to industrial problems may be given two interpretations: scientific production, the definition generally assumed so far, and scientific management. The need for the latter is evident in the affairs of the North British Railway Company, which show the inadequacy of accounting techniques and the difficulties of effective control. Even in the eighteenth century, when divorce between ownership and manage-

[1] T. S. Ashton, *The Industrial Revolution*, 19-20.

ment had not reached the extent fostered by joint stock enterprise, elaborate book-keeping was more often used to prevent fraud than to supply a tool for efficient management.[1] Critical calculations on how to determine profits or value assets were evolved only in the nineteenth century,[2] helped by the contribution of Scots to the growth of more advanced accountancy techniques, but action had still to be taken on the evidence provided, and that required an acceptance of the need for change and knowledge of the desirable form of change. In short, for scientific management scientific production had to provide alternative courses of action when established enterprises were failing, and it is to such achievement that the Scottish educational tradition may have made a vital contribution.

The issues at stake are illustrated in the account of the Lewis Chemical Works, which shows in a melodramatic form the outcome of an enterprising industrial venture in a situation where the appropriate combination of skill and scientific knowledge was lacking. The experience of the Lewis Chemical Works is an extreme, and so it may be thought a bad example. Only its date makes it a bad example. In the eighteenth century such a major firm as Carron Company, even when operating largely under the control of someone of the intellectual distinction of John Roebuck, frequently quivered on the brink of failure. Scientific eminence did not guarantee industrial success. Yet the interest of some of the leading figures in the intellectual life of Scotland in the industrial developments of the country cannot be gainsaid. Those of Francis Home, of John Roebuck, and of the triumvirate of Watt, Anderson and Black have all been cited. Their contribution was direct and specific, but the Scottish intellectual tradition's contribution lies less in a series of specific inventions which had some industrial application and more in the emergence of a new methodology, a scientific method, which could perceive the advantages of new methods of production even when it was not always possible to produce convincing explanations of why that should be so. It is

[1] For a full discussion of the development and objectives of accountancy, see S. Pollard, *The Genesis of Modern Management* (London, 1965), 209-249.

[2] A. C. Littleton and B. S. Yamey (eds.), *Studies in the History of Accounting* (London, 1956), 11-12.

possible that the scientific method may be linked to the Newtonian approach to the physical world, adapted by Scottish thinkers and applied to social phenomena. Whether they succeeded in transferring the method is a moot point, but they held firmly to the belief that it was possible thereby to produce an explanation and understanding of the totality of any physical and social system. Rational explanation was called for, and on that basis appropriate courses of action could be determined.[1]

Such an approach, an acceptance and a rational evaluation of change, encourages industrial improvement, but it was more likely to encourage some industrial skills than others. Though the methodological approach may properly be described as scientific, it was not one which led by itself to the emergence of skill in those industries which required a high level of abstract scientific knowledge. Scotland developed its chemical industry, and was able to exploit its scientific knowledge because of the proximity of the growing textile industries, but any abstract scientific lead, as in chemicals, was not retained, and the industrial tradition which emerged was less abstract, more obviously applied, and was most evident in the growth of an engineering, or – to take an example from an entirely different field – a medical tradition. The late eighteenth and early nineteenth centuries, the generations immediately after the great age of the Enlightenment, produced a galaxy of talent of both Scottish engineers and Scottish medicals. That emphasis was to continue, perhaps somewhat paradoxically in light of the frequently expressed criticism of the rarefied academic nature of Scottish education. It is evident in the Scottish universities, even in the age of industrial success, when some of the earlier closer links between the universities and industry were breaking. Apart from the medical schools, which were in a category of their own, Edinburgh had its chair of agriculture from 1790 and Glasgow its chair of engineering from 1840, with a most distinguished occupant in Macquorn Rankine from 1855. These educational moves, though not always immediately successful or welcomed in the universities, complemented the form of Scottish industrial enterprise, or at least, the absence of any abstract scientific contribution to industry from the Scottish universities in the nineteenth century did

[1] A. C. Chitnis, *The Scottish Enlightenment*, 93f.

not disturb the existing pattern of industrial growth.[1] Even such a luminary of the Scottish universities in the nineteenth century as Lord Kelvin applied his talent in the traditional industrial forms.

The beneficial effects of this tradition were evident in the eighteenth century, in the earliest phases of modern industrialisation, for then, with the notable exception of the chemical industry, the mechanical arts made the main contribution to industrial change,[2] and that was the field in which the Scots were skilled. The deficiencies of the Scottish tradition became more marked, and so a matter for greater public concern, only with the growth of a greater body of scientific knowledge in the nineteenth century. The fault did not lie wholly with the industrialists: '... science teaching in schools in Scotland ... is deplorable',[3] and the same critic thought that the universities were no better. The Glasgow chair of engineering was a royal foundation, not greatly welcomed by the university and its first occupant's lectures not greatly favoured by students. But if the fault did not lie wholly with the industrialists, it lay with them in part. Some early attempts to encourage industrialists to support technical training in the Andersonian University failed and criticism of the level of technical knowledge in Scottish industry was expressed to the Royal Commission on Scientific Instruction in the 1870s. The root cause of the deficiency lay in the traditional bias of Scottish education towards the maintenance of the broadly based curriculum and its philosophical emphasis, with the result that many of an increasing range of scientific subjects were not taught and some of those which were, such as mathematics, were taught in ways 'irrelevant to modern problems and developments'.[4]

Whatever the benefits of the Scottish educational and intellectual tradition, it was not conducive to the emergence of the knowledge or skills needed in those industries requiring a high level of abstract

[1] M. Sanderson, *The Universities and British Industry, 1850–1970* (London, 1972), especially 163–4.

[2] For a full discussion of the relative importance of these contributions see A. E. Musson, *Science, Technology and Economic Growth in the Eighteenth Century* (London, 1972), 60. See also G. N. Clark, *Science and Social Welfare in the Age of Newton* (Oxford, second edn., 1949).

[3] T. Purdie, *The Relation of Science to University Teaching in Scotland* (St Andrews, 1885), 10.

[4] G. E. Davie, *The Democratic Intellect: Scotland and her Universities in the Nineteenth Century* (Edinburgh, 1961), 150.

scientific knowledge, the science based industries in the language of the present day. Hardly surprisingly, the considerable Scottish contribution to the establishment of the chemical industry in the eighteenth century declined in the nineteenth century, when Scotland remained tied to old processes. The industry's final extinction, though long delayed, was foreshadowed when the Solvay process superseded the Leblanc process in the manufacture of alkali, for its application was suitable to the natural resources of Cheshire and not of Scotland, and in due course all alkali production in Scotland came to an end. The loss of the early lead in the chemical industry may have been unavoidable because of the comparative natural advantage of Cheshire, but it had a special significance. The chemical industry was in a field where scientific effort was needed.

Any adverse consequences of failure in science based industries was not immediately evident because the basis of the widespread success, and the transformation of the industrial structure in the nineteenth century, rested most of all on the production of low cost or semi-manufactured goods. The dangers arose only when the unique basis of the success in that field was eroded by the diminution in the supply of natural resources and possibly of cheap labour, both appearing as international competition intensified and making the need for low comparative costs of production more necessary than ever. Then an alternative strand of industrial growth was needed.

The decline in natural resources is easily demonstrated in geological terms. The production of iron ore was 3,000,000 tons in the 1870s, less than 600,000 in 1913, and petered out between the wars. Coal production did not decline. It increased to meet buoyant export demand, but, as in the production of iron ore, output of the more easily mined and of the geologically more valuable grades did fall, notably the splint coal of Lanarkshire. The general decline was matched by a critical particular deficiency of the resources needed for the new advances in steelmaking before 1914. At first the new processes, the Bessemer converter and the Siemens-Martins open-hearth furnace required supplies of pig iron smelted from non-phosphoric or hematite ores, of which Scotland had virtually none, and so supplies had to be imported, chiefly from Spain. Later in the 1880s the basic process of steelmaking enabled other ores to be used, but to switch from producing acid to producing basic steel was not an easy course to adopt, and in any case the demand for Scottish steel was for acid steel, for plates in the shipyards. While Scottish supplies of all ores were declining the basic process enabled overseas competitors to exploit rich and hitherto little used resources. For Scotland there was no way of avoiding importing ore from overseas and even of some special coals from England.

The decline in the availability of cheap labour cannot be demonstrated so easily. The wages census of 1886 had shown that in most cases the computed average wage earnings for Scotland were generally below those for the U.K. as a whole. The next survey, of 1906,[1] of actual earnings as well as of computed earnings, the only one to be made in Scotland until the 1950s, shows earnings often topping those for the U.K. For all men, in iron and steel manufacture, earnings in Scotland were 36s. 11d. a week and 35s. 4d. in the U.K.; in engineering and boilermaking, the Clyde was 31s. 10d. and the U.K. was 31s. 11d.; in shipbuilding, the Clyde was 33s. 2d. and the U.K. was 32s. 10d. Qualitative evidence provides confirmation of the probability of an upward, converging trend of both rates and of earnings. The elastic supply of labour from Ireland was greatly lessened, so much so that by the late nineteenth century employment in the coalmines was being offered to labour recruited in the Baltic and Eastern Europe. And, increasingly, wage rates were negotiated on a national basis, particularly during the two wars. The move of wage rates and earnings into conformity with those of the U.K. especially in the early twentieth century came at a time when the trends of international unit wage costs and of productivity were operating against the U.K.[2] Hence the move towards conformity operated adversely against Scottish competitive ability, nationally and internationally, unless there

[1] *Reports of an Enquiry by the Board of Trade into the Earnings and Hours of Labour of Workpeople in the U.K. in 1906*, Cd. 4545, 1909, LXXX; Cd. 4844, 1909, LXXX; Cd. 5086, 1910, LXXXIV; Cd. 5196, 1910, LXXIV; Cd. 5460, 1910, LXXXIV; Cd. 5814, 1911, LXXXVIII; Cd. 6556, 1912-13, CVIII. Moves towards convergence can be studied in *Reports on Standard Time Rates of Wages in the U.K.* from 1900, Cd. 317, LXXXII, 335 and subsequently; less satisfactorily in *Reports of Changes in Rates of Wages and Hours of Labour in the U.K.* from 1893, C.7567, LXXXI, Part II and subsequently. An illustration of how negotiating machinery led to convergence is in *Evidence to the Industrial Council in connection with their Enquiry into Industrial Agreements*, Cd. 6953, 1913, XXVIII, Qs. 2, 753-5.

[2] E. H. Phelps Brown and M. H. Browne, *A Century of Pay* (London, 1968), 137.

was a compensating increase in Scottish productivity. In general, there was no such increase if the evidence of net production per head as calculated in the first census of production of 1907 is followed.[1] The areas of high earnings and high net production were those of high-quality production – the specialist producers – on which basis Scotland was still able to maintain its competitive position. In the heavy industries – mining, further processing of iron and steel, engineering and in shipbuilding – few major generalisations are possible. Only in mining was there an unequivocal coincidence of higher earnings and higher net production, and the failure to evince such a coincidence in the latter sectors of the heavy industries was more marked on the Clyde, the area of major employment, and the area so central to the continued prosperity of Scottish industry.

The certain loss of natural advantages and the possible loss of cheap labour affected the producers of the low-cost semi-manufactures particularly adversely. The other main strand of Scottish industrial success lay in the achievement of the specialists, the highly skilled, and so, if necessary the high cost and high price producers, which in Scotland in the late nineteenth century meant shipbuilding above all else, and cheap steelmaking in the train of shipbuilding. That was the order of growth. In the nineteenth and twentieth centuries, shipbuilding prospered with improvements in propulsion (sail, steam engine, steam turbine, diesel engine) and in construction (wood, iron, steel). The Clyde's success in shipbuilding was based primarily on the improvements in propulsion, on the area's existing skill in engineering, and in a supplementary or secondary way on the local availability of cheap iron and then of cheap steel. The success of the marine engineers, leading to further development in shipbuilding and in steel, was only one aspect of engineering success, which was evident in other fields as well, in locomotive engineering, and in the production of specialised machinery. Even when the generalist producers of the semi-products, coal and iron, even steel, for all its attachment to shipbuilding, were encountering competition before 1914, the specialist producers remained prosperous at least superficially. The pattern of their markets changed and they became increasingly dependent on supplying the less developed

[1] *Final Report on the First Census of Production of the U.K.*, Cd. 6320, 1912.

parts of the world, notably India and other parts of the Empire. The prosperity was not only precarious but sometimes superficial, since markets were by no means secure, and some major specialist producers in the heavy industries were neither profitable nor successful by the beginning of the twentieth century. But any precarious or superficial elements in the prosperity before 1914 were ignored and the record tonnage of ships launched on the Clyde in 1913 was taken as symptomatic of the apparent security and success of the specialist producers in Scottish industry. And from the specialists there was always a demand, of sorts, for coal, iron and steel, even if comparative costs in these industries were less favourable than some of their rivals overseas. By 1914 the prosperity of Scottish industry rested on success in the specialist strand of industrial production[1] and no longer on the earlier strand of success in providing the world markets with unskilled semi-products such as cotton piece-goods or pig iron.

The specialists generally enjoyed their more favoured position before 1914 because of some inelasticity in the demand of their customers, as for higher quality textiles or because of the desire for some form of specially designed engineering equipment, be it ships or locomotives. But two distinguishing characteristics of the growth of the specialist producers among the heavy industries – the first applicable to all, the second less widespread – influenced much of the subsequent history of Scottish industry.

The first, more obvious, and applicable throughout the nineteenth century, was their dependence on demand for investment and not for consumption, with the inevitable result that demand fluctuated more violently, giving the pattern of fluctuations which affected the major Scottish industries of the nineteenth century and so affected the attitudes of Scottish industrialists that methods of tackling periodic depressions in the nineteenth century, and the expectation that a period of prosperity would inevitably follow a period of depression, affected their policies in the inter-war years, when conditions were so different. The second characteristic, which emerged in the later years of the nineteenth century and in the early years of the twentieth, at a critical time when Scottish producers were encountering increased competition, was the way in which

[1] A. Slaven, *The Development of the West of Scotland, 1750–1960* (London, 1975), 182.

some major Scottish industries, and in particular some major Scottish firms, became so dependent on demand for their products from the public sector that their continued prosperity was a by-product of public policy, which had a variability all its own. The best example lies in the dependence of some shipbuilding firms on the Clyde on Admiralty orders. Of thirty-nine launches from John Brown's between 1908 and the outbreak of war, twenty-one were naval vessels.

When the modern Scottish industrial structure was being formed in the eighteenth century its progress depended on agricultural improvements; when it was established its continued prosperity rested on overseas demand, and latterly on demand for investment goods, again much of it from overseas or from the public sector. Until 1918 these characteristics produced few immediate problems, but they placed much of Scottish industry in a precarious position for the future. The qualities which the heavy industrial bias lacked are equally obvious, though any regret at failure of industrial growth in other fields became a matter of concern only when the earlier basis of expansion collapsed. The specialist form of industrial production was not geared towards the industries based on scientific knowledge, not towards light industry, and not towards the domestic consumer market. The Albion Company, the one lasting success in car manufacture in pre-1914 days, specialised in the manufacture of commercial vehicles from 1913. Some of the earliest ventures into the new industrial fields came from foreign enterprise: Nobel at Ardeer in 1873; Singer's at Glasgow, then at Clydebank in the 1880s. Perhaps the most important of all, was the lack of a light machine tools industry with its pervasive influence on growth throughout industry. The weight of the Scottish industrialist tradition – specialist or generalist – was against such growth, and before 1914 there was apparently no need for it.

Like so much else, the prosperity of Scottish industry was never the same after 1918, because after the immediate post-war boom, the basis of the prosperity of the skilled specialists was removed. It was some time after 1918 before the need for any change in direction of industrial growth was recognised. The industrial collapse was recognised, but the cures were to be found in whatever nostrum pleased the individual: wage cuts or not; the adoption of the gold standard or not; nationalisation or not. Only in the 1930s was a change in the industrial structure advocated, and then the very magnitude of the task seemed overwhelming, both quantitatively, as it was considered a permanent surplus of male labour in the west of Scotland alone of some 100,000 had to be reabsorbed somehow somewhere, and qualitatively as the transfer of skills involved meant a complete revolution in the industrial traditions of generations.

★

The success of Scottish industry may be characterised by certain features. Its unique sources of success in the age which transformed Scotland into an industrial society lay in the liberal endowment of natural resources which were exploited by an elastic, and probably relatively cheap supply of labour. The tradition of industrial specialisation which then developed was in many ways the continuation of that of the eighteenth century, reliance on specialisation in heavy engineering production, and so on one less attuned to the requirements of the modern industrial structure based on the application of abstract science. That tradition proved successful when there was no effective competition, but when the competition appeared, the Scots were unable to meet it. In the cotton industry, scene of Scotland's first modern industrial success, the inability of the Scots to compete led to the decline of that one-time international leading industry. Even before 1914 similar problems were besetting some of the heavy industries, the prosperity of which had masked the decline of the textiles. The engineering competence in these fields remained, but concentration on technical competence did not ensure economic success. Scottish costs had to be competitive. Once again the dangers were hidden as many of the traditional Scottish industries became dependent on export markets and on government contracts, so that by 1914 much of the heavy industry of west-central Scotland, which was critically important for so much of Scotland's industrial prosperity, was working for government orders or for markets in less developed areas. In 1914 the industrial tradition was one of which Scotland was proud, but, whatever its technical merit, it was not a tradition which held the key to future success in either its markets or its specialisation.

JOURNAL OF HENRY KALMETER'S TRAVELS IN SCOTLAND

1719-1720

edited by T. C. Smout, PH D

★

INTRODUCTION. Henrik Kalmeter was the first and possibly the most interesting of the industrial spies who came to Scotland from Sweden in the course of the eighteenth century.[1] His employers were the Bergskollegium in Stockholm, an official body charged with responsibility for the Swedish mining industry, and he was sent to report on the state of the mining industries (metalliferous and otherwise) in various parts of Europe, but especially in Great Britain. He landed here from Rotterdam in 1719, when he was 26 years old, and went to stay in Edinburgh with his uncle Krumbein, an immigrant music teacher who had lived in the city for at least a quarter of a century.[2] In the autumn of 1719 he visited London, but returned in August 1720 on the death of his uncle, and spent a further nine months studying and working in Scotland, before finally leaving for England and for France.

His original diary, in the Royal Library, Stockholm, ran to some 700 manuscript pages, and described his travels throughout Britain and Europe: what is published here is everything within the diary

[1] Sven Rydberg, *Svenska Studieresor till England under Frihetstiden* (Uppsala, 1951), gives an account of Kalmeter and the others. The only other traveller of this type to have received publication in English is E. Svedenstjerna. See *Svedenstierna's Tour: Great Britain 1802-3. The travel Diary of an Industrial Spy*, ed. M. W. Flinn (Newton Abbot, 1973).

[2] David Johnson, *Music and Society in Lowland Scotland in the Eighteenth Century* (London, 1972), pp. 11, 26-27, 30-31, 33.

that relates to Scotland, though Riksarkivet in Stockholm also contains an unpublished report from Kalmeter's to Bergskollegium dealing with the mines in some detail.[1]

The contents of the diary largely speak for themselves. It was written partly in Swedish and partly in English: I am profoundly obliged to Stewart Oakley for help in translating the former. Throughout the translation, however, the original spelling of proper names has been retained. The passages that were originally in Swedish are indicated in the text by being contained within the symbols ** **.

T.C.S.

[1] Rydberg, *op. cit.* p. 156, gives the reference as 'relationen daterad London 22/1 1720 i Bergverksrel. utl. RA Öm, Bergskollegiet Arkiv'.

13 July, 1719

Since now I have been so long time in Scottland, it is but reasonable that I should give some account of what I have seen in that country, with such particularities as I have got notice of, either trough my own travellings or information from other people. As for an exact geography and description of Scottland, it may be gotten out of several authors whose proper view it hath been to treat of it, that being out of my intent, as besides that, I am just now wanting those subisidys of Books which for that purpose are necessary. See Cambdens *History of Great Britain*, Meiges *the Present State of Great Britain and Ireland*, *Atlas Geographay*, the Vol. *Britannia Antiqua et Moderna*; whereof the part treating of Scotland is yet to come out.[1]

Scottland is distinguished from England trough the Rivers *Tweed*, and Esk, of which the last goeth out in Solway Firth, and so in the Irish Sea. The Scotts in England for that reason oftentimes *remember their friends beyond the Tweed* or *in the land of Cakes*, which name is given to Scottland of certain sort of bread made of oats and called cakes.

The length of Scottland from the South to the North, or rather the latitude is from about the 54 degree 30 min. to 58 35 min. which makes about 240 English miles, and the longitude or what I now call the breadth, is where it is broadest, not above 140 miles. The temperament of the air is very wholsome, as is to be seen of the age of several people that I have known there come above 100 year. I have seen people of 70, 80 and 90 years as frish as they were not above 50. In the winter it is not extraordinarily cold, nor in the summer too hot, except when it is still and calm, it is sometimes sultry weather. It is true in the mountanous parts it is more rough weather, as about the *Leadmines* where in wintertime the snow is oftertimes as high as to cover their small houses. And as the country is full of hills and mountains, so their is a great deal of wind,

[1] William Camden, *Britannia* (there were many editions: see for example *Britannia, abridg'd with improvements and continuations to this present time* (London, 1701)); Guy Miege, *Present State of Great Britain* (London, 1707); Herman Moll, *Atlas Geographus* (London, 1711-1717); *Magna Britannia et Hibernia: antiqua et nova* (both volumes published by 1720, in London).

especially as I have observed about Edenburg in the spring, which, I do believe, comes from the melting snow and exhalations raised then in more plenty than else; as well as from the small breadth of the country thereabout betwixt the two seas.

Their nourrishment consisteth most of flesh, of beef and sheeps and severall sorts of fowls, tho' they dont want fish too, furnished as well from the salt sea as sweet rivers; as salmons, truits, cod, ling, etc. Of the herings I'll get occasion to speak furtherdown.

Of the locks and rivers in Scottland may be seen the geographical descriptions; I shall only mind that it is said that Scottland hath not too much of water.

Lockness in Invernessshire is famous because it never freeseth but retaineth its natural heat even in the extremest cold of winter; and the many hills and rocks contribute very much to the fine springs and wells they have in plenty.

The River of Forth that cometh down from Sterling, passing that town and discharging itself into the *Firth of Forth* by Lith, is not very large, especially higher up, but is extraordinory usefull to the country for carrying up and down their goods, as the tide goeth up to Sterling, where it is very pleasant to see the many links and turns of this river, that town beeing distant from Allowa by land 4 miles, but by water 24. This river and that of *Clyd* which passeth Glascow are not very large, except near where they fall into the sea, but the largest and longest I believe that are in this country.

It is thought that in antient times the most part of Scottland hath been covered with woods, at least till the Romains come in, who destroy'd a great deal of them and whose footsteps you may see a little when you have crossed the water at *Queensferry* 7 miles from Lith, going to Alva in the ruins of the Vall erected of them to keep out the incursion of the Picts.[1]

Since that [time], the woods have been more and more cut down, partly, as it's say'd, to hinder the robbers and highwaymen from hiding themselves there, partly to improve the country for sowing and labouring, so that now in all the lower most part of it, you'll find no woods at all, except some in the Shire of *Annandale* and thereabout, whereof more hereafter, and the *plantings* which

[1] Whatever he saw it was not the Roman Wall, which of course runs south of the Forth.

severall noble- and gentlemen have erected by their country houses, as I shall tell when I come to speak of them that I have seen.

In the northern parts of the Highlands are, as they tell, very large woods of excellent fir, etc. and though Herman Moll in his mapps[1] takes it to be easy to make there some rivers navigable, for carrying from thence timber down to the seaside so that they should not have occasion to get it from Norway, yet severall people have told me that it is not, or may not be found practicable for the rock and hills. And I do believe, that neither the Scotts have a mind, or as they are now impoverished through the Union with England, are able to venture such expenses, nor will get any encouragement from England.[2]

From what is say'd, it may be seen that Scottland is distinguished in the *South* and *North* or the *Highlands*. And tho' some have told me, that these begin not far above Sterling, where you will see a row of wild and rough mountains betwixt them,[3] when I lookt to them from *Bagleir* about 12 miles from *Sterling* nothing but a terrible darkness was discovered, yet other[s], and rightly, say that the distinction betwixt the *Highlands* and th'other country is to be made by the languages, them in the lower parts speaking *Scotch*, but the other *Irish*, which is a language quite different from the English and Scotch.

In the lower parts or Shires of Scotland, although there is no want of mountains and hills where commonly is good feeding for sheeps, yet the country is very fertile and gives a great deal of corn as well for fournishing the country as sometimes for exporting, especially in the Shire of Fife and Edenburg, about *Glascow* and *Sterling*, etc. where you can see the finest fields of barley, wheat, oats and peas, but ry is very little sown in that country. For feeding the ground they make use of limestone which they spread over the ground

[1] *The North Part of Great Britain called Scotland* was published by Moll in London in 1714.

[2] Wood was, however, floated down the Spey attended by men in a currach and the York Buildings Company introduced rafting on that river after 1728. David Murray, *The York Buildings Company* (Glasgow, 1883), pp. 60-61.

[3] Kalmeter's English seems to stumble here: perhaps he means the Ochils interposed between the Highlands and Lowlands, or that the foothills of the Highlands towards the Trossachs were visible. 'Bagleir' is Balgair near Balfron.

mixed with dung or other rotten earth.[1] In the places near to the sea the[y] use for that purpose the dirt or *seaweed* that the sea throws up, and is after that gathered of the people. And 'tho they reckon themselves pay'd when they get 4 corns after one, and in some places but 3, yet sometimes the ground yields 6, 8 and 10.

The Highlands again have but very little corn amongst theyr hills, but as they are furnish'd and supply'd from the lower country, so they have fine feeding for *cattle* and sheeps, which are theyr greatest products, as I shall tell hereafter.

Scottland consisteth of 32 counttys or Shires, wherein the only and principale religion is the Calvinien, the people beeing called *Presbyteriens* because the Government of the Church or Ministerium consisteth of *Presbyters* as at Geneva, one of them being not distinguished from another through any degree of honour, only if he hath acquired himself some more reputation through learning or preaching. No student of Divinity is allowed to preach before he hath been examined before the Presbytery and so got liberty to it, till he may be promoted to any vacant Parish or employment. But as there is no occasion for anybody to bring himself up above the other, or to attain some post of honour as under the Episcopal Government, so there is none of quality or the gentry that breeds their children to that, the *steepings* beside that beeing very small, in that country seldom above 50 *pd.* Sterling, but in some towns, 100 and 140. (140 l. is the most that a priest gets in Edenburg, unless he gets some other position like a Professor's post at the College.) The ministers beeing also sons of boers and countrymen or ministers and sometimes of little learning and breeding are but very little estimed by the gentry.

It is so far off that they suffer any ornaments in their churches that they commonly are but very mean places, and enough taken care of if they are sometimes cleansed from the dust. Nor do they suffer any organs, their songs being begun and directed through their Presenters, which in some places causeth but a very rude and undisciplined sound.

They have no settled form or lithurgie, but preach and pray what

[1] Liming was the first important innovation of its kind adopted by the agricultural improvers. See T. C. Smout and A. Fenton, 'Scottish Agriculture before the Improvers – an exploration', *Agricultural History Review*, xiii (1965), pp. 62-64.

comes in their mind and as the spirit gives it, which sometimes, like water coming from a fire well, but running through bad channels, is lukewarm enough. The Lord's prayer is not used among them, and not accounted upon a minister as it is told me, having once utter'd himself in this blasphemy that if our Saviour ever was drunk in his wandring here, it was then when he made that prayer. Another said it was come from the Devil. Their Ceremonies in administrating the Sacraments are very short, as in the Baptising a child the minister stands in his chair pouring the water upon it, and praying some few words.

There is a *toleration* in the towns in Scottland, that the Episcopal people or they of the Church of England may have their *meeting-house*; but an extraordinary jealousie is betwixt them and the former, which not only cometh from the difference in the Church government, as I have heard once a Presbyterian Minister pray that God would defend them from Popery, *Prelacy* and other evils; but that the Episcopals in Scottland are commonly Torrys and Jacobites, but the other are Whigs and for the Hannoverian succession. (It is impossible to go into the questions of how the clergy have their Synodical Meetings, where all those of one Province meet together etc., and of how there is a schism between the Episcopalians here and in England, mainly concerning the right to the Crown.)

In Scottland are 900 Parishes of which some have but one, some 2 ministers. These elect some out of their members and send to the *General Assemblies* which is yearly kept the 14th day of May in Edenburgh, where they come together and elect a *Moderator* to whom they propose what they have to say, give their judgement of matrimonies, divorces, examine and create ministers, etc. The King sends allways a Commissionaire to that Assembly, who hath 1,000 pd.st. for it. *My Lord Rothes* was it this year, and his son that carryed the King's Commission before the Commissionaire, had 500 l. sterling. They sit down about a fortnight or 3 weeks. But how sometimes the Episcopals have prevailed in Scottland, as under K. Charles 2, James etc., and sometimes the Presbyterians as under Cromwell, K. William and now, that may be seen of their histories.

About the Laws, Government and Jurisdictions in Scottland see

Sir. G. Mackenzies Institutions of the Laws of Scotland.[1] As they had in former times their own King so they had their own Parliament till the Union with England and other Courts. But now in matters of *civil rights* the highest court is that of the *Lords of Session* who are 15 ordinary, and 5 extraordinary of the best nobility, who are allowed to sit to learn rather than decide. They sit at Edenburg from the 1 of June to the last of July, and the second time from the 1 of September to the last of December.

In *criminal affairs* is the *Justice Clerck* who hath 5 Lords of Session joined to him called *Commissioners of Justiciary*. They sit sometimes at Edenburg in the time of Vacance, and go sometimes about in the country at the *Curcuit Courts* as they call it.

The *Exchequer* or the *Commissioners of the Theasaury* judge what concerns the Kings Revenues.

The *Ammirality Court* judges in all maritime affairs, had before an high Admiral, but now a Vice-Admiral.

The *Inferior Courts* are first the Sheriff, one in every shire: he hath both civil and Criminal Jurisdiction.

In the Kings proper lands are *Stewards*, and in some towns and Bailliaries *Baillies*.

Justices of peace are appointed to advert to the keeping of the peace and what is relating to good neighbourhood. Such are in Edenburg and the places belonging thereto, and in the other touns. They have under them *Constables*.

The *Lord of Regality* is he who has the land whereof he is proprietor or superior, erected with a jurisdiction equal to the justices in criminal cases, and to the sheriff in civil causes, he has also right to all the moveables of delinquents and rebells who dwell within his own jurisdiction. Such a Regality must be granted in the Parliament.

Every *Heritor or Laird* may hold courts for causing his tennants pay his rents, and if he is the King's vassal or his land is erected in a Barony, he may judge such as committ Blood on his own ground.

The Dignities in Scotland are *Dukes, Marquesses, Earls* or *Counts, Viscounts, Knights Baronets* and they either hereditiary or for time of life, and *Gentlemen*. N.B. The Gentry in Scotland is commonly fine people and reckon themselves more civil to strangers then the

[1] George Mackenzie, *Institutions of the Laws of Scotland* (Edinburgh, 1684, and many subsequent editions).

English, as they likewise go more abroad. Their learning is most *in the Law*, which to study the better they go to Leyden. Them that travell farther see commonly Italy and France. Their women are civil and beautifull.

Before the Union, as I told, they had their own Parliament, consisting of 160 Peers, which were hereditary, and the Representatives of the Shires and Royal Boroughs were 155, which did not sit in two houses as in England, but in one house or Parliament.[1] But now in the Parliament of Great Britain they have only 16 Peers, all elective, and 45 Representatives, viz. 30 Barons and 15 Burgesses.

Because now this Union has made such a noise in Scottland, and so many malcontents, so it will be fit to speak a little about it. The rest may be seen in the *Memoirs concerning the Affairs of Scottland from Queen Annes accession to the Throne till the Union*, etc. whose author is a Scotsh Gentleman *Lockart of Carnwath*.[2]

It hath been observed, that since the Scots Kings accession to the English Crown (either that the Kings living still in England were not informed sufficiently about the affairs concerning the utility of Scottland, or, there being a natural jealousie betwixt the two nations, they followed more the interest of the English, who allways endeavour'd to keep the Scots low, and out of a condition to do them harm) Scottland hath been on the decaying hand, so that when at the Union of the two Crouns the Odds betwixt England and Scottland was computed but at *one to six*, at the Union of the two Kingdoms (anno 1707) it was at about *one to fifty*.[3] See the foretold book, pag. 400.

However the English not thinking themselves secure enough, so long as the Scots could withdraw themselves from going in to the

[1] Attendances in the Scottish Parliament were much smaller than Kalmeter suggests; *e.g.* in the first session of 1702, 38 peers and 81 representatives of the shires and burghs were present, and in 1706, 67 peers and 132 representatives of the shires and burghs voted on the first Article of Union. *Acts of Parliament of Scotland:* xi, pp. 3-5, 313-15.

[2] George Lockhart, *Memoirs concerning the Affairs of Scotland* (London, 1714).

[3] There was no computation at the time of the Union of Crowns of the relative wealth of England and Scotland. Before the Union of Parliaments, 'The ratio of wealth, as reflected in customs and excise revenue, was 36:1, and, as is indicated in the land-tax yield, 41:1; the overall figure is rather more than 38:1.' G. S. Pryde, *The Treaty of Union of Scotland and England 1707* (London, 1957), p. 44. But of course even this was a very imperfect measurement of the ratio between the national incomes of the two countries.

English measures, or perhaps carry on an understanding with their enemies, sought allways for an occasion to incorporate Scotland with England and so in a manner deprive them of their liberty. In K. William's time it was wrought upon, but succeeded in Q. Annes time in this manner. The Scots undertook a commerce upon, and sent Colonies to *Darien*, a country in the Isthme of America, where they built some places, as *Caledonia*, Scots Fort, etc. And as to such a business it was need for a large Fond, so a vast many people, even the servants at Edenburgh, were persuaded to contribute and give money to it, in hope to grow rich in sleeping. The English, who don't like to see Scottland too flourishing, look'd upon that improvement of Scottland as a thing disadvantageous to them; and so it was delibered in the English Parliament, first in K. Williams time, whether they should assist the Scots in that business or countermine them. And altho' some were for the first, seeing that it was a way to get in betwixt the Spannish territories, and that the trade would certainly after a time fall to the English, yet the last was resolved upon, and orders given to the Governor of Jamaica and th'other English places, not only to not assist the Scots with their ports and provisions, but to cross them as much as possible. In consequence of what, that business and trade must certainly be ruined and go to nothing, to the great loss of all them that were interested in it. That gained, the English in the beginning of Q. Annes reign proposed to the Scots that if they would consent to the Union with England, they would defray them of all their expenses and give them an *A'quivalent* for what they had spent upon *the African trade* then under this name it was called in Scottland. N.B. This Equivalent, for which England is yet indebted, is upwads of 250,000 l.[1]

[1] The Equivalent came in two parts: the first, a down payment worth nearly £400,000 sterling; the second, an 'arising equivalent' accruing from any increase in customs and excise revenue for the first seven years after union and of such part of the increase as would be used to meet payments on the English national debt thereafter. Of this, £100,000 had been paid over in specie shortly after the Union; the arising equivalent scarcely produced any funds in the short run, and the rest was met by exchequer bills and Equivalent debentures – effectively I.O.U.s created by the Government carrying 4 per cent interest. Those who held Equivalent debentures (on which no interest had in fact been paid by the state) formed themselves into an Equivalent Company in 1724. The capital of this company was then of £248,550, the exact amount of the debentures and presumably identical with the sum of £250,000 which Kalmeter says (rightly) had not been paid over. For this complicated question see H. Hamilton,

besides the debt to the sufferers of Nevis and St. Christosters which is 100,000 l.[1]

As this was a way to gain the mean sort of people, so the most part of the Nobility, Gentry and Presbyterian ministers, who one Sunday preached against and th'other for the Union, were not able to resist the power of gold plentifully bestowed upon them. And so after many debates and tumults the affair was concluded, the Union took its beginning the first day of May 1707, and the Scots Parliament joined with the English in a manner as it is say'd before, and called *the British.*

The advantage of this Union on the side of England, is that their forces are so much more powerfull and strong, joined with those of the Kingdom of Scottland, and on the side of Scottland, that as the Nobility is obliged to go up to London to search for preferrments, so the money is carried out of the country, the trade consequently diminished, and constrained by the English laws and customs, which in several cases are found not applicable to the Scots utility and incouragement of their commerce, and the Scots obliged to go in to all the wars and measures the English undertake.

The *Taxes* of the country or lands are pay'd in such a manner. Every ground, land or estate is valued for so much money as well in England as Scottland, and the Parliament of Great Britain imposes as much to be pay'd of every pound st. as their necessities require for that year, viz. 4, 3, or 2 schillings of every pound a year. Now according to one of the Articles of the Union, the[y] in England pay 6s. per pound, which is but very seldom, they give of

---

An Economic History of Scotland in the Eighteenth Century (Oxford, 1963), pp. 292, 297-9, and R. H. Campbell, 'The Anglo Scottish Union of 1707: II, The Economic Consequences', *Economic History Review*, 2nd series, xvi (1964), pp. 473-4.

[1] Parliament voted £100,000 to indemnify the sufferers of the French raid on Nevis and St Kitts in 1706 on condition that they resettled their lands devastated by the enemy. Richard Pares, *A West India Fortune* (London, 1950), p. 49. Cash, however, was not paid over for many years, but, as with the Equivalent, the Government provided debentures. There was a good deal of discussion on the topic in Parliament around 1720. *Journals of the House of Commons:* Vol. xix (1718-1721). Kalmeter must not be taken as implying that this £100,000 was owed in Scotland, though a proportion of it must have been, since some Scots were settled in Nevis and others had married heiresses of St Kitts – notably Colonel William Macdowell later of Castle Semple. See T. C. Smout, *Scottish Trade on the Eve of Union 1660-1707* (Edinburgh, 1963), pp. 98, 177. George Eyre-Todd, *History of Glasgow* (Glasgow, 1934), p. 150.

all Scottland 72,000 pd. Sterling, and that is called *a twelve months sesse.* When they in England pay 4s. of a pd. Scottland pays 48,000 pd. S. which they call *eight months sesse* because the taxe is payd in 4 termins every time for two months. 3s. per pd. in England make in Scottland 36,000 pd. 2 schill. 24,000 pd. and 1 sch. 12,000 pd. sterling.

Of that sum that Scottland is obliged to rise, *the Royal Boroughs* pay *the Sixth* part, their deputies coming yearly together and taxing every borough in a proportion as their trade and circumstances are. The citizens, that have no ground, pay for their houses, and tradesmen are taxed after their trade.

This is the ordinary revenue. As for the other, they consist in duties upon goods etc. which may be seen of the *Book of Rates.*

Before the Union the Scotts had all sorts of foreign money going amongst them, as rix-dollars of all countryes, etc. (besides that they coined their own rix-dollars or 4 marcs pieces, 2 marc pieces, 1 marc, ½ marc, 40 schilling pieces, 20s. pieces, 10 and 5 schill.) but since the Union the[y] have the same monies with England viz. Sterling, which in its fineness is this; when the finest silver after their way of reckoning hath 12 onces, which is a pound, the money and goldsmith silver hath 11 onces and 2 penny weight, and is all called Sterling. The Goldsmiths weighs their silver in deniers, whereof 12 make one once. The English goldsmiths silver is a little finer, their standard beeing rised, that they might not smelt money.

One Guinea of gold is 21 schillings.
½ Guinea ditto 10 sch. 6 pens.
1 Croun silver, 5 schil.
½ Crown, ditto, 2 sch. 6 pens.
1 Schilling, ditto, 2 sixpens or 12 pennys
1 Sixpens, ditto, 6 pennys of copper.
1 penny hath 2 halfpennys
1 halfpenny, 3 turnats.

1 pd. Sterling is 20 Schillings but is no coined money. The Scots have otherwise an other way of telling their money. A pound Scotts is 20 schillings; a schilling Scotts is 1 penny Engl. Their Halfpennys or Bawbys are lesser then the English, but go now together.

A marc Scotts is 13½ penies.

Scotland hath yet its own *Minthouse* at Edenburgh, but they have not coined much money since the Union,[1] only that the[y] re-coined all the Scotts money, tho' they may do it if they have silver; but they get the money from England and loose all the Scotts money, also the advantages a country may have from *coining*, which besides that is a sign of a nation's independance of an other. The Government maintains yet all the people (or servants) necessary for the mint, as the Governor, who is My Lord *Laderdeal*, a Master Guardian, etc., whose wages altogether is 1,200 pd. st. whereof 100 go to the reparation of the Minthouse where these people live.

The *Weights* in Scotland are as follows.

In any course (not fine) goods:
16 onces go to *one pound.*
2000 pound make a *tonne*
16 pound make a *stone.*

But in *gold and silver* and *bread and corn* they make use of the Troysh weight, whereof:

12 Onces go to one pound
20 pennyweight make one once.
24 grains make a pennyweight, which makes 480 grains an once.
16 *drops* make *likewise an once*, and 30 *grains* a *drop*, which also makes 480 grain, and consequently 5,760 grains make a pound.
17 stones and 2 pound or 274 pound make a Svedish Schippond, or as some say, 17 stones and 4 pound.

N.B. They have in Scotland 2 sorts of weights in course goods; the *Throne weight*, whereof they make use for weighing butter, woolle, etc. and hath 20 pound weight per stone. Th'other is the Amsterdamer weight, 1/5 part less, or 16 pound per stone, whereof I have spoken next before. Use is made of this weight in goods going out, as the lead oar, etc.

The Scotts yard is $\frac{1}{3}$ part longer than the *Dutch*, and since the Union equal with the English.

In counting or measuring the time they use the Old Style, which likewise is here observed, beginning the year with the first of January.

[1] No money was struck at the Edinburgh mint after the reign of Queen Anne. See Ian H. Stewart, *The Scottish Coinage* (London, 1955), pp. 120-2.

★

**I have taken some trouble to acquire knowledge about Scotland's most remarkable products; but it is seldom possible to obtain precise enough information to be able to indicate the correct quantities of what is in production at home, or of what is carried abroad. Therefore I will only mention something about each and all, as I found it myself or heard of it from others, that one may judge to some degree of the wealth and attributes of the country. (For more on this and other topics, see my second visit to Scotland.)

As I said before, the countryside in the Southern Provinces is exceedingly fertile, so that not only are the Highlands supplied from them with grain, but also a great deal is shipped out to Holland, France, Sweden, Norway, etc. As evidence of this I might mention that for the last three years about 70,000 bolls of grain a year have been sent out of Montrose, a town and port in Angus shire.[1]

Besides this they also have a great many cattle which provide the farmer with a livelihood where the land will not grow corn. And although everywhere in Scotland there is an abundance of sheep, for which the green hills and mountains give good opportunity for grazing, yet it can be said that the Highlands have most because it is their best-known product. Although their cattle are smaller than the English, yet, as they are sweeter and better flavoured, they are also in demand there, and so many are sent to England that the trade is thought to come to 40,000 pound sterling a year.[2]

(I should here note what the Dutch Gazzette stated at the beginning of the year 1720, that in the Parliament then sitting an attempt

[1] Montrose was the main corn-exporting port in the 1720s. Rosalind Mitchison, 'The Movements of Scottish Corn Prices in the Seventeenth and Eighteenth Centuries', *Economic History Review:* 2nd series, xviii (1965), p. 289.

[2] Compare this estimate of the cattle trade with the figures before the Union, when between 1697 and 1703 on average some £38,000 sterling worth of cattle were sent south, numbers varying from 60,000 to 11,000, and Clerk of Penicuik's estimate of 1733, when he supposes that £100,000 worth were exported, being 60,000 head. Kalmeter's and Clerk's figures can only be informed guesses. See 'Sir John Clerk's Observations on the present circumstances of Scotland, 1730', ed. T. C. Smout in *Miscellany of the Scottish History Society: X*, (1965), pp. 186n., 195n.

was made to show that every year coarse woollen and linen cloth worth 200,000 l. sterl. was sent out from Scotland into England, and that twice that value came back again in fine cloth and the like; this was attacked by others who said that in their opinion England was the only country from which Scotland gained a surplus in trade, the export and import being, moreover, uncertain because no customs dues are paid.[1])

The fisheries – especially the herring fishery – are also of great importance. The herring is taken not only by Dutch doggers in the North Sea but also in particular in the waters between Scotland and Ireland, where it goes under the name of 'Glascow herring'. These come in mostly in the month of June, when one may have them fresh, but it is incredible, and quite impossible to state, what quantities are salted for sale to Sweden and Norway in the months of September and October.[2]

A great quantity of salmon is also sent from Aberdeen, etc. to France, in particular (Salted cod is also sent in abundance from Scotland, and I might here mention that in the month of April a ship went from Lith to Stockholm with salted cod and malt, and returned with iron and boards: a merchant concerned informed me that for every ton of fish and malt they reckoned one skeppund of iron, which gave them a fine bargain).

Scottish salt is more widely known. It is made in several places on the Fyrth of Forth, such as Lieven, the Metthle, Deisert, Kirkcaldy, etc., in such a manner and in such quantity as will be described below.

I come now closer to my own activities, when I have occasion to speak of those of Scotland's products that are mined out of the

[1] This is a marginal note, obviously (from the date) added afterwards. The debate in question seems to have left little trace in the official records of Parliament, but was perhaps related to the petition of the London weavers to have weaving of all printed and stained linens prohibited in the interests of English silk and woollen industries, which called forth dozens of counter-petitions from Scotland asking for Scots linen to be exempted from any such sumptuary laws. See *Journals of the House of Commons:* Vol. xix (1718–1721).

[2] For the herring fisheries in the last years of the seventeenth century, see Sir Robert Sibbald 'Discourse anent the improvements may be made in Scotland for advancing the wealth of the Kingdom', N[ational] L[ibrary of] S[cotland], Adv. MS. 33.5.16, and T. C. Smout, *Scottish Trade on the Eve of Union: 1660–1707* (Edinburgh, 1963), pp. 219–24.

earth, minerals, metals and the like. First among these comes coal, which is most indispensible to Scotland, both as a fuel and as a means of working their other products. Nature has provided coal in several places where it was so much the more necessary for want of wood, as in the southern provinces: in the north of the country where little coal is found they either have timber, or are able to use peat to some extent, or can import coal from those places where it *is* found. One can, however, also judge from the small supply that there is in several places, and from the many unsuccessful attempts that have been made to discover more coal, that in time shortage might arise, especially as a few places which now yield abundance of coal should decrease their output, most of which I shall mention below under the dates when I saw them. I have heard the same opinion expressed by the Earl of Liven,[1] who on these grounds considers it so much the more essential to encourage and continue the planting of pinewoods, which they began in many places about thirty years ago.[2] The best coal is found in the province of Fyfe around Wemys and the harbour they call the Metthle, which as it lies close to the sea, enables them not only to transport the coals with little expense to the saltworks and there to make use of the smallest (which could not be sold in the country), but also to ship out a good deal to Holland, for which purpose the Dutch doggers put in here in large numbers. This coal is also reckoned to be as good as the English, if not better, since it is not so heavily impregnated with sulphur, and therefore not thought so harmful to the chest.[3]

Their 'charcoals', as they call them, are of several kinds, pine-charcoal and that of other woods all going under the same name. They also burn their coal in a slow fire for charcoals,[4] as well as their peat, which they cut out of the mosses, allow to dry, and store

[1] David, third Earl of Leven and second of Melville, b. 1660, d. 1728, commander-in-chief in Scotland in Queen Anne's reign. He was living quietly on his estates and in some financial difficulty at the time of Kalmeter's visit. William Fraser, *The Melvilles* (Edinburgh, 1890), i, pp. 302–6.

[2] M. L. Anderson, *A History of Scottish Forestry* (London, 1967), i, chapter X, traces the first attempts at re-afforestation to the seventeenth century, particularly to its closing decades.

[3] For the highly esteemed qualities of Scottish coal as domestic fuel, see J. U. Nef, *The Rise of the British Coal Industry* (London, 1932), i, pp. 118–19.

[4] In this context Kalmeter means 'coke'.

away for use. They use this charcoal in several smelting processes because it produces a fiercer and purer fire.

The planting of fir-woods, which they commenced some time ago and which has been carried out in several places, has given rise to the question as to whether this planting might not be so improved that in time they will not only be able to provide some supply of fuel, but also of the timber and boards which now they obtain mainly from Sweden and Norway. Although several gentlemen have such plantations on their estates, among which the largest is My lord Liven's 500,000 trees at Mellirn, his house in Fyfe, yet it is evidence that the trees are either small and young, or else kept only for pleasure and decoration, so that they produce only a little useful material and fuel from twigs that are cut off to assist the preservation of the trunk. In many places there are enough barren marshes and hills which could be utilised in this way, but it would be another matter to plant enough to supply all their want of fuel and materials, particularly as the old woods will very soon be felled, and when they have been destroyed the young woods will not be fully grown, since this generally takes a long time here and the trees will be thirty or more years before they come even to a very ordinary size.

The manner of planting is as follows. They take fir-cones which fall or are shaken down from the trees, and lay them out in the sun to dry, when they open of their own accord and the seeds fall out. They are then sown in a garden like other seeds,and after a year or two the young trees are transplanted to a place they have taken in for the plantation, generally leaving ¾ of an ell between each, and a fence around them. (Note the mild providence of Nature, which repaid the mountainous nature of the country and the infertility above ground with the riches below.)

I have heard several who would judge, either from the situation of Scottland, lying close to and on the same ground as England, or from their own experience, that the former must be as well provided with all the different kinds of minerals as the latter, such as sulphur, alum and the like, and even in the time of K. James I, letters patent were given for the future prospecting and working of these in England, Scotland and Ireland. However that may be, it is certain that at present no such works are undertaken or flourishing in the country. (Mineral waters or healing wells they have in several places, as at New Aberdeen and two miles from Perth,[1] which are said to be very good, and are in use every year; at Kinghorne opposite Lith is a mineral spring, etc.)

As for metals proper, it is clear that until now very little has been done in Scottland. But four or five years ago, a silver-mine was discovered at Alva (of which more below)[2]; it was fairly rich, and the work was richly rewarded, so that it then caused a great stir in the country, and awoke the desires of several who thought they had some metal on their land to try their own luck. As a result, copper veins in particular have recently been discovered at many places, as I shall mention below, with the date and place of each, and its possibilities. Time must show how these will turn out and succeed, but I cannot forbear to mention that there are few which are thought to hold any promise, and I have been told that some years ago the Scots were just as enthusiastic for discovering mines as they are now, but that after four or five years the urge was suddenly lost, either because they did not in that time make the expected profits, or because they had no encouragement from the public.[3] And for several reasons I cannot but believe that though these new attempts prove there must be metals hidden in certain places, little can be expected from them, considering the ignorance of the people in such matters, the scarcity of money in Scottland, and of fortune among people who might wish to be enterprising in this way, as well as the small encouragement that the English government gives for improving Scottland. Moreover, seeing that trade with Sweden and the Baltic has now become more secure and free, and that in England copper works are coming more and more into operation, they must find it too inconvenient to develop such works in Scotland, especially as consumption within the country is nothing, and manufactories are unknown.

In former times, iron works also appear to have been in operation

[1] *I.e.* Pitkeathly 'medicine well' near the Bridge of Earn.

[2] See p. 38 below.

[3] R. W. Cochran-Patrick, *Early Records of Mining in Scotland* (Edinburgh, 1878) (henceforth cited as Cochran-Patrick, *Early Records of Mining*), demonstrates that there were bursts of prospecting activity on several occasions in the sixteenth century, and in the period 1603-1616. There also seems to have been a revival of interest in the years just before and after 1680.

in the west of the country,[1] but to have been closed down either through fuel[2] shortages or other inconveniences, so that it is certain that there are now no ironworks in Scottland except that in the parish of Cannaby 12 miles from Carlisle, in the province of Annandale, where there is a smelting house and 4 forge-hammers built on the Duke of Booklooks land about 12 years ago, which is now run by a merchant in London named Dod, and Mr Boock.[3] But as it was too costly to transport ore by land from England, and they had no other source, they are not going so strongly, being kept going only with old iron such as horse-shoes and similar scrap, that they buy up in Holland and in the countryside around, and from which they for the most part make castings, such as ovens and the like. Their smithy work is now of little or no value. These things were told me by a man who managed the said Duke's affairs.

(There are also a few forge-hammers on the southern side of the Fyrth of Forth, where the smithy work is nevertheless slight, and only consists of sheet for the saltpans and the like, as with the forge-hammers at Dalkis.)

Consequently, Scottland has to be provided with iron from Sweden which was made very clear by the fact that in those years when trade with Sweden was prohibited[4] they all obtained Swedish iron just as before, either fetching it secretly from that country themselves, or buying it up at Königsburg.

The price for Swedish iron has recently been ½ Crown (or 30 pence) per stone, when previously it was supplied at under or a little over 20 pence.

There are two lead-works of value in Scottland, at Leadhills and at Vaunlockhead. Both shall be spoken about in their place. I have not been able to find any particular opportunity for others, except that in Angus on an estate called Glenask 20 miles from the sea there is supposed to be very good lead ore, but as an Englishman who

[1] For those at Letterewe and elsewhere see W. I. Macadam, 'Notes on the ancient iron industry of Scotland', in *Proceedings of the Society of Antiquarians of Scotland:* xxi.

[2] Swedish 'kul'.

[3] This ironworks seems to have been unrecorded before. There was no recollection of it in the *Statistical Account* (xiv, 407ff.) so it was probably relatively short-lived.

[4] Trade with Sweden was forbidden by the British Government in 1717 and 1718 when Anglo-Swedish relations deteriorated almost to the point of open war.

began work there some time ago came to grief through accidents it was then closed down and still remains quiet.[1] At an estate called Rankillor in Fyfeshire I was shown several stones that contrary to expectations were found to hold lead though only a little (about 1/16 part); but silver, which in ordinary lead ore is generally found more abundantly, was here present up to 40 or 50 ounces per ton (which, as said, is reckoned at 20000 skålpund).[2] At Leadhills, the lead does not yield above 14 ounces or less per ton. In an old English book called *The Antient Law Merchant*[3] I have found a silver-mine mentioned which was discovered in 1607 18 miles from Edenburg towards the sea, on the land of one Thomas Hamilton, that yielded 22 ounces of silver from every 100 of ore, but the author believes it was abandoned through carelessness.[4]

At Linlithquo, a place ten or twelve miles west from Edenburg, there were silvermines discovered and worked in the time of Q. Mary of Scottland, but these lay abandoned until recently, when a company began to prospect in the district again, though so far without any particular success. This company comprises Sir John Erskine,[5] who has the silvermine at Alva, his brother, Provost

[1] This was in the 1670s: shortly after Kalmeter's visit to Scotland the mine was briefly opened again, from 1724 to 1731. T. C. Smout 'Lead-mining in Scotland 1650-1850', in P. L. Payne (ed.) *Studies in Scottish Business History* (London, 1967) (henceforth cited as Smout 'Lead-mining in Scotland'), pp. 117, 119.

[2] This estate was the property of Thomas Hope of Rankeillour, for whom see p. 25. It lay three miles west of Cupar.

[3] Gerard de Malynes, *Consuetudo, vel lex mercatoria; or the ancient law merchant.* There were several editions: that in N.L.S. is dated London, 1684, but the work was written in the early seventeenth century and was a target of Thomas Mun's *Englands Treasure by Foreign Trade*, written circa 1622.

[4] This was the Hilderston mine. See S. Atkinson, *Discovery and Historie of Gold Mynes in Scotland* (Bannatyne Club, 1825), and Cochrane-Patrick *Early Records of Mining*, pp. 117-65.

[5] This is the first of several mentions of Sir John Erskine, third baronet of Alva, whom Ramsay of Ochtertyre aptly described as 'the prototype of those men of speculation who of late years have done some good and much mischief to their country without benefiting themselves or their families.' From 1715, when silver was found on his estate (see p. 38 n. 1 below) until his death in 1736 he was involved in every form of speculative mineral mining and prospecting in the country. All were unsuccessful in the long run, for though he was 'thought very learned in that matter' he 'had more wit than wisdom and more fancy than judgement or discretion'. He was also an enthusiastic Jacobite who only got his estate back after 1715 because it was believed he had valuable secrets about his silvermine to reveal to the government, a pioneer of agricultural improvement (he introduced red clover to Scotland), and a projector of a canal from the Devon to his coal mines. In 1716 he was active in the negotiations

Campbell of Edenburg, a man named Minie, and an Englishman called Peck. They have combined to prospect and work metals.[1]

In the aforesaid old book there is also reference to gold sand found in a stream on Crafford Moore, about one mile from Leadhills where the leadmines are, being 22 carats in fineness. In a mountain close by, gold was discovered in Q. Elizabeth's time, and similarly some years ago there was a German here who gathered some gold grains out of the stream when the rain washed the sand down. But I believe it must have been of very little worth, because such an 'important' thing was thus abandoned.[2] Nonetheless, the aforementioned company now has a further search in mind.[3]

What other mining is carried on in Scotland can be seen below, but I will mention here what I could ascertain in this country about Ireland – namely that out in the country 50 miles from Dublin there is supposed to be a silvermine which is not very old, but which brings in about £700 sterl. a year for its owner. At Mackielin, a little town in Downshire, there are some ironworks belonging to a Mr Hackets.**

★

Since I have spoken of the general nature and circumstances of this country, I shall now go down to some particulars, and shortly tell what in one or other place I have seen remarquable, but first give a short view of *Edinburgh*, which is the capital city of Scotland situated in Edenburg shire, and fully under the 56 degree of latitude.

---

between Charles XII and the Pretender in an effort to encourage a Swedish invasion of Scotland. The materials for a study of this extremely fascinating man exist in the Paul MSS and Erskine Murray MSS in N.L.S.; meanwhile there is the character sketch by Ramsay of Ochtertyre in A. Allardyce (ed.), *Scotland and Scotsmen in the Eighteenth Century from the Ochtertyre MSS* (Edinburgh, 1888) (henceforth referred to as *Ochtertyre MSS*) ii, pp. 110, 309-10.

[1] Of these characters, John Campbell was provost of Edinburgh on three occasions between 1715 and 1724, and Daniel Peck had been engaged on copper mining in Scotland as early as 1714. See below, p. 37.

[2] Cochrane-Patrick, *Early Records of Mining*, *passim*, contains many details of these early gold-mining adventurers of whom Bevis Bulmer is the best known. See also S. Atkinson, *Discovery and Historie of the Gold Mynes in Scotland* (Bannatyne Club, 1825).

[3] Sir John Erskine had a lease of minerals on the Shortcleugh Water (the gold stream) from the Earl of Hopetoun in 1719. N.L.S., MS 5098.

The town is very old, and as its situation upon hills and mountains and far from the sea is not very commendable in itself, so it is say'd that the many invasions of the English in antient times devasting the country hath caused the people to gather themselves together in this place, which on one side they surrounded with walls, as it is yet seen, and on th' other side was covered with a 'lock' (lake). Whereto came the excellent situation of the place to build a castle upon a rock at the west end of the town, where it now stands, commanding all the town and neighbouring country, tho' the rocks on the south side of Edenburg seem to give occasion to trouble the toun from thence, if such a case should happen. The rock where the castle standeth is high on all sides, and there is no *entree* to the castle but from the toun. The thesaurie, the crown and th'other regalia of Scotland are kept there; the malefactors and prisoners of state are there imprisoned. In the last rebellion the Jacobites in vain attempted to surprise it in night-time.

The toun is not broad, having only two streets, one all along with another, but long with the suburbs about a Scots mile, and extraordinarily populous, as there is occasion enough to, the houses being commonly 6, 7, 8 storys high, and some 10, 12 and 13.

Yet there is no doubt but there was more people before the Union of Crowns and Kingdom of Scottland and England, when the kings lived there and the Parliament. Since that time the multitude of people and consequently the trade hath very much decreased,[1] as the toun perhaps should be ruined if the Session and the other Courts that are kept there should be transported to some other place, wherewith they have threatened them sometimes.

This decreasing of trade hath made, that there is a vast number of poor people whose *gagnepain* is nothing but to sell ale and other liquors, whereof an incredible deal is drunk, the toun being filled with all sorts of tradesmen whose multitude is hindersome to themselves. I have observed that the lack of money is greatest among the Jacobites, who are strong in this town, and for that reason longed for a change of Government, expecting a better fate through it.

[1] There is no evidence that Edinburgh's population declined after the Union. George Chalmers, *Caledonia* (new edition, 1887), ii, p. 881, gives the population of the city as 30,192 in 1706 and as 47,790 in 1755, but the origin of the first figure is admittedly obscure.

At the foot of the Canongate (Via Canonicorum) in the eastern suburb is the kings palace, called the Ebbe,[1] where the Scots kings lived. It is an old, large and magnificent building, but there is now nothing to be seen except the gallery with the pictures of the kings of Scotland.

Round about this house is a small district where any man feared to be imprisoned for his debts at Edenburgh may retire and be free from his creditors attacks, but may not venture to come over that district. Such people are called (in jest) 'Ebbe Lairds'.[2] Churches are at Edenburgh about 12 or 14, in one place 3 under one roof.[3] The Parliament house at Edenburg where the Lords of Session sit down is not to be forgotten. Of the hospitals is best that of George Heriot a Gentleman, who having no heirs and being a rich man erected his house, a fine building with gardens, and his fortunes to an hospital for about 150 boys who are there taught in the Arithmetick and writing, and afterwards employed by sea or to other trades.[4] Besides that are 2 Maiden hospitals, one maintained of the Merchants, th'other of the Tradesmen.

The Magistrates at Edenburg consisteth of a Prevost (*Borgmester*) that is altered every two years, 4 Baillies and a Dean a guill who is annual too, and hath to do with the affairs of merchants, buildings etc. before this he judged of bills of exchange or money, but now it goeth to the Parliament[house]; Town Theasurer, etc. Their revenues are of the houses and other things that I can't know only that *the Plack*[5] of that is $\frac{1}{3}$ part of a penny, *of a Pinte of ale* (that is about one Swedish *kanne*) is say'd to amount to 100,000 pd. Scots a

[1] The 'Abbey' – *i.e.* Holyrood.

[2] 'The environs of the palace afford an asylum for insolvent debtors'. Hugo Arnot, *The History of Edinburgh* (Edinburgh, 1779), p. 309.

[3] That is, St Giles, divided into the High Kirk, the Old Kirk and the Tolbooth Kirk. 'The preaching in each of the churches had a character of its own and attracted different types of hearers'. J. Cameron Lees, *St Giles, Edinburgh* (Edinburgh, 1889), p. 257.

[4] Heriot's Hospital was not, as this passage implies, ever the home of George Heriot. It was not commenced until five years after his death in 1623.

[5] This was the Imposition, a duty of 2d. Scots a pint on beer or ale brewed or sold within the city (*i.e.* 1s. 5d. sterling, not 1s. 3d. sterling as Kalmeter says). It is doubtful if it really yielded £100,000 Scots a year, as tacksmen generally accepted the farm of the tax for something in the region of £60,000 Scots a year: on the other hand there were allegations it was sold too cheap. *Extracts from the Records of the Burgh of Edinburgh, 1701–1718* (Edinburgh, 1967), esp. p. xxxv.

year, or 8,333⅓ pd. Sterling, whereof may be seen the consumtion of that liquor yearly.

The Colledge in Edenburg: see Chamberlaines *the Present State of Great Britain* pag. 451.[1]

A mile from Edenburg on the east side and to the sea is *Lith*, a town and seaport, where a little water falleth in to the river of Forth, which is there 7 miles broad, and giveth also occasion to a seaport where they yearly have a good trade upon the Baltick Sea, Norway, France, Hamburg, etc. The port is not very large, but fenced with valls against the storm of the sea. The tide is there about 8 foot the nipptide, 9 and 10; and the springtide 12 and 13. In the town is to see the custom house, the storehouses of deals, iron etc. and the glassworck belonging to Mr Weihtman and Befour, where they only make bottels, which are reckoned very good and strong, and are there sold for 20 pence a dozin. They take thereto ¾ parts of woodashes, them they buy from London, ¼ of the refusals of the ashes of soap-making, and as much sand as the ashes may require. The 'seawear' (a kind of wrack or big reed thrown up by the sea) burnt, till it comes to a very hard body, and broken glass of bottels, is likewise mixed with it. This is all warmed in a furnace before they put it in the pots, where it is smelted about 10 or 12 hours before they begin to draw the glass. There is likewise a saw-mill near to the town.[2]

The 24th of April s.d. I went from Lith over the water to see the shire of Fyfe, to Kinghorne a little town and port on th'other side, and from thence to *Faulkland*, one of the Scots kings houses built of king James the vth A[nn]o.1537. It is a large building with a tower upon to see the country, which is there about very fertile. It belonged allways to the prince of Scottland, and is just situated under the two high mountains called the *low mounts of Fife*. This is 10 miles

[1] John Chamberlayne, *Magnae Britanniae notitia, or, the present state of Great Britain . . . the North part call'd Scotland* (London, 1708). In Uppsala university library there is an example of this book with a note in Kalmeter's hand. 'London in October 1723. The Author of this Book Dtor Chamberlayne died in London the 2d day of November 1723'. Sven Rydberg, *Svenska Studieresor, till England under Frihetstiden* (Uppsala and Stockholm, 1951), p. 156n.

[2] For early history of Leith glass-works (founded 1664 at the Citadel of Leith, and 1699 at North Leith) and the saw-mill (founded 1695), see W. R. Scott, *The Constitution and Finance of English, Scottish and Irish Joint Stock Companies to 1720* (Cambridge, 1911), pp. 189-90, 195.

from Kinghorne, which is 7 miles from Lith. The 25th to Rankillor, a gentlemans house 4 miles from Faulkland.[1] It is a proper and well furnish'd house, surrounded on all sides with plantings of fir, which gives a fine prospect. (This Ranquillor was very excited about some stones which were found on his ground, containing a little lead and silver.) It was built by this gentleman's father, who was Lord of Session and first begun with plantings.

The 27th, I saw My lord Livens house, Mellvin, 1 mile from thence, which is a new large and fine building[2] and hath, as I sayd before, a planting of 500,000 firs, but all young.

The 2 of May I went to Lesle, 6 miles from Rankillor. It is a very fine house with a court with a vast number of apartments, all richly furnished where amongst especially the gallery is to be seen, filled up with fine pictures and 208 foot long. The house belongeth to the Earl of Rothes and was built of his grandfather, duke and Chancellor of Scottland.[3] The Earl was now Sheriff of Fyfe, Vice Admiral of Scottland and Commissioner to the General Assembly. The gardens and plantings are fine, the latter beeing not so very large, but the oldest I have seen.

The 4th of May from Rankillor 6 miles over hills and barren places to *Kenmore*, a little town whereabout I saw the coalworks of Mr Durie and My lord Wemyss, which, with the saltpans I shall speak of father down, since I may get occasion to take another vieuw of them. The 6th I was at Wemys 4 miles from Kinghorne, a fine house with gardens and plantings[4] pleasantly situated by the sea and belonging to the Earl of Wemys together with the town of the same name and the country thereabout.

[1] The laird at the time of Kalmeter's visit was Thomas Hope, who became President of the Honourable Society of Improvers when it was founded in 1723. His interest in minerals was no doubt due to his kinship with the Earls of Hopetoun with whom he remained in close touch. J. A. Symon, *Scottish Farming Past and Present* (Edinburgh, 1959), p. 302, and MSS at Hopetoun House.

[2] Melville House was of advanced classical design and built between 1697 and 1701. J. G. Dunbar, *The Historic Architecture of Scotland* (London, 1966), p. 102.

[3] The orignal house was substantially destroyed by fire in 1763, leaving the wing containing the picture gallery (only 157 feet long according to the Ancient and Historical Monuments Commission). The remains were rebuilt in 1767. *The Royal Commission on Ancient and Historical Monuments and Constructions of Scotland, Eleventh Report . . . Fife, Kinross and Clackmannan* (H.M.S.O., 1933), p. 188.

[4] Wemyss Castle was a late medieval tower substantially altered and added to by the Earl in 1670, when the terraces and gardens were laid out. *Ibid*, p. 284.

The same day I went to Lith and Edenburg, and returned back to Lesle 7 miles from Kingthorne the 8th, and Rankillor the 9th, where I stay'd till the 12th, when I went back to Edenburg, having in the meantime seen Cooper, a country town 2 miles from Rankillor, which is the *head burgh of Fyfe*, where the Sheriff holds his court once a year. It is situated by a little water that by St. Andrews 5 miles from thence falleth into the sea.

Thus I have for this time taken a look of the shire of Fyfe, which is a very fertile and plentifull country of corn.

**On May 25th, I travelled from Edenburg to visit the lead-mines, which are the best, and indeed the only ones, in Scottland, passing first through *Edenburg – or Lothian-shire*, which is a good, level and fertile country, then through *Twedaleshire*, where the country at last begins to get more mountainous, to *Bigger*, a town where I visited a place half a mile away, which give occasion for a little mining for copper, a thing they began some few years ago, but immediately abandoned through ignorance in that matter, though it seemed to me that there were better opportunities here than in many places where I saw them prospecting in Scotland.

On May 26th, I came to *Leadhills*, the town where the mines are situated, 33 Scottish miles from Edenburg, in Craufurd Lindsay parish of *Clydsdale*: the country round about is very mountainous and infertile, apart from some grazing for sheep on the hills, and the weather, especially in wintertime, is so appalling that the snow often covers the huts where the people live.

The mines lie on the Earl of Hoptoun's land, and he operates them himself;[1] they came into the family in the time of his grand-father, who received them through marriage with the daughter of an Englishman named Founds, to whom they had belonged earlier.[2] In this earl's father's time they were thought to be rather diminished,

[1] For the history of these mines see T. C. Smout, 'Lead-mining in Scotland', pp. 103-35, and for the geology see G. V. Wilson, *Memoirs of the Geological Survey, Scotland, Special Reports on the Mineral Resources of Great Britain*, Vol. xvii, *The Lead, Zinc, Copper and Nickel Ores of Scotland* (H.M.S.O., 1921) (henceforth cited as *Special Report . . . Lead*), pp. 30-43.

[2] Thomas Foullis, a goldsmith of Edinburgh, had lead-mines in Lanarkshire from about 1578 onwards, and apparently was the first to exploit the Leadhills area systematically for lead alone. His niece became sole heiress, and married Sir James Hope in 1638. Smout, 'Lead-mining in Scotland', 104. There is no indication he was English.

but he then so improved them that the present earl came into the considerable fortune he now possesses.

I have not been able to discover how old they are, except by depending on the conjectures of the people, who put their age at about 300 years: the oldest document about them in existence is a Deed of Gift from King James V, who lived between 1530 and 1540, from which it may be seen that even then they had been worked for some time;[1] likewise, the great extent of the work that has been carried out in them serves as sufficient testimony to their antiquity.

Although there are lead veins here and there all over the district, and the land everywhere provides opportunities for prospecting, yet there are principally three being operated; the first, called the *Reckhead Veine*,[2] or the Highworcks, runs exactly north and south; it was first discovered under a rubble-heap within the town, and climbing up the mountain side, where they now follow it for about a Scottish mile with several 'levels' or tunnels, of which the deepest where they are working at present, is 45 Fathoms from the surface, a fathom being reckoned at 2 yards. The ore vein itself, which on one side has a white sparr and on the other a narrow streak of bluish clay, always runs in a horizontal position, with an overhanging fissure, sometimes wider, sometimes narrower; what is now being worked is $1\frac{1}{2}$ ells wide. Occasionally the fissure intervenes and cuts off the ore, but then the ore is certain to be found again by itself. The best and richest lead-ore comes from this working: according to people at the work, it generally yields 2/3 or $\frac{3}{4}$ parts pure lead or, in other words, about 70 per cent.

The second vein, called '*Browns Veine*', runs in the same way up from the town, between the two others, from north to south but veering a little towards the east, so that some think it joins the Reckheads Veine. It is 23 fathoms deep.

The third, which is called the *Levrickha Veine*,[3] also comes up from the north, bending first a little to the west, and then to the

[1] Cochrane-Patrick, *Early Records of Mining* records no such Deed of Gift relating to lead-mines in the area, though James V (who effectively reigned from 1528 to 1542) was clearly interested in encouraging the exploitation of gold and silver and it is quite possible such a deed once existed. As early as 1239 the monks of Newbattle had a lease of mines in Crawfurd Moor. *Ibid*, xxxiv.

[2] *I.e.* Raik Vein.

[3] *I.e.* Laverock Hall Vein.

south, which gives some men reason to think it may join the first two. The depth is now 32 fathom. This ore is the richest in silver.

Besides these, there is the *Watboth Veine*[1] which runs from east to west and cuts off the so-called Levrickha Veine. The manner of working is as follows. They follow the vein horizontally with tunnels of the same width as the vein, and sometimes as high as a man: but when the vein becomes deeper with the mountains increasing height, they sink narrow shafts down until they find the ore, and then go in again with another tunnel, and so on, one above the other; in this way it happens that some ore is left in the roof, which they try to recover in some places by breaking through the tunnels. The work is carried out either by boring, or with hammer and chisel. Every 30 or 40 fathom they drive down shafts from the surface, where the winding is done by certain workmen with handgear. The water collecting in the mines is led through the same tunnels (where one must often wade up to the knees) down to the town, where it runs to the smelting houses which otherwise have no water.

The fissure is hard for the most part, but sometimes they need timber for supporting the tunnels, and this is obtained from Annandale 12 miles away, consisting of birch and mast oak. The wood is believed to have been abundant in the past, but it is now more reduced. They agree for a certain piece of woodland at a certain price, fell it themselves,[2] and cut the timber into suitable staves or pieces as they need it: it is transported to the mines on horseback, paying 15 pence[3] for every load of eight stone.

The chips are sold to the people in the district, and the bark is used for preparing leather, for which a great deal is sent to Ireland.

Abraham Wattsson, the overseer at Vaunlockhead 1 mile from these mines, has recently paid £150 sterl. for a certain wood containing 1100 oaks as well as other young trees.

The workmen, who do not exceed one hundred in number without the breaker-boys and watch-boys, have free housing but must rest content with five or six pence a day, and carry the ore themselves to the foot of the shaft.

[1] This vein cannot now be identified.

[2] For details of such transactions see J. Gladstone, 'The Natural Woodlands of Galloway and Nithsdale', *Forestry*, xxxiv (1961), pp. 174-180.

[3] Swedish, stiver.

When the ore comes to the surface, they take the best of it, which by hammering can be made so pure that no dross remains with it, and lay it out on the mine-hills in heaps, some big and some small: from here it is sent away to Lith, the harbour one mile from Edenburg, where 2½ stivers are paid for every stone of 16 lbs. weight.[1]

In Rotterdam there is a company of merchants who, by a contract with My lord Hoptoun, ship out all this lead ore at their own risk and expence from Lith to Holland, where it is ground up very fine, and used in the manufacture of all sorts of porcelain vessels, and for that reason it is called 'Potters Ore'. My lord Hoptoun formerly had a crushing-mill at Lith,[2] but as the Dutch found it was not so useful for them, they increased their price for the ore, or in some other way procured its ruin.

The quantity of this 'Potters Ore' exported is reckoned, one year with another, at 400 tons annually, each ton containing 2000 lbs. weight. The Dutch pay 7 shillings and some stivers for every 100 lbs. Now, if the total expences are reckoned at 2 shillings and these odd stivers, which is putting them at their highest, there remain 5 shillings over as certain profit on each 100 lbs. which makes £5 sterl. per ton, and at 400 tons, £2000 sterl, although Mr Secretary Pringle who manages My lord Hoptoun's accounts and affairs, told me of 6 shillings profit on every 100 lbs weight.

The inferior ore is first of all broken up with hammers by the boys, then washed, and carried down to the smelting houses. There are three of these, of which My lord Hoptoun only uses one, finding it better to export the ore to Holland. The other two are now used by an Englishman called Mr Lothian[3] who has a contract with the Earl so that he takes two stones and My lord the third, the former meeting all expenses one with another, and supplying pure lead to

[1] The road ran via Biggar, where lead was unloaded from local carts on to those of the Leith carriers. Smout, 'Lead-mining in Scotland', p. 110.

[2] The mill – a windmill – was built in the late seventeenth-century, but not used before 1704 – when repairs to it were the cause of a lawsuit between the Earl of Hopetoun and the wright-burgesses of Edinburgh. T. Chambers, *Domestic Annals of Scotland* (Edinburgh, 1861), iii, pp. 290-1.

[3] George Lothian had come from Cumberland to carry out smelting under contract, and later obtained a concession to work part of the mine. Smout 'Lead-mining in Scotland', p. 118.

My lord. Of these two smelting houses, one is an ore-hearth where the ore is smelted, and the other is a slag-hearth where the slag which comes from the first is resmelted: but they can always be altered, and adapted to what work is required. Besides these, a refining house has recently been built to extract silver from the lead.

The foundation of the ore- or smelting-hearth is laid with stones not over one quarter high, upon which is laid the hearth, being made of iron of the thickness of two hands, and of roughly this shape:

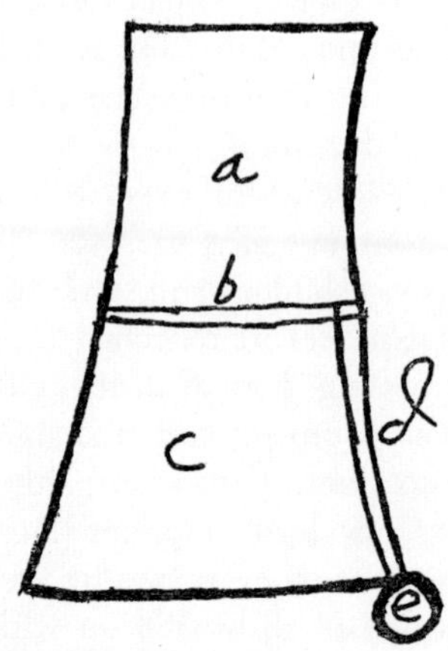

'a' is the first bed of the hearth, where the lead is extracted from the ore: it is 2 or 3 fingers deep.
'b' is a girder sloping outwards to stop the lead running out in all directions: it is 2 fingers high, over which the breast just hangs, an opening being left there of two hands (or rather six inches), where the slag is drawn off and where peat always lies to maintain the heat.
'c' is the forehearth on which the slag is collected and the peat is lain.
'd' is a narrow gutter sloping a little downwards, where the lead runs down to a pan
'e' which stands on the floor directly below and which is always warmed with peat under and inside it.

Such a hearth can be used for more than 20 years, if it is a good one, before it cracks. Behind and just above the hearth lie the so-called 'bearers', also made of iron, one over the bellows pipe and one below, for which a suitable hole is left. On the sides are the so-called 'keys', of which there are two on each side made of iron, as well as on the breast, being at the joints smeared with a mixture of clay and sand. A hearth thus constructed is about 16 inches high and long and eight inches wide – that is, over the breast: from the pipe it is ten inches deep.[1]

When the smelting begins, they first fill the hearth with peat, set fire to it, and begin to blast until the hearth is properly hot: then they put on a shovel or two of coal, and 2 or 3 shovels of that slag which was left after the last smelting. When this is smelted down and the aforementioned slag put on, they always throw 4 or 5 peats on first, and a shovel with coals, or more if they are not good, or if the ore is hard: and then they add two shovels with ore already broken and washed, as we have said, and mixed with a small quantity of lime, about one spadefull to an ordinary wheel-barrow of ore, or a little more if the ore is hard to smelt.

However, as the ore is fairly quickly smelted down in the hearth, the top gutter must be opened every now and then with a small chisel, to allow the lead to run down into the pan: and the slag, which steadily increases, must also be drawn out under the breast. When the pan is full, the impurities floating on the surface are skimmed off, and the lead is poured with an iron ladle into a long iron mould standing on one end of an iron balance which on the other end has a heavy weight of the same size as the required ingot or 'bar', which is here 6½ stones. If the ore is good, these ingots are produced at the rate of ten per shift, of which there are two in each day; the master is paid 12 pence per shift, but the servant gets 8 pence. On the bottom of the iron-mould are engraved My lord Hoptoun's arms or marks as the owner, and now Mr Lothian's also as the manufacturer of the lead.[2] The slag which has been worked is broken, washed and put into the same hearth three or four times,

[1] This resembles the small blast furnaces introduced by the Germans into sixteenth-century England, adapted for native conditions. For a description of smelting in this period see Robert T. Clough, *The Lead Smelting Mills of the Yorkshire Dales* (Leeds, 1962).

[2] Kalmeter's rough sketches of these arms have not been reproduced.

as stated, until it is obvious that no more can be extracted from it here, when it is sent on to the slag-hearth.

The slag-hearth, of which the back and bottom are made of iron but the remainder of stone, is of the same size as the former, but a little deeper, and otherwise different in that it does not have any gutter or channel, but the lead runs out underneath into a forehearth built of clay and sand, and fairly deep, on top ofwhich both the coal and the used slag lies to keep it warm: it is poured from that into an iron mould with a ladle, making here about three bars or lead ingots per shift. For this hearth they do not use the same fire as in the former, but they first burn their coal to small 'charcoals' or tinder,[1] as they call it, with which the hearth is first filled, and then 5 or 6 shovels of the broken and washed slag are added. When it gets going, they usually put on two similar shovels with tinder, and two or three with slag, and thus carry on as before, only they draw the hearth to clean it once a shift, instead of once a week [as] in the former process.

As all lead normally contains silver, and as this here is reckoned to hold between 8 and 14 ounces for every 2,000 lbs., they have therefore recently constructed a refining house to extract the silver in the following way.[2]

The crucible was made of boneash and surrounded with an iron band worked to such a size as required, and laid on two iron bars inserted in a wall some way above the ground. On one side there was a blast-furnace from which the flame of the fire fell through a hole, into the surface of the lead, and kept it all at a strong heat in order to separate the silver. The lead is first smelted in a pot or pan, and then poured with a ladle through a hole in the wall which otherwise has a cover over it, into the middle of the crucible. At the back of the wall there was a bellows which, with its blowing meanwhile made the flame work all over the lead, throwing it along so that it fell to the ground through a hole between the iron band and the beam of the test in a glitter, or, as they call it, a 'litterige',

[1] This appears to refer to coke.

[2] What follows is a description of the cupellation process, which had been known since Roman times (they also used bone ash, as described here) and which was essentially unchanged until the Pattinson process of 1833. See *A History of Technology*, ed. C. Singer, E. J. Holmyard, A. R. Hall and T. I. Williams (Oxford, 1957), ii, pp. 43-45; iv, p. 137.

which was then reduced to lead again in an oven with a slow fire.

Be that as it may, this crucible, which was the first, did not succeed because there was a hole in the base of the test through which everything ran out. Later on I met a workman in Newcastle who was a refiner here, and he told me that they obtained 9½ ounces of silver from every 2,000 lbs. of lead.

How much of this lead is sold yearly in bars is impossible to state accurately, because the ore is not equally plentiful and rich, but the lead made on the Earl's own account comes to about 20,000 stones, which make 3076 bars, or, as is often claimed, 4,000 bars. The expenses are not large, as the consumption of coal, peat and lime is slight, especially of the last, besides which they are found near by except for the coal, which must be fetched eight miles,[1] though they do not use as much as a horseload per shift, paying 8 pence for it, 3 for the coal and 5 for carriage.

One may also estimate the expense from the following: the workmen often make a contract with the Earl, undertaking to produce pure lead, for which they receive 2½ pence for every 16 lbs, but paying for no tools, coal, or the like, only giving their work in the mine and smelting houses. Alternatively they agree with the Earl to make pure lead, and to pay all their own expenses except tools: then they get 4, 5, or 6 pence for every 16 lbs pure lead at the smelting hut, depending on the richness and abundance of the ore in the place where it is being extracted. They reckon this arrangement more advantageous for them if they can get it, especially if the ore is good.

If one now reckons on lead delivered at Lith, 6 pence expenses for every 16 lbs., and these 16 lbs sold for 18 pence, although when it is sold in smaller quantities it is worth 20 pence, then the Earl makes a further £1,000 sterl, which with the former £2,000 adds up to £3,000 sterl. a year. That much one can safely reckon, seeing that here the profit is put at its lowest and the expense at its highest, quite apart from the ⅓ part which the Earl gets from the aforementioned Mr Lothian, and others who have contracts. However, as well as the above sum, one must reckon those expenses which are

[1] *I.e.* from the mines at Sanquhar in Dumfriesshire. Smout, 'Lead-mining in Scotland', p. 109.

spent on one or two servants, whereof there are four overseers, a minister of religion, and a servant in Lith who receives and dispatches the lead, and also on the maintenance of the works, all of which does not come to £2,000 sterl. a year. I ought, however, to mention that the Earl's income in cash from this work is generally estimated at between 30 and 40,000 merks Scots, which makes about £2,000 sterl.

Barely a mile from these mines, there are also leadmines at Vaunlockhead, on the Duke of Queensbury's land.[1] They are of the same type as the former, and have been worked in the same manner from old times, except that here there is no 'potters ore' sent away, and everything is in worked lead: the output amounts yearly to over 3,000 bars. (The ore is generally richer in silver than that at Leadhills.) All the lead is refined: they think their expenses well paid when they get 9 ounces of silver from each 2,000 lbs of lead, although, as we have said, they can get between 9 and 14 ounces. It is certain that the lead at these and the previous mines is the best and softest one could desire.

(The king, or 'the Crown', has nothing from these and the previous mines, nor are any customs paid on export, on account of the Deed of Gift which their owners have for them;[2] if, however, any nobler metal should come to light, it would fall to the Crown.)

These mines are run by a company of London merchants who keep an overseer there, giving the Duke 1/7th part for his land, besides the ¼ part which he has as a member of the company with them.[3]

On 11th July, I travelled from Leadhills to Hamilton, 20 miles; Hamilton is a fine little town belonging to the duke of that name, who has a beautiful house with a picture gallery, gardens and

[1] For a general account of these mines, see T. C. Smout, 'The Lead Mines at Wanlockhead', *Transactions of the Dumfriesshire and Galloway Natural History and Antiquarian Society*, xxxix (henceforth cited as 'Wanlockhead'), pp. 144–58.

[2] See *Acts of Parliament of Scotland*, xi, pp. 466, 486; *House of Lords Manuscripts, 1706–1708* (Historical Manuscripts Commission, H.M.S.O. 1921), p. 583, for these exemptions which do not, in fact, spring from a single deed of gift but from several distinct grants.

[3] This was the London (Quaker) Lead Company, formally known as the 'Governor and Company for smelting down lead with pit-coal', who held a lease at Wanlockhead from 1710 to 1775. Smout, 'Wanlockhead', pp. 148–9.

plantations there.[1] The land round about is extremely fertile. From there, 8 miles to Glascow in Clydisdaleshire, which is a very well situated and delightful place, ten miles from the sea, though the water that flows through the town enables small ships to come up with the ebb. They have a fine trade there, and send ships to the West Indies. The herring-fishing round there is important. In the town one may view the beautiful, wide street, the long bridge over the river, the Town Hall, Merchant Hall, three Sugar-houses, and the University or their College, which comprises ten professors and was founded in 1451.

On 2nd June, I travelled to *Baglier*,[2] a place in Sterlingshire 16 miles from Glascow, through a very harsh country of mountains and mosses. There I visited a prospecting that had been made for I know not what, except that there was a white sparr running into the mountain.

On 3rd June, to *Desler*,[3] a gentleman's house, and then to *Sterling*, 12 miles. The town is small and old, and there is nothing to see except the castle which was constructed by K. James V on a cliff commanding the surrounding country. It is for that reason very strong, especially as the 'passage' from the north of the country, or the highlands, to the south of the country, runs through this place. In former times the *insignia regni scotiae* were kept here. One obtains from here a beautiful view of the countryside, which is very fertile and delightful by reason of the River Forth, which here meanders about with many bends. The bridge over it is famous.

Then to Menstri, a gentleman's house, 3 miles: here on 4th June I visited three new copper prospectings which, however, seemed to me to be of little value, partly on account of the mean appearance they had in themselves, and partly because the road to it is much too difficult, leading through several hills and mountains, where one could not get up and come down without great trouble.[4]

[1] Hamilton Palace, associated with James Smith the architect who also worked on Melville House, Yester House and Dalkeith Palace (all visited and admired by Kalmeter), has been completely demolished. Dunbar, *op. cit.*, p. 102.

[2] *I.e.* Balgair, three miles east of Balfron.

[3] *I.e.* Dasher, outside Kippen. There is a farmhouse but no 'gentleman's house' there now.

[4] There are abondoned mineral trials not far from Menstrie Castle on a vein of quartz and barytes. *Special Report . . . Lead*, p. 143.

(From these mountains I saw the place Cherraymoor, where an action was fought with the rebels in 1715, succeeding no better for them than that at Glenshill in the north of the country in the year when they were forced to withdraw.)[1]

Not far distant they have also begun to work on a gentleman Manner's land on a copper-vein, but with what 'appearance' I cannot say, since I did not view it myself.

On 4th June to Blair, a small place in *Clackmanhan* or *Menteith* shire, one mile from Menstri and three miles from Ava, where I then (as well as once afterwards) visited two copper-veins newly discovered there.[2] The first, which lies close to the town and mainly to the west, is situated high up on a mountain: they went in there on account of the green sparkle and white sparr, or rock, and thus discovered a copper-vein turning towards the north-west, which they followed with a tunnel to about 4 or 5 fathoms and then once again sank 2 or 3 following the line of the ore. Although it was plentiful at first, so that they got something from it, it is now found in smaller quantities as the vein itself grows narrower. Nevertheless it was very good, yielding between 20 and 25 per cent.

Less than half a mile to the east another copper-vein was discovered about two years ago, after several searches in the mountain, although it was high up and situated below a mountain peak; they have now gone in there about 12 or 15 feet. This was the best that I saw, in respect both that the ore was very good, at least as good as the former, and that the vein, running due north both at the bottom and in the field, was $\frac{3}{4}$ of an ell wide and yielded abundance of ore. Furthermore, as a rock striking in from the east gave them occasion to go in on that side, they then found another narrow vein there:

[1] The skirmish at Glenshiel was fought on 10th June, 1719, *i.e.* the week after Kalmeter viewed the site of Sheriffmuir. This marginal note must, therefore, have been added later. Kalmeter would have had a particular interest in this, as it had originally been the intention of Charles XII to combine with Cardinal Alberoni to invade Britain and give support to the Jacobites, but Swedish policy was transformed on the death of Charles XII in December 1718 leaving the Spaniards to venture alone. They sent 307 men and two frigates to back a Jacobite rising as a feint for a major invasion of England, but the project petered out. P. Hume Brown, *History of Scotland* (Cambridge, 1911), iii, pp. 156-8.

[2] This mine and the next is not clearly described in *Special Report . . . Lead* unless the trials at Menstrie or some of the shafts associated with the Alva silver-mine refer to this. See *ibid*, pp. 143-4.

unless this was only a wedge jutting in there and distinct from the first one, it was thought from its strike towards the north-west to join the first at this point. The same tunnel was driven in 4 or 5 fathoms because of a vein revealed there, consisting of a loose greenish earth that contained copper and ran to the east.

Now, though I cannot really see what permanency can be promised from a vein strike in a field so high upon the peak of a great mountain, yet there are other opportunities that give Sir John Erskine and the aforementioned company[1] who work both these veins, the inclination to push the work: for instance, there is water flowing down between the mountains in a narrow stream that could easily be used to drive a wheel for a smelting house. Such 'burns', as they are called, are found all over Scotland between the hills, and provide water that is not otherwise over-plentiful. There is also coal within two or three Scottish miles, and also the River Forth within three miles for the transport or export of their produce.

On the same day I travelled three miles to Allowa, a little town in the same shire, which belonged formerly to the Earl of Mar, who also had a splendid house there that is now forfeited to the Crown because he was the leader in the last rebellion against King George, and had to flee the country. The house was consequently empty, and there was nothing there to see except a chair which, to show the antiquity of the family, was said to be 700 years old. But the garden is beautiful, and decorated with exquisite statues.[2] Otherwise, one may view the town, and harbour, and the adjacent saw-mill with the customs-house.[3] A quarter of a mile away K. Robert the Bruce's house is to be seen.[4]

Not far from the town are coal works, which are in full operation and of considerable extent, furnishing the country round about with coal.

On 5th June to *Alva* in Stirlingshire, two miles, to the house and

[1] See pp. 20-21 above.

[2] Alloa House, home of the Earl of Mar, was destroyed by fire in 1800. The gardens had been laid out by John, Earl of Mar, in 1706 in the French manner and had a considerable influence in Scotland. *New Statistical Account*, vii, Clackmannan, p. 17.

[3] For an account of how all these establishments in Alloa had grown out of Earl John's care for his town, see T. C. Smout, 'The Erskines of Mar and the development of Alloa, 1698-1825', *Scottish Studies*, vii (1963), pp. 59-61.

[4] *I.e.* Alloa Tower.

estate of Sir John Erskine, Knight Baronet, on whose land, half a mile from the house, lies that silvermine which recently caused so great a stir in Scottland on account of its richness. An Englishman named Peck, who came up to Scottland to look for metals in several places, had in 1714 taken the opportunity of a narrow strip of white sparr, or rock, running up right across a high mountain, to go in there prospecting, and when he had hardly come one yard, a gland of silver was discovered which was not only rich in itself but also contained pieces or lumps of solid silver which I have seen myself. However, since such mines are *regale*, they found it expedient to work so quietly that no-one heard anything in particular about it, and they smelted the best of the ore as well as they could at home in the house, in great pots or crucibles with lead, also refining it: this I heard from an Edinburgh goldsmith who said he had witnessed one such smelting when they obtained 6 or 700 ounces of silver. However, the rebellion came to Scottland in 1715 and 1716, and Sir John Erskine took part in it, so that he was later forced to retire from the country along with many others. But when he heard that he ran a risk of loosing his estate, he made a proposal to the government through his friends that if he could be granted a pardon he would reveal a rich silver mine, and this he obtained. He and his mines were afterwards left free except that he should pay the crown one tenth of the silver he could work, and certain people are sent from the mint at London to make an examination at the place.[1]

Consequently, they also began to extend the work at four places just above each other, obtaining a considerable quantity of ore of several sorts, until these gave out completely. At the time I was there nothing was to be seen of them, although the work continued and they had entered 10 or 12 fathoms with their tunnels, blasting with gunpowder where the rock was hard.

[1] This account is borne out by the Paul MSS in N.L.S., which further explains that James Hamilton, an English workman who had been employed by Sir John to refine the ore before the latter went into the rebellion (with six servants and a tenant), and had then been made overseer of the mines, made off in March 1716 with a sample of the ore which he took to London and showed to the Lord Mayor. Hamilton spoke of 433 oz. of silver refined in eight days, and of 40 tuns of ore packed in barrels and buried near the house. It is not very clear how Sir John got his estate back as the secret had already been revealed by the workman. N.L.S., MS. 5160.

Processing the ore takes place in a different manner, and as I have not yet had the opportunity to investigate it I shall only repeat what I heard from My lord Rothes, that they obtain 7 shillings from one pound of ore, which makes about 14 per cent by their reckoning: others say 5 shillings from each pound, which is 10 per cent. I must also mention what the king of England is supposed to have said when he was informed of the richness of the ore, that it was not a real vein, but merely a pocket – which also turned out to be the case.[1] Nevertheless, the aforementioned owner has begun to build a smelting and refining house where a stream comes down below the mountain.[2]

On 12th June, I travelled from Alva to Kinross-shire, 10 miles: it is among the best houses in Scotland, with beautiful plantations and gardens, and belongs to Sir Thomas Hope.[3]

On 13th June, to Rankillor in Fife, 10 miles from Kinross.

On 16th June, to Craigghall,[4] which [also] belongs to the aforementioned Sir T. Hope and has considerable plantations of timber.

On 18th June, to St Andrews, 7 miles from Rankillor in Fife, which has formerly been the seat of the Archbishops in Scotland and a great place, but can now scarcely show any signs of its past splendour. One may view the ruins of the castle there, and the walls of the beautiful cathedral church that was 7 foot longer and 2 foot wider than St Peter's church in Rome. In the Town Church may be seen a handsome epitaph over the last archbishop, Scharp, who was murdered by the Presbyterians in 1679. The harbour is nothing remarkable, as it lies open to the sea and is shallow, for there is little trade there.

The University consists of three colleges:

1. The College of St Salvator, with one principal, three professors of philosophy, one of Greek and one of humanity.

[1] Sir John Erskine, however, said 'I was drawing such sums out of the mine that I could not help looking upon the Elector of Hanover as a small man'. *Ochtertyre MSS*, ii, p. 110n.

[2] A document of 1729 refers to the Alva mines 'for silver, copper, lead and other minerals' with 'a smelting and refining house with furnaces and stamping mills'. N.L.S., MS. 5098.

[3] This of course is the great mansion built by Sir William Bruce for his own use in the years from 1686, the finest house of the finest classical architect before the Adams. Dunbar, *op. cit.*, p. 97.

[4] Another Bruce house. Dunbar, *ibid.*

2. The College of St Mary, with one principal, one professor of theology, one of oriental languages, one of ecclesiastical history.
3. The College of St Leonard, with one principal, three professors of philosophy, one of Greek, one of humanity, and also one librarian: but the library was nothing remarkable, having mainly old books, and these in no quantity.

On 23rd June I started by return journey to Edenburg from Rankillor, and travelled 14 miles to *Brunt Island:* which is a little town just opposite Edenburg on the other side of the Fyrth of Forth. It has a small but very good harbour, where the greatest ships can lie. There is a mill there worth seeing, as it is worked by seawater coming up with the tide, running into channels and then begining the mill into operation with the falling ebb.[1]

One mile away on an estate called *Newbiggin* I visited a cave or cavern on the beach, where *petrificata coneretiones nitro-calcaria* are to be found.[2]

On 24th June (Heaven be praised!) I came successfully back to Edenburg.

On 30th July I travelled again from Edenburg over the Fyrth of Forth at Lith to visit the saltworks on the other side. Although such works are found on both sides of this water I cannot mention them all, there being 85 pans in operation on the Fife side alone:[3] I will therefore only discuss those at Metthle and Liven, because they have the same character as the others, and because one may judge the manner of making salt from their differences.

[1] Tide mills were not very uncommon in England and Wales, but this appears to be the only record of such a mill in Scotland. See Rex Wailes, 'Tide Mills in England and Wales', *Transactions of the Newcomen Society*, xix, (1937-8), pp. 1-33.

[2] 'Fossils of the vegetable kind are found, but not in great abundance, at the quarries at Newbigging, and at the old sandstone quarries near the coast.' *New Statistical Account*, ix, Fife, p. 408.

[3] There is a brief but useful survey of the Scottish salt industry by Ian H. Adams, 'The Salt Industry of the Forth Basin', *Scottish Geographical Magazine*, lxxxi (1965), pp. 153-61. Kalmeter, however, gives a picture of prosperity after the Union which conflicts with the impression conveyed by Dr Adams. Kalmeter's picture is confirmed by the studies in the British salt industry by Edward Hughes, who points out that the Forth industry was much more prosperous than that of north-east England after the Union due to, and not in spite of, the English salt duties imposed after 1707. For two generations after the Union, northern England was flooded with Scottish salt which paid less than a third of the tax paid by the north-east English salters. E. Hughes, *Studies in Administration and Finance, 1558-1825* (Manchester, 1934), pp. 413ff.

After leaving Kinghorn, one goes two miles to the town of Kirckaldy, which is a good mile in length all along the shore: there are five salt pans here. One mile away is Disert, another town with a harbour (like the former) and with 8 salt pans belonging to My lord Saintclair.

From here to Easter and Wester Wemyss is two miles. In the latter is the house belonging to the earl of that name, who has 8 salt pans there. From thence two miles to the *Metthle*, which is 7 miles from Kinghorn. The Metthle, as the place is called, is a harbour where vessels put in to fetch both coal and salt. There are only a few houses there where the work-people live, and both the work and the houses belong to the aforementioned Earl of Wemyss.

About half a mile away are the coal works that also belong to the aforementioned earl, and are operated for a great distance underground in several 'levels', or wide tunnels, for which the coal gives opportunity by lying horizontally. A pump has been constructed for draining the water, drawing it up into the shaft and then leading it away through subterranean channels into the sea.

Some of these coals go for use in the country, some are shipped out, and the smallest which cannot be sold, are used in the salt pans. It is certain that coal-works like these, which are found up the whole coast round here, not only provide an opportunity to set up salt pans and work them more easily, but also yield a good trade with the Dutch doggers, besides supplying the country.

At Metthle there are 8 salt pans, and they each have a fire cistern or well filled by salt water, coming up with the flood tide through channels or watercourses: from these cisterns it is then pumped or drawn up into the channel that leads to the pan.

At Wemyss there is a windmill that draws up the water. A sieve is placed in front of the wall of the channel to prevent any impurity entering. The pan itself is 18 foot long and 9 foot wide, and is made of iron plates one ell or more long and one quarter or more broad and half an inch thick: these are fastened together with strong nails, and supported with bars to prevent their weight buckling them. The pan is 18 inches deep, and is filled with water to 15 inches. It is smeared inside with lime, which makes the first salt seem less white. The wall in which the pan is set has an opening underneath which is just as wide as the pan, exactly like the arch of a bridge.

Here they throw in the aforementioned small coals, and heat the pan with their flames. In front of that, a little space is left through which a chimney leads out the smoke, and there the men go in to throw on the coal that all lies on the sides, but casts its flames both directly under the pan and on the sides. There is a little door in front of that little space that is always shut up again, and is left open only when they wish to allow the pan to cool a little. The pan is generally cleaned and lime-washed once a month.

When the pan is thoroughly heated, the water is allowed in, so that at first it becomes very hot and begins to foam, and to cast up impurities in a thick white scum: to help this process they take a handfull of ox or cow's blood, or the white of an egg or two, and work it in with the salt until it becomes like water, and then they throw it into the channel with the water so that it flows into the pan and makes all the water in the pan foam and cast up impurities like this. When they see that it is foaming well, the scum is drawn off with a narrow board (specially made) and thrown away. As well as this they also put three or four small tubs into the pan which by themselves collect all the coarse impurities that could fall to the bottom, as well as that lime which gets loose from the pan, and this is used with clay instead of sand for building. So even if one throws a penny into the pan, one finds it again in one of these tubs.

When the water is so well boiled that salt begins to be visible on the bottom the pan is refilled, and the work thus proceeds as described until the pan has been filled four times, which takes about 36 hours in the first instance, but not so long when the pan gets warmed up. Towards the end, a weaker fire may be applied, and when all the water has been made into salt they begin to 'draw' the pan, that is, to draw all the salt together and lay it in a specially prepared place, until it is measured by the servants at the salt warehouse from which it is despatched by weight.[1]

That one may now judge something of the sale, etc., of the coal and salt at other works, there follows here an estimate of their costs and prices at *Metthle:* though it should be noted that the Earl of Wemys has a concession from the crown by which he pays smaller export dues than do the other works, and which means that

[1] It is worth comparing this account of the technology and costs of the industry with some of details given by Hughes, *ibid*, pp. 403ff., for contemporary English works.

the Dutch, Bremeners, etc., put in here in such numbers that they are compelled to wait some time for their loading.[1]

The coal is sold as follows. Sea-coal, or that which is shipped out, fetches 10½ pence for every 18 stone, which is somewhat more than a Swedish *skeppund:* beside the expense of bringing it on board. The same weight of coal (18 stone) sold within the country fetches 6d. 18 stones of small coals sold in the country fetches 4d. The same 'load' or burden (18 stone) of those small coals that go to the pans is reckoned also at 4d.

The salt-maker pays for each dozen of these loads or burdens, nine firlots and a pack of salt, which makes 518 lbs of the English weight which is used here and of which 14 lbs make a stone. Now if the saltpans at each work consume 9 dozens of these loads, the saltmaker supplies the owner each week for each pan, about 20 bolls, 2 firlots, 1 peck of salt, or more precisely 8 dozen loads of coal are reckoned for 19 bolls of salt, the ninth dozen being allowed free for firing the pan.

The salt-maker receives twopence for each boll, and pays his two workmen himself. Apart from this he has any extra salt he can make from the aforementioned coal, and a certain quantity of meal.

The price for each boll of salt when it is sold, as best as can be reckoned, is usually more or less about 3 shillings sterling, which makes £2 17s. 0d. on 19 bolls, or on 20 bolls 2 firlots 1 peck at 3 shillings per boll, £3 1s. 10¼d. But the expenses of bringing the coal up and transporting it is reckoned at 22 pence on each dozen loads, which makes 16s. 6d. on 9 dozen. Similarly the expenses for making the salt are reckoned at 16s. 6d., which together is £1 13s. 0d. Therefore the owner makes a profit each week on every 9 dozen loads of coal – £1 8s. 10¼d. N.B. A boll is 224 lbs English weight, a firlot or bushel is ¼ of that, or 56 lbs, and a peck is 14 lbs.

The customs dues, or revenue that the Crown has from the salt, which is watched over by servants appointed by it who also see that nothing goes out into the countryside untaxed, is as follows.[2]

[1] There is no reference to this in the lists of private rights kept intact at the Union. *House of Lords Manuscripts, 1706–1708* (Historical Manuscripts Commission, H.M.S.O., 1921), pp. 583–90, but this does not altogether rule out the possibility of the earl having such a concession.

[2] For details of the duties see Hughes, *op. cit.*, esp. p. 414.

The 'gross duty', as it is called, is 4s. sterl. on each boll (or 4 bushels), though with 3d. drawback when the salt is dispatched, which makes the 'neat duty' 45 pence for 4 bushels. This tax is paid by the man who buys the salt, and whenever it is sold within the country, but when it is exported it pays only 1½d. on the 4 bushels.

On 31st July I visited the salt pans at Liven, a little town half a mile from Metthle, belonging to a Mr Durie who has a fine coal-works less than a mile away with a shaft 18 fathoms deep, though the tunnels themselves strike in far and wide and are over 30 fathoms deep.

There are 6 saltpans here, only 4 now being in use. They differ from the former in that under the pans they have what are called 'branders', or iron sheets of the same length as the pans with holes in them, so that (in the same way as in a blast furnace), they hold coals burning upon them and allow the flames to play under the pan. Above the iron pan there is another pan of lead, much smaller but deeper, into which the water flows from the channel. In the wall between the iron pan and the lead pan there are some holes through which the heat of the fire under the iron pan comes to keep the water tepid in the lead pan until it is ready to be siphoned into the salt-pan.

This method with the lead pans is not held to be as good as the previous one, it being supposed that the gentle heating in the lead pan causes the finest and most volatile part of the salt to be carried away in the vapours, for which reason they try at Metthle to work with a strong fire from the start. Furthermore, the water here is not so briney as it is at Metthle because a little river of fresh water flows in here: for that reason, too, when an east wind drives the water up to Metthle it is not found to be so briney there as it is otherwise. It is also observed that salt from Liven often becomes moist and damp again when it is put into a bowl, for this is less easy to see in a large heap: but it does have this advantage from the sweet water coming in there, that it is generally whiter than the other, though not so salty by about one third. Otherwise the process is the same as the one described before.

On 1st August I returned to Edenburg.

On 7th August I visited *Prestonhall:* 6 miles from Edenburg in

Wester Lothian shire:[1] It is a very pleasant estate with plantations and corn fields around. The same day, 3 miles to *Dalkis:* where one may view the town of that name, and especially the splendid house which the Duke of Monmouth, or Brooklook in Scotland, has built there.[2] Not far away this duke has another beautiful house,[3] and the income that he receives from these and other estates in Scotland is estimated at £12,000 sterl. a year, and £5,000 in England in addition. On 8th August, 4 miles to Edenburg.

On 15th August I began to journey from Scotland to England, and travelled at first in company with my uncle to *Haddington:* a little place 12 miles from Edenburg where the only means of support and trade consists in grain, the country round being fairly fertile. The town is situated in East Lothian shire, whereof it is also what they call the 'head borough', or the place where the Sheriff holds his court.

(4 miles from Edenburg one passes a little town called Musselbruck where there is some manufacture of cloth, made here but sent to London to be dyed, an art they do not so well in Scotland.[4] 3 miles away is a place called Prestonpans where a great many of the salt works are, belonging to several different people.)

On 16th August, 3 miles to *Jester:* a beautiful house belonging to the Marquis of Tweddale,[5] and though it is not yet finished it is still worth seeing for its beautiful plantations of timber all around, and for its gardens.

On 17th August, I travelled from Haddington, and after taking leave of my uncle, went 14 miles to Kockburns peath, passing, a quarter of a mile away, the water that divides the aforesaid shire

[1] Prestonhall is in Midlothian.

[2] Dalkeith Palace, built for the Duke of Buccleuch by James Smith in 1701, and containing decorations by Grinling Gibbons. Dunbar *op. cit.*, pp. 102-3.

[3] It is not clear which house he has in mind: the Buccleuchs had other homes, but in the Border counties.

[4] The flourishing character of the Musselburgh stuffs industry in the early eighteenth century is testified to in the *Old Statistical Account*, xvi, p. 13.

[5] Yester House, started by James Smith and Alexander Macgill shortly after 1714 for the Marquess of Tweeddale, but not completed until the time of William and Robert Adam many years later. Dunbar, *op. cit.*, pp. 103-4. The plantations had been begun shortly after 1660, and must have held many fine mature trees at the time of Kalmeter's visit. Some of them are still there.

from Berwick shire or the Mers. The country round there produces grain and cattle, but lacks coal.

On 18th August, 14 miles to *Berwick*. (On the way one passes a bog seven miles long where hardly anyone lives, and the people round about burn peat for want of coal.)

*

On 16th July (1720), I returned to Edinburg, 26 miles through the provinces of the Mers of Berwick shire and Lothian, of which the former is full of mountains on that side.

During the time I stayed in Edinburgh, I travelled from time to time to visit the countryside. Thus on 17th September I went to Rankillor in Fife, where they still work in vain to discover metals, as I have mentioned before. I returned again on 19th September.

On 21st September I travelled out to the Hirsell, the house of the Earl of Home in the Mers, six miles from Kelso. On the way I visited Newbattle, the Marquiss of Lothian's house 4 miles from Edinburg; it is a very old house, but very well situated by a water, and with plantations and similar adornments. The gallery with the paintings is handsome. The skull of the learned and celebrated Buchananus is on view in the house.[1] I returned on 23rd September.

On 6th October, I accompanied Colonel MacDougall[2] who was going to London as far as Prestonpans, 6 miles from Edinburg, and on the return journey visited Pinkey, the Marquiss of Twedale's house, an old agreeable building with handsome avenues.

On 10th October, once more from Edinburg to Newton, a gentleman's house in Clydsdale, 32 miles from Edinburg.

On 11th October to Leadhills, 3 miles away, and then a further 8 miles through a wild country of mountains and mosses to Pen-

[1] What was claimed to be George Buchanan's skull was obtained from Greyfriars burial ground by John Adamson, Principal of the University of Edinburgh, 1623-1651; after his death it became the property of the University of Edinburgh and in 1890 was 'preserved in the Anatomical Museum'. P. Hume Brown, *George Buchanan* (Edinburgh, 1890), p. 354. Whether it was on loan to Newbattle Abbey in these years, or whether Newbattle had a rival skull, is not clear.

[2] He cannot be identified with certainty, but may possibly have been Col. William Macdowall who in 1727 bought the Castle Semple estate with West India money. George Eyre Todd, *History of Glasgow* (Glasgow, 1934), pp. 141, 150.

breck,[1] an estate in the shire of Ayre or Kyle where there is new work on a vein of iron ore which certainly appears good in itself, but since there is no wood at all in the district and transport is very difficult as the place lies more than 20 miles from the sea, I cannot see what they will accomplish here.

About 2 miles away I was informed they have an opportunity of lead ore.

On 12th October, I travelled from here about 10 miles to Sanchar, a 'Royal Borough', though a little place, in Nidisdale: here I was made a burgher, as earlier I had been at Edinburgh,[2] and from there I went 6 miles between dreadful mountains to Vaunlockhead, and finally to Leadhills.

On 13th October, the work at Leadhills was in the same condition as it was before, except this year the lead ore has been found in great abundance, so that the earl has built two more smelting houses, and Mr Lothian one.

On 14th October, I travelled over forbidding mountains 6 miles to Trolos,[3] an estate on the border of Clydsdale and Nidisdale, where a vein of blue clay with the fissure on one side gave good hope that lead ore would be found.

On the return journey I visited two veins which are reputed to contain lead across Lawder mountain,[4] which is supposed to be the highest in southern Scotland, and from the summit of which we had a view of all the surrounding high mountains.

On 14th October [sic] from Leadhills back to Newton, where we saw some places on the way where the aforementioned company have made prospectings for lead by a contract with My lord Hoptoun, but so far without success. On 16th October we came finally back to Edinburg again, and on the way I had the pleasure

[1] Presumably Glenbuck, where there is a pocket of haematite associated with galena and barytes in the vicinity. M. Macgregor *et al.*, *Memoirs of the Geological Survey, Scotland. Special Reports on the Mineral Resources of Great Britain, Vol. xi, The Iron Ores of Scotland* (H.M.S.O., 1920), p. 210.

[2] There is no record of a Kalmeter, or any similar name, in *Roll of Edinburgh Burgesses and Guild Brethren, 1701–1760*, ed. Charles B. Boog Watson (Scottish Record Society, 1930).

[3] This is in the same parish as Leadhills, but *Special Report . . . lead* does not refer to mineral veins in the vicinity.

[4] *I.e.* Green Lowther, 2,403 feet: it is, however, exceeded in height by Broad Law, 2,723 feet, eighteen miles to the north-east.

of seeing more mountains at one time than ever before. Since they have no corn there, their occupation consists of sheep, which are here quite small but good to eat, the hills being covered with grass where the animals go out of doors even in winter.

On 4th November I travelled out to Dryden, Mr Lockhart Carnwath's house 4 miles from Edinburgh, to visit the engine he has had installed in his coal works in the same way as that at Newcastle, to draw up water by using the smoke of warmed water, or more correctly, by making a vacuum.[1] The shaft is 30 fathoms deep.

One mile away we saw Rosslin chapel, an old church built in Catholic times with exquisite work under the roof and especially round the pillar near the altar. Immediately below lies Rosslin house, belonging to the family of that time, and in old times a place fortified by both nature and art. The tower has fallen now. It lies on the very top of a high mound, surrounded by water, and is extraordinarily pleasing. The same day, back to Edenburg.

It is practically impossible to obtain adequate information about the nature and quantity of the goods which Scotland obtains from other countries or exports of her own, because there are no such books kept in the customs house which could intimate the shipping at each harbour, and also because the trade with England cannot be judged with certainty, as no customs dues are now paid between the two countries. Nevertheless I ought to mention what I obtained regarding trade with my own fatherland from a merchant who lived in Stockholm for some years and had Scottish orders there when most Scottish trade was run to that place. The goods sent from Scotland to Sweden are as follows:

1. Herring: 6 or 700 lasts are thought to go to Sweden one year with another, and *1* of them to Stockholm.[2]

[1] This would have been a Newcomen-type engine, and only the second or third steam engine to be erected in Scotland, being preceded by one at Stevenston in Ayrshire in 1719 and possibly by one at Airth in Stirlingshire, the date of which is given as *circa* 1720. See Baron F. Duckham, 'Early applications of steam power at Scottish collieries', *Industrial Archaeology*, vi (1969), pp. 70-73. This engine has not been recorded before.

[2] The Sound Toll Register recorded 440 lasts of herring shipped from Scotland to Sweden (and paying toll at Elsinore) in 1715, and 811 lasts in 1716. In other years levels were well below this, *e.g.* only 250 lasts on average, 1719-1721. *Tabeller over Skibsfart og Varetransport gennem Øresund, 1661-1783*, ed. N. Bang and K. Korst (Copenhagen and Leipzig, 1939-1953), Bind ii.

2. Salt cod in barrels, and some dried cod or ling.
3. Some small salt, when other salt is expensive in Sweden. A little is always sent to Malmö and Carlscrona. Otherwise the greater part of the Scottish salt is disposed of at Danzig, and some at Bremen. (N.B. It is forbidden to salt herring in Scotland with Scottish salt, as it is not strong enough.)
4. Some coarse Musselborough and other stuffs. Some shalloons are also generally smuggled in.
5. Corn or malt is seldom sent to Sweden except when there is a dearth there.
6. Tobacco sometimes comes from Glascow, but not in any quantity.
7. Some Scottish linen is also regularly smuggled in.
8. It is forbidden to export wool from Scotland, but some nevertheless goes to Sweden, generally in peace time through Norway.
9. A little lead sometimes goes the same way.

The goods chiefly sent from Sweden to Scotland are as follows:
1. Iron: the quantity can be judged from the enclosed paper,[1] bearing in mind that at that time most came from Stockholm, but later on some was shipped from Norrköping and Gefle, and especially in wartime from Göteborg, which perhaps lessened the shipping from Stockholm to Scotland. Besides this, it happens that Scottish ships going to Danzig and unable to take on a full loading of clapboard and other things there are in the habit of sometimes taking on 1 or 200 or more skeppund of iron.
2. Copper sheet was then also sent from Stockholm, up to 20 or 30 skeppund for the coppersmiths, sometimes rising to 30 or 40 skeppund in kettles and brandy pans, mostly for Dundee, though not so regularly each year: the Scots are now mostly provided with these articles from England.
3. The quantity of brass wire shipped from Stockholm to Scotland in the year 1704 can also be seen in the aforementioned paper, and there is no doubt some was also sent from Norrköping to Scotland.
4. Tar and pitch was then sent more to Scotland than later, when Carolina tar came into use.
5. Boards, from Stockholm, Göteborg, Saltkullen, etc.

[1] This paper is now missing; it must have related to the year 1704 – see item 3 below.

During this time, I attended Doctor Crawfords College of Chemistry,[1] and I learned the art of gilding in Edenburg, for which see what I have gathered together elsewhere.

In Leith, I visited the soap-manufactory belonging to a Mr Douglas.[2] They take potashes and lime crushed very small, mix them together, and steep them in quantities of water in cisterns designed for the purpose for about 24 hours, until at last it comes to the required fatness and thickness in the final cistern. Then they take it out and pour it into a great lead pan where it is boiled with train-oil and tallow for about a couple of days, and then poured into firkens where it is allowed to cool, and so is ready.

By the same building, and immediately alongside, there is the sugar-house belonging to Mr Richard Morrow and partners.[3] The sugar arrives coarse, just as it is made in the Barbadoes etc., from whence it goes to Glascow, and then overland to Leith. It is refined in the following manner.[4] It is boiled with clean water in large copper pans so that it may cast up all impurities in a scum on the surface, to which end they throw in a lot of raw eggs three or four times, and when the pan starts to bubble up or over, they throw in a very little butter or tallow to calm it down again. The liquor is purified, which can happen in a couple of hours, it is poured out and boiled in another pan, and then poured into specially made clay moulds shaped like a sugarloaf, stirred round six or seven times with a special stick, and then left until it is slightly

[1] Dr James Craufurd was made the first Professor of chemistry at Edinburgh University in 1713 (and in 1719 he was given the chair of Hebrew as well). When he was appointed the chair had no endowments and 'the Counsell declared he is not to expect any sellery as professor'. No doubt he set up this establishment to keep himself alive. *Extracts from the Records of the Burgh of Edinburgh 1701–1708* (Edinburgh, 1967), p. 259; Alexander Grant, *The Story of the University of Edinburgh* (London, 1884), ii, pp. 392–3.

[2] Douglas's soap works in Leith dates from circa 1695. W. R. Scott, *The Constitution and Finance of English, Scottish and Irish Joint-Stock Companies to 1720*, iii, pp. 135–6, 195.

[3] This was the concern founded by Robert Douglas in 1677. For an account of it, see T. C. Smout, 'The Early Scottish Sugar Houses 1660–1720', *Economic History Review*, 2nd series, xiv (1961), pp. 243–4.

[4] Noel Deerr, *The History of Sugar* (London, 1950), ii, p. 464, explains that until the middle of the eighteenth century the art of refining sugar was treated as a 'mystery', and not until a French publication of 1764 was any detailed description given, though partial accounts had been made in 1637 and 1698. This gives Kalmeter's account of the practice at Leith special value.

stiff. These moulds are then put over other pots, and as there is an opening in the narrow end of the mould, a hole is made in the sugar loaf with a piece of iron to enable the syrup to run out into the pot, the sugar being covered with clay. From this syrup they distil what is called 'rum', a kind of brandy, in large pans. When the clay is dry the sugar-loaf is removed: the best part is kept for cooking sugar or coarse powder sugar: the worse is cut off and, with the aforementioned scum or with the finer syryp, is reboiled and poured into smaller moulds from which comes the best syrup that is either sold or (as said) reboiled for sugar. When the clay covering the mould is dry, it is laid on once more to precipitate all the fluid or syrup from the sugar loaf, which is left from 4 to 6 weeks until the sugar is dry, and then it is ready.

Sugar candy is made in the following way: the liquor after the first boiling is poured into a specially-made and rather large copper mould, also shaped like a sugar-loaf, in which narrow hoops like barrel-hoops are set fairly close to one another, these hoops being threaded crosswise with twine tightly wound over, on which the sugar sets, and is then much easier to break into pieces. These moulds are placed in a room to dry, there being an oven or stove which warms the room for this purpose.

Here follows a list of the principle markets in Scotland, and what their manufactures are:[1]

St Johnstown or Perth: the market there for linen, 25th July.

Dumferling: for all kinds of linen and ticking, for serge-cloths, covers, etc. 15th November.

Anderkeeding in Fife: for the same kinds, 1st August.

Dumblain in Perth shire: for all kinds of woollen fabrics, 10th October.

Kelmarnock in the shire of Ayre: for fine sarsers.

Sterling: for the same.

Landrik in Clydesdale: for woollenstuffs, 6th November.

Marybowl in the shire of Ayr: for plaidings, which are stuffs which womenfolk use for covers etc., and sarsers of all kinds, 1st August.

[1] The main interest of the following list is the large part played in the markets by woollen cloth, which quite belies the common story that the woollen industry was ruined by the Union of 1707. For a good survey of the true condition of the woollen industry at this time see C. Gulvin, 'The Scottish Woollen Industry, 1603-1914', Edinburgh University Ph.D. Thesis, 1969.

Dumfries: for woollen stuffs, plaidings and sarsers of all kinds, the first Wednesday in February.
Thornhill: for stuffs and sarsers in Nidsdale.

The wool comes most notably from Galloway, Nidsdale, Clydsdale, Annandale, Twedale, Forrest and Tevedale, the price usually ranging from 7 pounds scots, or about 11 shillings 8 pence sterl. to 4 shillings sterl., per stone, which for wool is reckoned at 20 lbs. weight. Galloway and Tevedale wool is reckoned to be the finest.**

JOURNAL OF HENRY BROWN, WOOLLEN MANUFACTURER, GALASHIELS 1828-1829

edited by C. Gulvin, PH D

★

INTRODUCTION. Henry Brown was born in 1796, being the eldest son of William Brown, a Galashiels weaver/clothier known locally as the 'Baron'. William is listed as a member of the Galashiels Weavers' Corporation in 1789[1] and he set up in the woollen trade on his own account in the Netherhaugh, Galashiels, early in the next century. His sons, Henry and James, appear to have begun their manufacturing business on these premises about 1818 and gradually expanded their operations, successfully weathering the problems of the late 1820s recounted in this document. In 1835 Henry and James Brown moved to Selkirk, where the wide haugh alongside the River Ettrick afforded a splendid site for the erection of Ettrick Mills, the first of any note in the burgh. By 1850 their factory had doubled in size, the firm having become one of the leading producers of tweeds in the country. When James Brown died in 1859 his two sons returned to Galashiels and established a successful business at Buckholm mill there. Henry carried on at Selkirk with his own sons but died within a year of his brother in 1860, his sons then carrying on business at Ettrick Mills until 1883.

The manufacture of coarse woollen cloth had been taking place in the Border village of Galashiels for centuries when this document was being written. The earliest mention of the craft extant

[1] R. Hall, *History of Galashiels* (Galashiels, 1898), p. 287.

is in a charter conveying the barony to the Crown in 1622.[1] Until the second half of the eighteenth century, however, woollen manufacturing was prosecuted only on a local basis, the weavers merely working up yarn for private individuals in the locality, a practice known as 'custom weaving'. Gradually these operations expanded as the market widened for the cloth of the district known as Galashiels Grey, an imitation of the Yorkshire Kersey cloth. Wool consumption at Galashiels then increased from a mere 722 stones (24 lbs. = 1 stone) in 1774 to 4,944 stones in 1797.[2] Gradually, too, other cloths began to supplement the manufacture of Greys, notably 'Drabs' and 'Blues', the latter using woad and, increasingly, indigo for dyestuffs, so that by giving more attention to the colour and finish of their products the Galashiels clothiers were in receipt of the bulk of the prize money offered by the Board of Trustees in Edinburgh for the manufacture of cloths, and, according to Henry Brown, had increased their wool consumption to about 14,000 stones annually by 1828.[3]

By the late 1820s, however, the traditional Galashiels cloths were under attack from several quarters. In the first place Yorkshire wool-dyed blue cloths made from fine imported wools were successfully competing with the Galashiels piece-dyed blues in both quality and price. At the same time a more fundamental fashion shift was beginning which was within a few years to displace blues of any description from their dominant position in the woollen trade. Demand was moving in the direction of novelty cloths with bolder colouring, mixed yarns and fancy patterns which later became the basis of the 'Tweed trade' in southern Scotland, affording Brown and his fellow manufacturers a degree of prosperity which they could not even dimly perceive in 1829 as they struggled to find a product that would sell profitably. Thirdly, the economic backcloth to Brown's labours in the late 1820s was the general recession which struck the British economy in those years. Wool and cloth prices fell sharply and Brown had to employ all his managerial and entrepreneurial skill to survive the crisis of 1829 in which about twenty of his fellow clothiers failed.

[1] D. Bremner, *Industries of Scotland* (Edinburgh, 1869), p. 189.

[2] R. Douglas, *General View of the Agriculture of Roxburgh and Selkirk* (Edinburgh, 1798), pp. 329-31.

[3] 29 July, 1828. Below, p. 77.

Henry Brown thus comments frequently on the problems associated with his business and the reader sees little hint of the better times to come in the 1830s. On the contrary he participates in Brown's struggle to counter competition and economic recession by improving his manufacturing techniques and enhancing the overall quality of his cloths by careful selection of wools and dyestuffs and by painstaking experimentation in the subtle arts of dyeing and finishing. The extensive passages dealing with the difficulties associated with these techniques serve to remind us of the skills required of a clothier in the woollen trade of that period, just as the passages concerning the purchase of raw materials show how reliant he was upon local agriculture on the one hand and international trade on the other.

Despite his perseverance Henry Brown was unable to deal effectively with Yorkshire competition in better quality wool-dyed blues, and he was forced ineluctably into manufacturing for the lower end of the market as the year 1829 progressed. At the beginning of the journal, in the spring of 1828, Brown was experimenting in making cloth from imported Spanish merino wool at 42s. per stone, purchased in London and dyed in-the-wool rather than in-the-piece – an obvious attempt to emulate the West Riding cloths that were competing with him in the Scottish market. At the same time Cheviot cloth was being produced from wool costing up to 16s. per stone for sale at 3s. to 4s. per yard. Prices were already falling however, and by the later months of 1829 these quality cloths had largely given place to cheap blues, duffle cloth and plaiding, the latter selling at less than 1s. per yard at times. It seems to Brown that the improved Galashiels cloths were no longer economic in the face of Yorkshire competition and that a reversal to coarse goods was the only sensible path to follow. Yet, ironically, and certainly unbeknown to Brown, the aristocratic tweed trade was to emerge from this same cheap plaiding which economic circumstances were forcing upon him in the depression of 1829.[1]

Given that Henry Brown and his brother James were shrewd and able craftsmen it is fair to ask why they could not deal more

[1] See C. Gulvin, *The Tweedmakers: A History of the Scottish Fancy Woollen Industry* (Newton Abbot, 1973), chapter 3.

effectively with the threat to Galashiels cloths posed by the manufacturers of the West Riding. The reasons Henry Brown himself offers in the journal are probably the correct ones – a lack of superior finishing, the unsuitability of local machinery for the production of fine cloth and the growing practice of breeding the local Cheviot sheep (from which he derived the bulk of his wool) for mutton rather than for wool, which led to a deterioration in the quality of the wool. The enquiry into the British wool trade which reported in 1828 revealed that Cheviot wool was no longer suited to the manufacture of superior cloth;[1] an Edinburgh wool merchant wrote in 1830 that the introduction of so many different breeds of sheep into Scotland, 'although it may have increased the carcass, has much deteriorated the quality of the wool, so that we now require to import the wool of other places, in order by mixing with our own to make our Scotch wool fit for the manufacture of cloth . . . the kind for the manufacture of cloth is deteriorated and will not now make cloth worth more than 3s. per yard'.[2]

One alternative for Henry Brown, as he himself realised, was to purchase more imported fine wool, but for the reasons mentioned earlier and due to the lack of wool-broking facilities in the Borders before the establishment of Messrs. Sanderson & Murray at Galashiels in the 1840s, this was hardly a practicable course to take. Thus he continued to purchase mainly Cheviot wool from local farmers but made it into cloth of medium and coarse quality, sorting it himself into a number of different grades depending from what part of the fleece the wool was taken. Thus rather than secure wool supplies from afar Brown, often in conjunction with another Galashiels manufacturer, travelled to various farms in the Borders and Northumberland to negotiate the purchase of his wool direct from the farmer rather than through an intermediary. A rough price would be agreed upon which would later be altered or confirmed by prices prevailing at local wool fairs.

[1] Report of the House of Lords Committe on the British Wool Trade, *Parliamentary Papers* (1828), VIII, p. 515. *Cf.* R. M. Hartwell, 'A revolution in the character and destiny of British wool', in N. B. Harte & K. G. Ponting (eds.), *Textile History and Economic History, Essays in Honour of Miss Julia de Lacy Mann* (Manchester, 1973), pp. 320–38.

[2] S[cottish] R[ecord] O[ffice]. Letter from Mr Craig, Merchant, Edinburgh, quoted in the *Report of the Special Committee of the Board of Trustees on Premiums*, 1830, p. 28.

Like many of the entrepreneurs of the industrial revolution who ushered in the age of capital through the medium of the small family firm, Henry and James Brown were men of humble social and financial status. The majority of the Galashiels clothier community to which they belonged had been weavers or dyesters serving the needs of the locality. The Galashiels Manufacturers' Corporation, first formed in 1777, and referred to in Brown's journal as the 'Clothiers Club', was an institutional expression of the need of would-be clothiers to cooperate in the purchase of manufacturing equipment, the renting of premises and the provision of power and machinery. Joint activity of this nature was still common in the 1820s, evidenced by Brown's joint purchasing of wool with other manufacturers, by the sharing of wool-preparation machinery, by the frequent occasions on which money was lent and borrowed among the clothiers and by the collection of outstanding customers' debts by one entrepreneur on behalf of another when on journeys to other parts of Scotland. The clearest example of the need to cooperate with other manufacturers in order to pursue business at this stage is shown in the way the firm of J. & H. Brown was organised, as demonstrated in the insurance valuation of 1828 set out in the journal.[1] Henry and James' father, William Brown, had set up in business in Nether Mill, Galashiels about 1804[2] but had soon linked up with James Bathgate with whom he shared buildings, water power and probably wool-preparation machinery, though each 'partner' pursued his own business. By 1828 William Brown still owned some of the property but rented it out to his sons Henry and James. Premises and manufacturing machinery were still shared with James Bathgate & Co., but the journal offers no indication that their actual businesses were combined. Indeed, when Henry Brown attempted to show the annual turnover of a number of the Galashiels clothiers he listed Bathgate quite separately to himself. Thus though the Brown brothers began business about 1818 they had had to erect only a dyehouse by 1828. Entry into this branch of the textile industry could be achieved with the minimum of capital outlay for fixed investment, while working capital could be obtained either through the local informal credit network by

[1] 13 November, 1828. Below, p. 87.

[2] SRO. Caledonian Insurance Company, Fire Book 1805, Policy No. 255.

borrowing from fellow manufacturers and friends, or more formally through local banks and their agents. These circumstances, therefore, placed woollen manufacture within the means of men of humble financial status, who, by frugal living and the regular ploughing back of profits into their businesses, could elevate themselves socially and financially. Thus Henry and James Brown were in a position to erect their own substantial premises in Selkirk by the mid-1830s.

This ready access to finance, facilitated by the inland bill of exchange and the practice of discounting, was crucial in lubricating the wheels of trade between Brown and his customers on the one side, and the wool farmers, drysalters, etc., from whom he purchased the bulk of his supplies, on the other. Credit was vital, as often several months elapsed between relatively heavy expenditure on dyestuffs and wool (Brown's own calculations reveal that wool represented at times upwards of 50% of the direct costs of production), and the receipt of the proceeds of his sales. Thus the ability to give and to take credit by means of the bill of exchange that could be discounted cheaply, was important for the preservation of liquidity in the woollen trade. When sales were dull, however, and bills matured – a combination of circumstances which presented problems of liquidity in Galashiels in 1829 – the conduct of business became more difficult and Henry Brown was forced to plan his production with great care. He and his brother survived the crisis but, as the journal shows, many did not come through unscathed largely, in Brown's view, due to mismanagement and too liberal a credit market.

The important rôle played by credit in the Border woollen trade was partly a function of the system of representation and distribution that was employed. In the 1820s the merchant wholesaler was not yet a figure of significance in the Border cloth trade, except perhaps in Glasgow. The clothier usually acted as his own representative and salesman selling direct to retailers. The Browns had a sizeable body of customers in many towns and villages of Scotland who were visited twice-yearly in the spring and autumn with the new season's cloths. These 'journeys' gave opportunity to take orders and also to collect outstanding debts from previous sales which had often taken place months before. Thus the terms and conditions upon which the woollen trade was conducted effectively tied up capital for long periods of time. The fact that credit could not be obtained on the London wool market to match that taken by his customers was probably another reason why Brown and the other Galashiels manufacturers did not more readily switch from Cheviot to imported wools.

Henry Brown's journal affords a portrait of the Galashiels woollen industry at a crucial time in its development. In many ways it was still technically primitive and organisationally rigid and clumsy, lacking the flexibility needed for new departures in products and methods of manufacture. It was still in a transitional stage between a domestically organised craft industry and one of wider commercial and technological horizons. In 1828–29, when this journal was being penned, its very survival seemed threatened, though in fact, as noted above, it was on the threshold of unprecedented prosperity. Its future lay with hard-working craftsmen such as Henry Brown, who, by a careful cultivation of the techniques of woollen manufacturing and finishing, by his technical flair,[1] and by his meticulous attention to the details of his business, fostered the creation of a woollen industry which achieved international renown for much of the remainder of the nineteenth century.

The first allusion to the Journal's existence is contained, in the editor's opinion, in David Bremner's *Industries of Scotland*[2] published in 1869. It was discovered in 1966 among the family papers of the late Brigadier E. Craig-Brown of Edinburgh and was kindly lent to the editor by his daughter Miss B. Craig-Brown, who also graciously gave permission for it to be permanently lodged at the Scottish College of Textiles, Galashiels. My thanks are also due to Dr F. Kidd, Vice-Principal of that college for guidance on some technical matters.

C. G.

[1] Henry Brown, together with William Walker, invented in 1842 one of the most popular forms of intermediate feed used on woollen carding machines, which became universally known as the 'Scotch Feed'. *Cf.* J. A. B. Mitchell, 'Brown's Patent Self-acting Feeder – the Prototype of the Scotch Feed?', *Scottish Woollen Technical College Bulletin*, No. 3, March, 1967, pp. 8-11.

[2] p. 156.

19 March 1828. Balance of £2 4s. 0d. to William Brown which settles for Rents due by us to him to Candlemas last. Lent to James Watson £2. Pd.[1]

26 March. Stock of cloths finished and finishing:

Sh[2]	8 Pieces[3]	sc nd	8 Pieces
er	14 ,,	sc	12 ,,
on	24 ,,	sec sc	16 ,,
nd	43 ,,	sec	15 ,,
nd on	14 ,,	Ditto	1 ,,
			157 Pieces

26 March. Calculation of the cost of 24 yds. of Dk. Blue Cloth from Wool at 11s. the stone:

1½st.[4] of wool	£0	16s.	6d.
Slubing[5] and oil		4s.	3d.
Spinning and Weaving		5s.	3d.
Dying and Dressing[6]		14s.	0d.
1s. 8d. yd.	£2	0s.	0d.

[1] An example of a type of entry which occurs many times throughout the journal and which, for the most part, have been edited out. It illustrates the informal credit network operating among the clothiers. Between March 1828 and December 1829 Brown lent a total of £540 to fellow manufacturers on some seventy different occasions in sums ranging from a few shillings to £40. In the same period he borrowed some £340 in this way. All debts were paid within a few weeks and no interest appears to have been charged.

[2] These symbols refer to the different grades of wool into which Brown sorted the fleeces purchased from the local farmer, except for the 'sh' grade which is Spanish merino wool. Brown explains his method of grading further below (see entry for 30 May 1828). Broadly wool from the shoulder of the sheep was the finest (the symbol 'er' may be derived from 'shoulder'); wool from the remainder of the back was second best; wool from the britch, belly and legs of the animal was the coarsest. Later a numerical method came to be adopted in the trade.

[3] A piece measured 28 yds. to 30 yds. in length. Weavers were paid by the piece. Note that this column actually totals 155 pieces.

[4] *i.e.* a stone of 24 lbs.

[5] Slubbing, to use the correct spelling, was a rough spinning process performed on a 'slubbing billy', which converted the slivers from the carding engine into a continuous length. Finer spinning then took place on the jenny or the 'mule'. Palm oil was used to make the wool easier to work. It was scoured out at a later stage of manufacture.

[6] Part of the cloth finishing sequence whereby a 'dress' finish is given to the cloth in which a gloss is imparted and the weave almost lost. It consisted of a combination of raising and singeing with a hot iron.

Calculation of the cost of 24 lbs. of Foreign wool[1] at 1s. 9d. the lb. into 24 yds. of Dk. Blue Cloth:

24 lbs. of wool	£2	2s.	0d.
Slubing and oil		10s.	0d.
Spinning and Weaving		10s.	0d.
Dying and Dressing	£1	10s.	0d.
3s. 10d. yd.	£4	12s.	0d.

Calculation of the cost of 30 yds. Dreadnought[2] from Cheviot wool at 16s. 0d. the stone (colour Drab):[3]

4 st.	£3	4s,	0d.
Slubing and oil		13s.	4d.
Spinning and Weaving		14s.	8d.
Dying and Dressing		17s.	6d.
3s. 8d. yd.	£5	9s.	6d.

27 March. Rent:	Machine House[4]	£1	0s.	0 d.
	Additional Garden		14s.	0½d.
	94 yds. Tenters[5]		11s.	9 d.
		£2	5s.	9½d.

To Frederick White Kelso for Reeds[6] 2nd Nov. last, £1 10s. 0d. Dis[coun]t 1s. 10½d.

[1] In this case Spanish merino wool (see entry for 6 May, below, p. 65). Little foreign wool was used in Galashiels at this time though it was almost totally to displace wool from local sources by 1850. As early as 1819, however, Galashiels manufacturers petitioned against a proposal to tax foreign wool imports, though they may at that time have been more concerned with any inflationary effect this might have on domestic wool: *cf.* Journal of the House of Lords, 9 Geo. IV, LX, 487. House of Lords Record Office.

[2] A densely-made coarse cloth.

[3] 'Drabs' were thick, coarse cloths of a grey/brown colour.

[4] *I.e.* a building containing the water-driven wool preparation machinery used to unravel the wool. It probably contained water-driven spinning machinery too.

[5] Tenters or Stenters comprised a large wooden rectangular frame erected in the open which was covered with small nails or hooks upon which the pieces of cloth were dried and stretched. Hence to be 'on tenterhooks'.

[6] The reed was the comb-like frame on the hand-loom through which the warp threads were passed to keep them separate so that the weft yarn could be readily woven in.

31 March. To 20 cwt. of coals[1] at 10d. To cash 16s. od. Dis[coun]t 1s. 8d.

1 April. We have been troubled for this eighteen months past with little light blue spots upon Dark Blues, after they were finished. We have had various opinions what could be the cause of them, and has never yet could detect it, we at present think it is with the webs[2] lying to-long wet, especially in that half dry, half wet state after they are first cutted; we find they stink very soon in that state; in laying out some of these today we have found two pieces No. 1341 & 1342 smelling, which we will notice if they are spotted. Refer to the 10 May.

3 April. Lent Jas. Sime & Son[3] £100: 7 Apr. pd. £20; 11 Apr. pd. £20.

It would require a sheet of Brown paper 40 In[ches] by 35 to be large enough to paper one piece.

11 April. Borr[owe]d from Jas. Watson[4] £100.

It is our opinion that neither us nor the other Manufacturers here can adopt making fine cloth dyed in the wool[5] for a good number

[1] An example of many such entries most of which have been omitted. Henry Brown's business, however, consumed about 60 tons of coal per annum at a cost of between 16s. and 19s. per ton, depending on the season. It was driven from the Lothians and used mainly for heating dye vats and drying stoves, and also possibly for domestic fires. Note that Brown had no steam engine at this time (*cf.* entries for 4 Oct. 1828, and 14 May 1829, below, pp. 82, 101).

[2] *I.e.* pieces, in this context. Brown appears to be using the term 'web' rather loosely as it usually indicates a piece length which has come straight from the loom and has received no further treatment.

[3] Another firm of Galashiels woollen manufacturers with whom Brown often co-operated in his purchases of wool.

[4] Watson is listed as a stocking yarn manufacturer in *Pigot's New Commercial Dictionary of Scotland* (1826), 657.

[5] Dyeing could be done either 'in-the-piece' or 'in-the-wool' at this time. Hank dyeing was uncommon. Brown mainly dyed 'in-the-piece', that is, after, rather than before manufacture. His cloths were usually of one solid colour so that yarns of various shades were not necessary. Dyeing 'in-the-wool' raised problems of fastness to washing because the webs were scoured and heavily milled or felted with water in the manufacturing process. Wool dyeing could also lead to uneven shading if different batches of wool were employed, leading to a lack of uniform colouring in the final product. Thus piece dyeing was safer and more appropriate for Brown's goods, though it, too, could raise problems (see entry for 21 May 1828, below, pp. 67-68).

of years yet, the state of the machinery being over coarse and Machine houses being divided[1] some will still make their cloth in the old way, these two causes with the prejudice of the Merch[an]ts to overcome will keep us back ten years at least but fine cloth has been and may still be made to a small extent, but it will be but small for a long time to come yet.

2 May. H[enry] B[rown] returned from London and Leeds being away 3 week and [one] day.

5 May. Cash taken to London	£210	0s.	0d.
Reveived from J. Blaikie there	12	0s.	0d.
	£222	0s.	0d.

Paid out for wool	£125	13s.	6d.
,, ,, ,, Indigo	70	0s.	0d.
,, ,, ,, Shawlls	5	7s.	6d.
,, ,, ,, Listing		13s.	9d.
Cash brought home	4	5s.	3d.
Expenses	16	0s.	0d.
	£222	0s.	0d.

In passing through Leeds[2] from London I realised the following information:

First – wool is dyed Blue entirely with Woad and indigo, no ashes[3] used nor boiled with redwood[4] nor cudbear.[5]

[1] *I.e.* shared with other manufacturers (see entry for 13 Nov. 1828, below, p. 87).

[2] Border woollen manufacturers felt they had much to learn from the West Riding particularly regarding finishing techniques. From the late eighteenth century the Board of Trustees for the Encouragement of Manufactures in Edinburgh gave a number of grants to clothiers to travel there with a view to improving their skill. In 1828 Brown was especially concerned about Yorkshire competition.

[3] Pearl ashes, or potassium carbonate, probably used here as an alkali in the scouring process. Indigo was a natural 'fast' dye and required no mordant to 'fix' it.

[4] Various redwood dyes were in use at this time, of which the most common was brazilwood, a 'fugitive' (non-fast) dye for reds, cheaper than cochineal but giving an inferior colour.

[5] Cudbear was a powder derived from lichens growing in Scotland. When used alone it dyed purple.

Second – the wool is put through a double scribbler twice and double carder once.[1]

Third – the weft is twined the contrary way of the warp and the weft is a little rounder than the warp and almost no twine upon it.

Fourth – they weave all wet and give two chaps with the lay.[2]

Fifth – they scoure all their raw threads with rollers which is a great improvement and Mills with soap of course.

Sixth – they raze[3] their cloth uncommonly well cutting them all dry.

Seventh – they press the most of cloth twice and sponges twice, press warmer the first time and the second time not so warm and then sponging slightly which give a neat finish.

The wool is all washed in cisterns the cloth all coolled after coming off the stenters and when they have brushed long, they cooll them again, they are very particular about this.

In press[ing] the plate is not too warm but they follow the press down 5 hours after it is set in, this ought to be particularly attended too and in fact so ought every manuf[actur]er. The manner in which they put in finish is by rolling upon a roller befor they are tentered and boils them, some a few hours other a day if the colour will stand it, blacks are all boilled befor they are dyed and it [is] said the effects of the boilling never leaves them. This reckoned a great improvement in finishing. The cloths are sponged all with steam. Dreadnoughts are all razed with teasles and well dry[?] beated.

[1] Scribbling was a rough preparatory process designed to unravel the wool by passing it between teethed rollers moving in opposite directions at different speeds. Carding took place on a similar machine (or increasingly on a different set of rollers on the same machine), with finer teeth which produced a roving suitable for slubbing see p. 117, n. 1, and p. 60, n. 5.

[2] The lay was the wooden batten with which the hand-loom weaver bear a course of weft yarn up against the previous course. The harder or more often this was done the denser the cloth tended to be. 'Chap' is old Scots for 'knock' or 'strike'.

[3] Raising made an important contribution to the finished appearance and handle of the cloth. Brown used teazels, *i.e.* the head of the thistle *Dipsacus fullonum*, rather than wires to raise the 'nap' of the cloth. The teazels were skilfully arranged either on a hand-held frame or on a circular gig which was then revolved while in contact with the fabric. If performed on dry cloth a pronounced pile was created very suitable for overcoatings; if done wet a smoother, 'dress' finish was obtained. Galashiels cloths at this time were probably not too finely dressed so that the cutting back of the raised pile was not done repeatedly as in the West of England trade.

Bottle greens are now dyed yellow first and then dyed Blue to such time as the shade pleases.

What they call true olives is dyed Light Blue first and if the fustic[1] is very good ½ lb. to the 1 lb. of wool, if middling 1 lb. of fustic to the pound of wool and one pound of Logwood[2] and about ½ lb. of copperas[3] to the 16 lbs. of wool.

Black are best dyed with hard water, they do not through so much as with soft water. No soap is used to clean blacks, all fullers earth.

6 May. The quantity of wool Bought at London:—

980 lb of Spainish at 1s. 6d.
283 ,, 10d.
432 German at 2s. 3d.

1695 net cash 5 per cent Di[scoun]t the expense of bringing home lost us this 5 per cent.

The six Spainish Sheet[s][4] should run about 8 lb. the sheet more which will be 48 lb. more of the 1s. 6d. and 10d. spainish.

10 May. Our ideas anent the causes of the light blue spotes upon our Dk. blues of the 1st April have failed and we now mean to boil them with bran[5] befor dying them in the thick state.

11 May. Bought from J. & R. Henderson at London in April last:

1 Chest E[ast] I[ndia] Indigo 221 lbs. at 5s. 4d.
1 ,, ,, ,, ,, 326 lbs. at 3s. 4d.

the first chest net cash, the other 4 Months Credit. Amount of Both Chests £113 5s. 4d.

13 May. The blue vats in Leeds is 7 feet broad by 7 feet deep. They

[1] A fast dye for producing yellow derived from a tropical American tree (*Chlorophora tinctoria*).

[2] Also derived from a tropical American tree (*Haematoxylon campechianum*) found mainly in the West Indies, and used for dark reds and blacks.

[3] A mordant made on an extensive scale from iron pyrites at Newcastle-on-Tyne. It was also used as a method of dyeing yellow.

[4] *i.e.* tarpaulins which contained the wool

[5] Used in the scouring process to soften the water.

are set with 7 cwt. of Woad and from 40 to 60 lbs. of Indigo according to quality.[1] Works out the vat in from 6 to 10 weeks.

There is 350 pieces of cloth put down in our book as finished since wool-time say 1 Augt. 1827.

14 May. We have 107 pieces in our shelves for by; 32 pieces ready to press.

Drawn from Geo. Craig[2] at 3 months payable at his house

	£100	0s.	0d.
Stamp and Discount	1	11s.	7d.
	£ 98	8s.	5d.

List of the different kinds of cloth that is finished and finishing:

Sec	4	p[iece]s	Black Gray
Sec	7	,,	Drabs
Sec	4	,,	L. Blues
Sec sc	3	,,	D. Blue
Sec sc	1	,,	Drab Dreadnought
Sc	9	,,	D. Blue
Sc	2	,,	L. Blue
Sc	4	,,	Drab Wool Dyed
Sc nd	16	,,	D. Blue
nd	16	,,	D. Blue p[ie]ce dyed
nd	15	,,	D. Blue wool Dyed
nd	11	,,	Drabs wool dyed
nd	4	,,	Black Mixture
nd	4	,,	Blue Mixture
nd on	12	,,	D. Blue pc Dyed
nd on	13	,,	D. Blue wool Dyed
on	29	,,	D. Blue wool Dyed

[1] Indigo here seems to be used to strengthen the colour obtained from the woad but gradually indigo came to replace woad in the dyeing of blues largely because much less of it was required to obtain a given colour. Four pounds of indigo gave as much dye as two hundred pounds of woad (*cf.* S. Fairlie, 'Dyestuffs in the Eighteenth Century', *Economic History Review*, 2nd Series, xvii (1965), 491.

[2] In 1825 George Craig is described as the agent of the Leith Banking Co. in Galashiels (*Pigot's New Commercial Dictionary of Scotland*, 657), but some of the entries in the journal suggest that he may also have lent money on his own account. He was also a Writer. Notice the low rate of discount at around 1½%.

on	2	,,	Drab wool Dyed
er	1	,,	D. Blue pc Dyed
er	12	,,	D. Blue wool Dyed
er	5	,,	Drab wool Dyed
er	3	,,	Olive pc Dyed
ra	4	,,	Drab Wool Dyed
raa	2	,,	D. Blue pc Dyed
sh	2	,,	D. Blue pc Dyed
	185	,,	in all

16 May. We have now given the cheviot wool a fair trial by dying it in the wool, Dk. Blue Cloths as low as 2s. 3d., 2s. 6d., 2s. 9d. and 3s. per yd. and finds that it makes the Cloth coarser like and does not Mill so firm as piece dying; reasons may be expected to be given why they look coarser and does not mill so firm this is not so easily done but it *is the case* and we therefore disaprove of wool Dying for cloth at or below 3s. od. per yd., that is, Blues.

19 May. The way the English Manufacturers account for wool Dyed cloths not appearing so fine as piece Dyed ones of the same wool, is that dying it in the wool makes it lose the natural sap and soft feel that wool has off the sheep back, and of course that natural sap makes it work better than any other thing ever found out yet.

We have proven without a doubt this day that Blue wool when first taken out of the vat if it is not allowed to get the air imediately a great part of it losses the colour and almost grows white therefore the utmost care ought to be taken to shake and rug the wool well down so as to get the air as freely as possible and it can not be too carefully done nor too soon after it comes out of the vat.

A new sole was put to our press this spring and as they generally decay in a few years by laying in the earth, we have for the purpose of an experiment kept the earth from this one by building and keeping it loos[e] to see if it will last any longer.

21 May. In every thing we do we are apt to err, and in Dying

Blue we ought to avoid the following, not to have the vat too weak, not to put too much wool in at a time, and not neglect shakin the wool well up immediately when it is taken out of the vat. Our vat is four feet wide by six feet deep and when we set it last (two weeks since) with 3½ cwt. of woad and 16 lbs. of indigo, we dye 30 lbs. of clean Spainish wool in it at a time which is quite sufficient; it is necessary too to die to a shade, that is have a small quantity of wool the same shade you wish the wool that you are dying to have.

24 May. The following are a few remarks on our journey to London last month which was principally to *see* if foreign wool could be bought there to enable us to make cloth as low as it has comed from England this last two years past, which has had a great tendency to cut up our trade, as the whole Manufacturers of this town has felt. We cannot well tell how the wool may turn out into cloth but it looks better than anything we have ever had to make our cloth to match the English.

Having only £200 with me to buy wool and Indigo it was doubtful whether the journey would pay the expenses, but the following statement will show:

Rate of J. Blaikie's profit on the wool 1,743 lbs.

	£28	9s.	10d.
547 lbs. of Indigo at 8d.	18	4s.	8d.
	46	14s.	6d.
Amount of expences	16	0s.	0d.
	£30	14s.	6d.

The Indigo looks well and the chest at 3s. 4d. looks better than what Geo. Paterson has bought at the same time at 6s. 2d. from the Downies Glasgow.

26 May. Marsh and Southey[1] were the most recommended. Marsh was the man we bo[ugh]t from and found him honourable and a real business man.

[1] London wool-brokers. John Marsh was situated at 9 King's Arms Yard, Coleman Street.

28 May. It would appear that when the woad is not properly pitched, or gets into the liquor, that it adheres to the wool and prevents the die from getting hold of it, this is proven by our present experience of dying Blue, as we have had it unequal and it was always the small pickels that was claped[1] that was lighter than the rest.

29 May. The coarsest Spainish must be striped thus: white, blue, white, blue, white, blue, Common Yellow. Next kind, White, Blue, Yellow, Blue, White, Blue, C[ommon] Y[ellow]. Next Kind, Yellow, Blue, Yellow, Blue, Yellow, Blue, C. Yellow. Next Kind, Yellow, Blue, White, Blue, Yellow, Blue, C. Yellow. To be equal proportions of yellow and white one In[ch] each but the blue which must be the same yarn as the weft of the piece and 1½ In[ch] ea[ch]. The yellow and white of these stripes was of Mowhair[2] which was got from England and looked very well.

30 May. Calculation of the cost of 24 yds. of Dk. Blue Cloth from this country Cheviot wool valuing it at 10s. the St[one] from which we value our different kinds at 14s. for on; nd on 13s., nd 12s., sc nd 11s., sc 10s., sec sc 9s., and sec 8s. Value of Indigo 6s.

on			
Slubing and oil	£0	7s.	3d.
Spinning and Weaving		8s.	3d.
Dying and Dressing	1	0s.	0d.
	1	15s.	6d.
1½ Stone of wool at 14s.	1	1s.	0d.
	2	16s.	6d.
25 per cent		14s.	0d.
	£3	10s.	6d.

24 yd. at 2s. 11d. [is] £3 10s. 0d.

[1] Old Scots for 'pressed down' or 'flattened', thus preventing the proper penetration of the dye.

[2] The fine white hair of the Angora goat.

nd on

Slubing and oil	£0	7s.	3d.
Spinning and Weaving		6s.	7d.
Dying and Dressing		18s.	0d.
	1	11s.	10d.
1½St. of wool at 13s.		19s.	6d.
	2	11s.	4d.
25 per cent		13s.	0d.
	£3	4s.	4d.

24 yds. at 2s. 8d. [is] £3 4s. 0d.

sec

Slubing and oil	£0	5s.	9d.
Spinning and Weaving		4s.	9d.
Dying and Dressing		11s.	0d.
	1	1s.	6d.
1½ St. of wool at 8s.		12s.	0d.
	1	13s.	6d.
25 per cent		8s.	0d.
	£2	1s.	6d.

24 yds. at 20¾d. [is] £2 1s. 6d.

The 25 per cent put on is:

10 per cent for profit
7½ ,, ,, ,, dis[coun]t
2½ ,, ,, ,, travelling expenses
5 ,, ,, ,, losses and unaccountables

Prices will be as near as possible:

sec		22d.	per	yd.	hips
sec sc	2s.	0d.	,,	,,	hip warp and next hip weft
sc	2s.	2d.	,,	,,	next hip
sc nd	2s.	4d.	,,	,,	D[itt]o and second weft
nd	2s.	6d.	,,	,,	second
nd on	2s.	8d.	,,	,,	D[itt]o and commonfine weft
on	3s.	0d.	,,	,,	commonfine

It is not worth while making finer Cloths than 3s. out of cheviot[1] while it remains about the present price and foreign wool as low. Coarse light Blues, Grays and Drabs may be valued at 2d. per yd. less than the above Dark Blues.

sec mark is hips; Sec sc is hip warp and next hip weft; sc next the hip; nd second; on commonfine. All piece Dyed Dark Blues.

In brushing our Cloths firm upon rollers and boilling them which is done before they are tentered to cool, we find to be a great improvement in laying down the wool and making the cloth firmer. We was the first to adopt this plan here nearly twelve month ago and no one of our manufacturers has as yet followed our example.

31 May. In tentering some of our cheviot commonfine wool dyed Dark Blues we still find them to look a great deal coarser than the piece dyed ones; they like wise cost 3d. to 4d. the yd. more than the piece dyed ones and does not look so well either when finished.

5 June. In case John Aimers[2] charge us to much for putting on a new sole on our press Wm. Roberts told us this day that he got top sides and sole, that is all the press but the nail, done for £5 10s. 0d. by Wm. Aimers.

6 June. Received from W. Brockie, Selkirk as balance of acct. £4 13s. 6d. of Turnbull & Brockies.

To John Blaikie 3s. for the commission and postage for the £12 got at London.

11 June. To Wm. Johnstone:

6½ yds. mixture at 2s. 3d.	£0	14s.	7½d.
2¼ „ D. Blue at 2s. 6d.		5s.	7½d.
3½ „ „ at 5s. 0d.		17s.	6 d.
	£1	17s.	9 d.[3]

[1] See above, p. 56 for a discussion of the falling quality of Cheviot wool.

[2] Aimers was a local millwright.

[3] The smallness of this order suggests this is a survival of 'custom work' performed for individuals in the district.

14 June. To J. & W. Cochrane for our share of a Bill for Highland Wool.[1]

	£5 18s. 0d.
On the 11th	1 0s. 0d.
	£6 18s. 0d.

16 June. To Thos. Sanderson for J[ames] B[rown], £1. Settled by a pair of boots to JB.

17 June. Price of Cheviot laid[2] wool for this last ten years:

In 1818 from	32s.	to 36s. 6d. per St. of 24 lbs.
1819	22s. 6d.	to 27s.
1820	17s.	to 23s.
1821	17s.	to 21s.
1822	15s.	to 22s.
1823	10s.	to 18s.
1824	12s.	to 19s.
1825	19s.	to 24s.
1826	10s.	to 15s.
1827	11s.	to 13s.[3]

Galawater etc. – Cheviot hills.

Price of Dk. Blue Cloth made from cheviot wool for this last ten years:

[1] According to this journal it was common for manufacturers to combine in the purchase of a farmer's clip, their businesses being too small to take it all or their requirements more diverse. This batch of wool was probably purchased at Inverness fair.

[2] 'Laid' wool had been smeared by the farmer with a mixture of tar and butter being an ancient practice designed to protect the sheep from damp and vermin. The recipe used locally is described in the entry for 7 Oct. 1828, below, p. 83. The process was sometimes called 'salving' and firms existed who specialised in the manufacture of salves designed to improve the quality of the wool, *cf.* the advertisement of Wm. Taylor & Co., Leith, in *Kelso Mail*, 5 Oct. 1829.

[3] These prices accord well with those given by Lord Napier of Ettrick Forest to the Committee on the British Wool Trade in 1828, *Parliamentary Papers* (1828), VIII, 515. Cheviot wool had reached a peak of 42s. per stone (24 lbs.) in 1810. The falling prices here, indicate a return to peace time supply conditions for foreign wool, a change in the structure of demand for Cheviot goods together with a general economic recession in the later 1820s.

In 1818 from	6s. 6d. to	3s. 6d. per yd.	
1819	5s. 6d. to	2s. 6d.	
1820	5s. 6d. to	2s. 10d.	
1821	5s. 6d. to	2s. 8d.	
1822	5s. 6d. to	2s. 6d.	
1823	4s. 9d. to	2s. 6d.	
1824	4s. 6d. to	2s. 4d.	
1825	5s. 0d. to	3s. 0d.	
1826	4s. 4d. to	2s. 3d.	
1827	4s. 0d. to	2s. 0d.	

Although these are about the highest and lowest prices it is not a very correct statem[ent].

21 June. I am persuaded that it is nothing else that caused the Light Blue spots upon our piece Dyed Dk. Blues than that they were not thoroughly wet before put in the vat to dye off after they are thick.

23 June. The report of Inverness market is that the laid Cheviot wool is selling at from 9s. to 10s. 6d. per St. of 24 lbs. which is from 2s. to 2s. 6d. the stone lower than last year.

24 June. From Henry Balintine for a balance of Indigo, £1 4s. 6d.
From Arch. Eliot 2 Dozen of deals 7 In[ches] Broad.
To Wm. Brown 15s. 8½d. which settles for Balance of Rent due at Whitsunday last.

26 June. We have one hundred and sixteen pieces lying finished in our shelves this day.

27 June. The clothiers here are generally complaining of their trade being worse at present than at any former period of their recolection; with us the demand is limited and the prices was never lower nor profits smaller.

28 June. For expenses at North journey[1] £4.

[1] For methods of distribution and selling in the Galashiels woollen trade see above, pp. 58-59.

7 July. Cash from journey	£132	2s.	od.	
D. McNie's Bill	76	11s.	od.	
P. Douglas ,,	24	os.	od.	
	232	13s.	od.	
Discount of Bills	1	15s.	3d.	
	£230	17s.	9d.	

From James Bathgate for carriage of press paper, 5s. od.

10 July. Drawn from Geo. Craig along with James Sime & Sons at 4 mos.

at 4 mos.	£140	os.	o d.
J. S. & S. Share	80	os.	o d.
Our share	60	os.	o d.
Discount and Stamp of our share	1	3s.	1½d.
	£ 58	16s.	10½d.

To Mr Simon Dodd:

Jas. Sime paid	for wool	£171	16s.	od.
,, ,, ,,	for butter	2	3s.	od.
J. & H. Brown	for wool	171	16s.	od.
,,	for butter	8	12s.	od.
		£354	7s.	od.

To expenses at Rink[1] 17s. od.

18 July. To expenses at [St] Boswells fair, 5s. od.

22 July. We undertook to make John McIntyre of Glasgow on the 1st of this month 60 pieces of Light Blue to be ready to send off yesterday which we accomplished and 4 p[iece]s additional, and as this is an undertaking greatly above what we are accustomed with we shall note down how we managed it; as we was working wool Dyed Blue upon our own machines we could not do a pound of it, but got about 42 Stone done at Robt. Sanderson's, 40 at Wm. Thomson's and 12 at Richd. Lees'[2]. We had 8 spiners and

[1] Rink is situated just south of Galashiels at the confluence of the River Tweed and Galawater. It was the site of the Galashiels wool fair.

[2] These men were other Galashiels clothiers who took work on commission when they had spare capacity at their mills.

2 dozen of weavers all upon them which finished that part very well.

The only errors we comitted were in not having the vat in good order when we began to die them and in not imploying another hand or two to help getting them milled, died and finished; we was particularly favoured with the weather as the rain came just in time to give us water for the Walkmill,[1] and the drought as favourable, the weavers and spiners being so plenty at the time in the twon[sic] helped us well; had these been as well imployed as usual it is most likely we could not have done them.

23 July. At St Boswell's fair there was little wool sold, laid chaviot from 9s. 0d. to 11s. 6d. per Stone, white unlaid from 16s. to 18s. Long white from 20s. to 24s.

23 July. Cloths on hand finishing and finished:

sec	5 p[iece]s	Drab
sc	2	Drab
sc nd	5	Dark Blue
nd	10	,, ,,
nd	2	Black Gray
nd	2	Blue Gray
nd	10	Drabs
nd	16	Wool Dyed Dk. Blues
nd on	12	,, ,, ,, ,,
nd on	7	D. Blue Piece Dyed
on	21	Wool Dyed Dk. Blue
on	2	Drabs
on	2	Olives
er	8	Dk. Blue wool dyed
er	2	,, ,, piece ,,
er	1	Drab
na	4	Drab
na	3	D. Blue piece Dyed
sh	1	D. Blue ,, ,,
sh	43	D. Blue Wool Dyed
	158	

[1] Or Fulling Mill where the cloth was felted to make it weather resistant.

24 July. Since the beginning of the year 1826 the Cloth Manufacturing with us has been miserably bad, and instead of making anything by it we have been lossing every day, which may be accounted for as follows: in 1823 and 1824 trade was very good and continued so in 1825, for in that year wool rose 7s. to 8s. the Stone and speculation increased throughout the whole of Britain and many other nations not excepted, to a most unprecedented height, but in the end of that year and beginning 1826 things took a different turn, distrust took place in London among the mercantile people and no less than about 100 of the English Banks failed and the panic was not long in reaching Scotland; and, although only one Scotch bank failed the failers of Merch[an]ts and depression of trade was very great, we ourselves had about 400 pounds of bad debts of which we lost upwards of 200 altogether; wool fell that year (1826) about 10s. the Stone and we had too heavy a stock on hand and, what was very remarkable, that panic in trade was followed by one of the worst crops ever witnessed which tended to depress the country still more and limit the demand for goods, and what was very surprising wool in 1827 raise from 1s. to 2s. the Stone and the country not being the least improven Cloth actually fell. Foreign wool being so very low enabled the English Manuf[acture]rs to send down cloths to Scotland from 3s. to 4s. 6d. the yd. which entirely cut up our finer cloth made from cheviot wool; all these things combined against us with another fall of cheviot wool this year of from 2s. to 3s. the Stone with another heavy stocks on hand of which we are obliged to reduce in price, it is astonishing that we are not all ruined.

25 July. For premims N. 1451–1452–1453–1454.[1]

29 July. Ordered from Robt. Usher, Newcastle, one Cask of Pearl Ashes to be delivered here free of carriage at 34s. 6d. the Cwt. ½ cwt. of Madder[2] at about 6d. or 7d. the lb. to be delivered free

[1] This entry refers to cloths being prepared for exhibition in Edinburgh under the auspices of the Board of Trustees for Manufactures there, who offered prizes (premiums) each year for the best cloths submitted. For the results of Brown's efforts on this occasion see entry for 10 Nov. 1828, below, p. 86.

[2] The madder root gave a fast, red dye.

here also, the ashes to be sent immediately. Invoice to be inclosed with the Madder and to say if he has got Heeming all settled which was given him.

Auld Sandy Small tells me this day that when he began the manufacturing which is upwards of fifty years ago he paid 7s. 6d. the stone for cheviot wool and a year or two after it was up at twenty. Some time before he began the manufacturing, the Highland wool was selling from 18s. to 48s. the pack[1] with a lb. [extra] to the stone and a fleece to the pack which was the way it was bought at that time. 30 to 40 packs a year was all that was manufactured in Galashiels at the time he began, the first Cloth made in Galas[hiels] was Gray ½ yd. broad which sold at 6d. the yd. James Mercer who is about 60 years old says that his father was the first who ever made Dk. Blue Cloth here, and he remembers quite well of his Mother showing a swatch of the first piece, many years after.

There will be from 10 to 1,200 packs of wool Manufactured yearly in Galashiels just now, we ourselves have Manufactured upwards of 70 packs in a year.

29 July. From John Moffat £1 4s. as balance of accounts.
To expenses at Langholm fair and Catcleuch,[2] £1.

6 August. We have at present 20 p[iece]s of Dk. Blue at and above 2s. 6d. per yd. for one below that price. At the same time it is evident that we should have exactly the reverse and it is certainly nothing remarkable that while we continue to act so contrary to our own judgement we *never can succeed in making money*.

7 August. The kind of Cloths we ought to make this year are principally piece Dyed Dark Blues from 20d. to 2s. 6d. the yd. and a few from 2s. 6d. to 3s. and a few coarse Grays Drabs and Lt. Blues made of cheviot wool. And likewise a few Wool dyed Dark Blues from 3s. to 4s. 6d. the yd. all made of foreign Wool, that is the Wool Dyed ones.

We have frequently had to regret having a number of Cloths on hand which were unsaleable and which can be ascribed to nothing

[1] A 'pack' of wool weighed approximately 288 lbs. or 12 stones of 24 lbs. each.
[2] Situated in Northumberland just south of Carter Bar.

else than not looking properly about ourselves so as to make no kinds of Cloth but what we was *sure would sell.*

9 August. We was confident some time since that it was nothing else that caused the light blue spots upon our Dk. Blues than that they were not well enough wet; but we have now boiled them with bran and still there are as many as ever so we at present know nothing about what is the cause of them.

Due to Thos. Sanderson	10s.	6d.
Paid	2s.	6d.
Settled	8s.	0d.

11 August. Four months after date we promise to pay to Mrs Thorburn, Cutpair, on order in the Leith Bank Office here thirty pounds St[erling] for value received in wool. J. & H. Brown. We paid the stamp.

We have this day weighed 8 pieces after they were finished for the purpose of seeing what difference they are between stout, middling, and light made cloths.

	lbs.	oz.
$29\frac{1}{2}$ yds. Dk. Blue on weighed	23	0
$28\frac{3}{4}$ " " " " "	20	13
$29\frac{1}{2}$ " " " nd on "	21	4
$29\frac{1}{2}$ " " " on "	23	8
30 " " " " "	23	11
$28\frac{3}{4}$ " " " " "	21	0
31 " " " sh "	20	10
31 " " " " "	19	11

The 23 lbs. piece and 23 lbs. 8 oz. and 23 lbs. 11 oz. are stout, the other three cheviot pieces Middling, the Spainish ones are lightish but will do. If Cloths are made too stout a price cannot be got to pay; if made too light the price has to be so much reduced that they will not pay either.

13 August. At Melrose fair yesterday there was almost no wool sold, the price of laid wool is averaging about 9s. in this quarter and about 11s. for the border; but it is some what remarkable that

we have not herd of any Englishmen that have bought a single parcel yet, who never but opened the Market till this year.

Our present method of Pressing is to give the plates a good heat, so to screw it down occasionally for the first two hours with the small dwang, and then to follow it down with the long dwang for other three hours, as hard as two men can do it.

18 August.	Order on the L[eith] Bank[1]	£88	16s.	5d.
	Drawn from „ „	25	0s.	0d.
		113	16s.	5d.
	Pd. Bill of	£100	0s.	0d.
	2 years papers to EA		10s.	1d.
	H[enry] B[rown]'s rent		11s.	3½d.
		101	1s.	4½d.
		£12	15s.	0½d.

26 August. We had some doubts of the coarse Indigo (price 3s. 4d. the lb.) turning out well in the working, but on trial, we find it to work well, and we think similar Indigo would be more profitable to work than finer; which is of this description – very light in the hand, (which is a perticular thing to attend too in low priced Indigo) and the clearer the blue the better.

30 August. To Darling for 20 cwt. of coals at 8½d.		£0 14s.	2d.
	Disc[oun]t		8d.
	Cash	13s.	6d.

[Stock of Cloths]

sec	12	p[iece]s Gray
nd	7	Dark Blue pc Dyed
nd	4	Drabs wool „
nd	12	Dk. Blue wool „
nd	2	Blue Mixtures
nd	2	Black Mixtures
nd on	11	Dk. Blue wool Dyed
nd on	5	„ „ pc „

[1] The branch office in Galashiels.

on	26	Dk. Blue Wool Dyed
er	7	,, ,, ,, ,,
er	3	Olives ,, ,,
er	1	Blue Mixture
naa	1	Dk. Blue pc Dyed
sh	1	,, ,, ,, ,,
sh	45	,, ,, Wool Dyed
sec sc	3	Dk. Blue pc Dyed
	142	

To HB's fortnight acct. to Cash, £1
To JB's fortnight acct. to cash, £1[1]

8 September. To expences at packing of Catcleuch wool £1 1s. 6d
To R. & J. Henderson's Bill for Indigo £95 12s. 6d.

15 September. Settlement with J. & W. Cochrane. J. W. C. to J. & H. B.

May 31	To Goods	£4	2s.	11d.
	Discount		6s.	5d.
		£3	16s.	6d.
	To $3\frac{1}{2}$ lbs. of Blue Nipans [?]		5s.	3d.
	9 lbs. of Blue Slubing		4s.	6d.
		£4	6s.	3d.

J. & H. B. to J. & W. C.

Aug. 25th to goods	£2	4s.	$7\frac{1}{2}$d.			
Dis[coun]t		3s.	$7\frac{1}{2}$d.			
	£2	1s.	0d.			
To 14 pieces pressed		14s.	0d.			
Horse Hire		16s.	0d.	£3	11s.	0d.
	Settled				15s.	3d.

[1] This entry is similar to many others, which have been omitted. It suggests that Henry and James lived very frugally if this represents their only drawings from the business. Later they took £2 each per fortnight, but half of this was often placed to their capital account. Here they are paying themselves less than could be earned by a skilled hand-loom weaver, although some entries suggest that occasional private purchases and expences were put down as a charge against the business.

For Drab sec 2 pieces:

	lb.	oz.
Bright Madder	1	—
Bark		8
Yellowood		2
Shumac[1]		8
Logwood		8
Copperas		12

22 September. To William Brown for Rents up to 12 Aug. 1828, £12 5s. 0d. which with £4 5s. 0d. formerly paid settles in full.

Rent: Machine House	£1	0s.	0d.
94 yds. Tenters		11s.	9d.
Additional garden		14s.	0½d.
Share of Caul[2]		6s.	9d.
	£2	12s.	6½d.

24 September. Ordered from Eagle & Henderson, Edinb[urgh], 1 Ream of Brown paper at 23s., 1 cwt. of Copperas at 7s., and ½ cwt. of alum[3] at 10s. 6d.

To Robt. Haldane for law expences, £11 11s. 0d. Law and justice ought to be but is not allied at all times and scarcely ever.

29 September. To A. Leslie for HB's garden, 10s.

Weavers are scarce just now and some of them have asked and has got more wages which is somewhat strange for in July last when we had a number of Light Blues to make extra from our ordinary manufacture we got easily 20 weavers who was all very slack of work and could have got easily a good deal more.

30 September. Lent John Aimers £10 10s. 0d. Pd.

[1] Powdered shumac acted as a mordant and was derived from a shrub found in the Middle East and the Iberian peninsula.

[2] The caul, or cauld, was a small dam in the damway cut from Galawater to the millwheel which permitted a head of water to build up sufficient to drive it.

[3] A commonly used mordant obtained from the shale removed from mines.

Granted to John Aimers a Bill at 4 months of	£38	14s.	0d.
Machine House acct.	£12	0s.	0d.
Jas. Bathgate's acct.	£ 6	14s.	0d.
J. & H. B. acct.	£20	0s.	0d.
	£38	14s.	0d.

4 October. We have been laying in 10 or 12 carts of coals thinking they will be a good deal dearer in a little as they generally rise at this season of the year price 9d. [cwt]. 22 Oct. – 10½d., 25 Nov. – 11d., Jan. 1828 – 10d.[1]

6 October. To packing wool at Lumsden and Oldtown:[2]

Expences	£1	1s.	1d.
Stamps		13s.	9d.
Twine		2s.	8d.
	£1	17s.	6d.

Weight of Robert Usher's cask of Ashes G[ros]s	95 lbs.
Tare	14 ,,
	81 ,,
Invoice weight	97 ,,
Deficient	16 ,,

at 32s. the cwt. 7s. 4d.

We have not had as few webs on hand this two years past, there is only 41 in our shelves.

Sent to Porteous & Smith, Edinr., a piece Casimere[3] Drab we got to refinish.

[1] See entry for 14 May 1829, below, pp. 101–2, for an explanation of fluctuating coal prices.

[2] These places are situated just south of the Carter Bar border, Oldtown being near Otterburn.

[3] A twilled cloth sometimes referred to as Kerseymere. It should not be confused with Cashmere.

7 October. Price of Cheviot Laid wool since 1750–1796:[1]

	s.	d.		s.	d.
1750	6	2	1774	7	9
1751	7	0	1775	8	0
1752	6	0	1776	8	9
1753	5	6	1777	8	8
1754	6	0	1778	6	10
1755	6	0	1779	5	0
1756	6	0	1780	5	9
1757	6	0	1781	6	0
1758	6	8	1782	7	4
1759	8	4	1783	8	4
1760	8	4	1784	9	0
1761	6	0	1785	9	9
1762	5	3	1786	9	9
1763	6	0	1787	11	8
1764	6	6	1788	12	0
1765	7	0	1789	12	6
1766	7	0	1790	13	6
1767	7	0	1791	14	6
1768	6	8	1792	17	0
1769	7	0	1793	14	6
1770	6	8	1794	14	0
1771	7	2	1795	18	2
1772	8	2	1796	23	4
1773	7	6			

Wool kept high from 1796 to 1818, some of the best lots of the border wool sold at 50s. some even at a little more.

The proportion of Tar and butter which the farmers of the Cheviot hills lays their sheep is 10 lbs. of butter to one Gallon of tar which 20 sheep is laid with.

Richd. Turnbull took up the under blade of the Yankee[2] to

[1] These prices appear to have been copied from J. Hogg, *The Shepherd's Guide* (Edinburgh, 1807), 326-7; *cf.* R. A. Dodgshon, 'The Economics of Sheep Farming in the Southern Uplands during the Age of Improvement, 1750-1833', *Economic History Review*, 2nd Series, xxix (1976).

[2] A revolving cropping machine which replaced shearing by hand. The 'yankee' cropper was introduced to Galashiels in 1819 by James Paterson who was recom-

sharp; which John Hislop or one of his men sharped it in about an hour. We mention this to see what he charges for it when he presents his acct.

John Dun says he can sell Copperas at 7s. 6d. the Cwt. and allum at 18s.

James Richardson: July 30 To Goods	£75	10s.	6d.
Oct. 7 By Cash and Dis[coun]t.	£52	13s.	7d.
	£22	16s.	11d.

13 October. To John Young for carriage of Lumsden wool, £1 4s. 0d.

To be laid to the Machines and among hand finishing:

6	pieces	sec	12	pieces	sc nd
14	,,	sec sc	10	,,	nd
18	,,	sc	6	,,	on
			66	principally for Dk. Blues	

15 October. The demand for Gala[shiel]s Cloth that is mostly Blue from 22d. to 2s. 6d. and 3s. has not been as good for this three years; Mr Kaye for J. & W. Campbell & Co., Glasgow, has been here twice within 3 week seeking goods and could not get himself supplyed of Dk. Blue. Of the above pieces we have sold since the beginning of March 450 pieces.

16 October. We have made this summer about 50 pieces of wool Dyed Dark Blues from foreigne wool which has turned out to our expectation. We made a good few last year too which looked all remarkably neat and came as near to the English as ever was made in Galashiels. Yet for us to attempt making a trade of these kind of cloths is quite ridiculous under the present circumstances and the best kind of cloths we can make anything like a trade off is Dk. Blues Dyed in the piece from 22d. to 3s. the yd. none higher and even but few at 3s., mostly about 2s., 2s. 2d., 2s. 4d., 2s. 6d.

---

mended by Sir Walter Scott for a premium from the Board of Trustees for Manufactures. His amusing letter to the Board is contained in T. Craig-Brown, *History of Selkirkshire* (Edinburgh, 1886), Vol. i, 571.

We look like having a good trade this year the reasons for which are very obvious; we depend almost on home consumption for our cloths and we have had a most favourable crop of everything. Cattle and sheep has been selling well; at last Falkirk tryst there was a rise on cattle and sheep since the tryst before of 10s. a head on cattle and 2s. on sheep which amounted in all to £24,000 and in fact the way these have been selling all year is a little fortune itself to Scotland. Potatoes has not been knone to be such an abundant crop for this many years and, while we have an excellent crop of corn, victuals has been rising owing it is said to other countries. With all these things in our favours we have cheap wool, and Indigo not high, stock very low in the twon and a good demand that is for those low kinds of Dk. Blues which is made from cheviot wool and which the twon can do best in. With these prospects we ought to do as much as we can.

22 October. J. & W. Cochrane has got a pack of Teazels which contained 150 of bunches.

Out of 50 stones of Blair wool which we consider very tarry there is 28 pieces except weft for one. They stand good lengths too.

We have only 26 pieces on the shelves.

We have bo[ugh]t a 1,000 St. of wool this year which is 83 pack 4 St.

25 October. Milled this week:

2	Dk. Blues on	
10	DB	sc
4	LB	sc
2	Drab	sec
6	Grays	sec
24		

31 October. To carriage of Old Town wool, £2 3s. 0d.

Out of 283 lbs. of Spainish at 10d. the lb. we have 330 yds. of Cloth which costs 8½d. the yd.

Expense of Making a piece from foreigne wool Dark Blue:

Motling[1]	£0	1s.	3d.
Dying		13s.	0d.
Oil & Slubing		11s.	0d.
Spining & Weaving		12s.	0d.
Wages		17s.	0d.
26 lbs. wool at 10d. lb.	1	1s.	8d.
	£3	15s.	11d.

3 November. We have not been so much plagued with the light blue spots upon our Dk. Blues this some time past; the reason we ascribe preventing them is that we are more careful in wetting them and in letting them lie wet before dying them off.

10 November. Word has comed about the premiums[2] and R. Walker gets the first of the 5s. 6d. R. Gill & Son and J. Rutherford and us gets the second divided. R. Walker and J. & W. Cochrane gets the first of the 4s. 6d. divided, R. Gill & Son and us the second divided. J. & W. Cochrane gets the first of the 3s. 6d. and R. Walker the second.

R. Walker, £40. J. & W. Cochrane, £23. R. Gill & Son, £8 10s. J. & H. B., £8 10s. Jas. Rutherford, £4.

Jas. Roberts 2 lots, James Hunter, John Gledhill and R. Lees 1 lot each, get nothing. We succeeded well last year but terrible deficient this, our cloths were far too light made and not low enough cut. R. Walker and J. W. Cochrane made far too heavy to pay, but it is evident that nothing but *very stout* Cloths will do for Premiums.

12 November. How the different kinds [of wool] are marked:

Hips	no string[s]
Next the hips and hip weft	1 ,,
Next the hips	2 ,,
Next the hip and second weft	3 ,,

[1] *i.e.* blending two or more different coloured yarns together to produce a mottled effect. As he was using foreign wool it would be dyed in-the-wool.

[2] See p. 76, n. 1.

Seconds	none
Second and Com fine weft	1 ,,
Commonfine	2 ,,
Com. and Superfine weft	3 ,,
Superfine	none

13 November. Coppy of Insurance.[1]

William Brown's Dwelling house	£140
wearing apparel and furniture belonging to William Brown and James Brown	£60
Presshop and wareroom adjoining	£30
press and press papers belonging to Wm. Brown	£20
Indigo	£30
Woollen Cloth belonging to J. & H. Brown	£120
a small stove occasionally used in the wareroom	—
Half of the factory of Jas. Bathgate & Coy. belonging to Wm Brown	£100
Machinery therein belonging to Wm. Brown	£150
Woolen goods in the process of Manufacture belonging to J. & H. Brown	£50
a stove applied to the wheels in time of frost	—
Weaving shop belonging to Wm. Brown	£40
Dyehouse adjoining belonging to J. & H. Brown	£20
Working utensils £20 in weaving shop and wool in said weaving shop and Dyehouse belonging to J. & H. B.	£170
a stove occasionally used in the dyehouse	—
Henry Brown's Dwelling house	£70
furniture and wearing apparel	£30

£200 at 1s. 6d. [per £100]		£0	3s.	0d.
£200 at 2s. 6d.	,, ,,		5s.	0d.
£300 at 7s. 6d.	,, ,,	1	2s.	6d.
£250 at 2s. 6d.	,, ,,		6s.	3d.
£100 at 1s. 6d.	,, ,,		1s.	6d.
£1050	Duty at 3s.	1	11s.	6d.
		£3	9s.	9d.

[1] The insurance policy here sheds light on the organisation of the business. The fact that William Brown has no goods in the process of manufacture, but still owns

17 November. The 26th Nov. is our day with the stove.

22 November. Milled this week

6	pieces	D. Blue	nd
8	,,	,,	sc nd
2	,,	,,	sc
2	,,	Drab	sec sc
18			

26 November. To Wm. Brown, £1 4s. 6d.

for our share of two pigs	18s.	8d.
for drying at stove	4s.	0d.
for two barrels	1s.	10d.
£1	4	6d.

28 November. To George Roberts 12s. for stocking yarn to Mr Valence which with 4s. for ditto formerly settles for 47 lbs. of wool got 20 Aug. last.

For advertisements, 1s. 9d.

2 December. Settled with Jas. Sime & Co. for carrying and expenses of all transactions with them in wool for this last season, and also settled with them for gray paper which was due them.

3 December. Among our hands at present in a finished and finishing state:

2	p[iece]s wool dyed Dk. Blue at	7s.	0d.
6	,, ,, ,, ,, ,, ,,	5s.	6d.
4	,, ,, ,, ,, ,, ,,	5s.	0d.
15	,, ,, ,, ,, ,, ,,	4s.	6d.
4	,, ,, ,, ,, ,, ,,	4s.	3d.
17	Cheviot [wool dyed Dk. Blue]	2s.	10d.
9	,, ,, ,, ,, ,,	2s.	6d.

buildings and machinery, suggests that his sons took over his business previously. William does not appear among the list of clothiers set out in the entry for 25 May 1829 below. James and Henry Brown appear to own no machinery. At least some of the weaving has been centralised as evidenced by the weaving shop. Henry possessed his own house but James appears to have lived with his father.

6 piece dyed Dk. Blue	3s. od.
10 ,, ,, ,, ,,	2s. 10d.
5 ,, ,, ,, ,,	2s. 8d.
6 ,, ,, ,, ,,	2s. 6d.
18 ,, ,, ,, ,,	2s. 4d.
8 ,, ,, ,, ,,	2s. 2d.
7 ,, ,, ,, ,,	2s. od.
4 Light Blue at	2s. od.
1 ,, ,, ,,	22d.
2 Drab ,,	3s. od.
2 ,, ,,	2s. 2d.
2 ,, ,,	22d.
4 ,, ,,	20d.
18 Grays ,,	20d.
2 Olives ,,	2s. 6d.
152[1]	

13 December. J. Brown's acct. for three weeks past £3

Cash £1 5s.
acct. £1 5s. £3

19 December. From John Young £17 15s. od.

for premium £8 10s.
for cloth sold £9 5s. £17 15s. od.

20 December. Milled this week: Last week:

Milled this week		Last week
2 pieces D. Blue	on	12 on; 4 nd on
12 ,, ,, ,,	sc	10 sc nd
4 ,, Duffle[2]	sc	6 sc
6 ,, D. Blue	sec sc	4 sec sc
2 ,, Drab	sec sc	4 Drab sec sc
4 ,, Gray	sec	4 Grays ,, ,,
30		44

[1] Note the heavy emphasis on the cheaper cloths. Only about a quarter are priced at 3s. per yd. or above (*cf.* the lists given on 25 Sept. 1829, 27 Nov. 1829).
[2] A dense, coarse cloth with a thick nap or pile.

To the Machines this week:

13 St. of sec
27 St. of sc
11 St. of sec for listing.

3 January 1829. Jas. Br[own's]. fortnight acct. £2

Cash	£1	
acct.	£1	£2

Bought from John Blaikie[1] the other day about 500 St. of cheviot wool at 9s. 3d. the St[one]. Farmers acct. payable by Bill at 4 Mo[nths]: dated 2nd Feby. first 1829.

5 January. From Geo. Paterson, 25 yds. Gray for No. 1690, 26 yds. sc

Wool done at the Mill last week, 30 St. nd; 9½ St. sec.

For Dying Drab:[2]

Bright Madder	1 lb.	0 oz.
Bark	1	0
Shumac		8
Logwood		8
Cudbear		2
Copperas		8

Taken to Robt. Sanderson between 22 and 23 St. of on.

10 January. We have only 35 pieces finished cloth in our shelves.

State of trade: Trade has been and is very good, every Manufac[ture]r has been particularly bussy this last 6 month caused by an actual demand for goods.

12 January. To Buckholmside[3] 34 St. 12 oz. including 3 sheets of sc wool to slub.

[1] Blaikie appears to have been a local dealer in wool.

[2] This is a different recipe to that stated in the entry for 15 Sept., above, p. 81.

[3] Another mill in Galashiels.

Expense of making 32 yds. of Plaiding:

rather better than a stone of wool	£1	0s.	0d.
Slubing		4s.	0d.
Oil		1s.	0d.
Spining		1s.	2d.
Weaving		3s.	6d.
Scouring, etc.		2s.	4d.
	£1	12s.	0d.

The net cost is 1s. the yd. It would appear to be a very bad trade for the greater part of plaiding sells below that price.

13 January. The light blue spots that we was so much plagued with upon our piece Dyed Dark Blues has disappeared and which we think is owing to wetting them properly in the dam before they are returned on the vat. After sinded[1] in the dam we let them lie all the night folded up.

14 January.	Wool received from John Blaikie weighed this day	303 St. 22½ lbs.
	2 sheets formerly got supposed to contain	36 St.
		339 St. 22½ lbs.

15 January. The above wool is from Ettrick Water, price 9s. 3d. and in the weighing and handling it yesterdey we thought it both coarse and dirty, and are of opinion that Boarder[2] wool is one fourth more value, being so much cleaner and finer.

20 January. Milled last week 26 pieces.
To our machines this week 44 stones.

[1] *i.e.* rinsed.
[2] By this Brown seems to mean wool purchased from the Northumberland side of the Border.

21 January. Wool received from John Blaikie this day:

	St.	lbs.
	169	12½
formerly received	339	22½
	509	11
Farmer's weight	489	
	20	11
2 sheets not weighed supose	1	13
St.	22	

26 January. Sent to John Richardson, Crieff, 22 yd. Black which we got to refinish.[1]

29 January. Paid James Mitchell for the Machine house acct., 7s. 6d.

Received from him, for 12½ lbs. of iron 1s. 6d.

It is every day more and more visible that no tradesman ought to be imployed without first stateing what the job will cost; for they are all given to over Charge most unsonsciounably especially Millwrights and Smiths. Many a pound we have lost by not looking tightly after them, Smiths charging 6d. lb. for iron that cost them only 1½d. lb. with very little work upon it.

2 February. Milled last week 26 pieces. [Dk. Blues and Drabs].

Granted a Bill at 4 months to John Blaikie for 488 St. of wool at 9s. 3d. amounting to £225 14s.

Discounted in the N.[2] Bank Bill of Porteous & Smith Edinr.	£26	5s.	0d.
Bill of H. Hall & Co.'s Aberdeen	50	0s.	0s.
	76	5s.	0d.

[1] Dyeing black was a difficult art requiring several immersions in a vat containing a mixture of dyes such as indigo, woad, and madder. Copperas was often used as a mordant to give a glossy tinge as was the juice of the bark of the alder tree. Richardson was one of Brown's listed customers so it appears he was not satisfied with a piece sold to him.

[2] Probably the National Bank at Jedburgh.

Dis[coun]t on Edin.	4s.	4d.			
Abern. Postage	1s.	6d.			
Commission	2s.	6d.			
Dis[coun]t	10s.	2d.			
	18s.	6d.		18s.	6d.
			75	6s.	6d.
Paid John Aimer's Bill			38	14s.	od.
			£36	12s.	6d.
Received J. Bathgate's share			12	14s.	od.
			£49	6s.	6d.

5 February. Settled Robt. Sanderson's slubing acct.	£14	19s.	9d.
Dis[coun]t		19s.	9d.
Cash	£14	os.	od.

6 February. Rent: Machine House	1	os.	od.
94 stenters		11s.	9d.
Garden		14s.	o½d.
	£2	5s.	9½d.

Jas. B[rown's] fortnight acct. Cash	£1
Acct.	£1
	£2

H. B[rown's] fortnight acct. To cash	£1
To acct	£1

Yesterday to James Hogg for his wool	£39	16s.	od.
Luckpenny[1]	1	os.	od.
	£38	16s.	od.

The chest of 3s. 4d. Indigo is now done, and it has turned owt very well, better than was expected.

[1] A small sum returned to the purchaser for luck and goodwill.

7 February. Bought from R. & S. Henderson Glasgow the other day a chest of Indigo of 344 lbs. at 5s. 4d. lb. subject to 5 p. cent dis[coun]t payable at the beginning of March.

It appears clear to us from our experience that Indigo of a violet copper and light in the hand is the most profitable for our use.

Wool slubed at our own Machine house last week: 26 stones sc
18 ,, sec
—
44 ,,

14 February. At the Clothier's Club[1] last night, Walter Cochrane informed the members that they had made an experiment with a certain quantity of white wool; the half of which they (J. & W. C[ochrane]) made into Cloth, the other into Plaidings; and if they could sell the plaiding at 1s. the yd. for which they only got 11d., they would be anabled to sell the Cloth, which quality was commonfine Dark Blue at 2s. the yd. They would be as well paid with the one as the other.

It would appear from that statement that the Plaiding trade is yet a great deal worse than making Cloth. Both the Plaiding and Cloth was stout made, the Plaiding could sell at no more than 1s. while the Cloth could bring 2s. 6d. the yd. if not 1d. or 2d. more.

Milled this week 46 pieces [all Dark Blues].

It is my opinion although we are at present making about 20 pieces of Dk. Blues a week that on the first of August we will not have what we consider a large stock below 2s. 6d. the yd. We may have more than we required at 2s. 6d. and above but I do not think we will have 40 pieces finished below that price on the 1st. of August next, that is to say of dark blues.

It was discussed at the Club meeting last night what the Manufacturers of this place, under their present circumstances could best manufacture, and it was unanimously agreed that the articles made from cheviot wool, viz. stocking yarn,[2] Plaidings, Bazes, Cloths,

[1] *I.e.* a meeting of the Galashiels Manufacturers' Corporation, a body founded in 1777 which still exists.

[2] Brown's interest in stocking yarn may reflect the relative prosperity of the Hawick hosiery yarn and stocking trade at this time.

Flannels[1] and any other articles that could be made from cheviot wool. The reasons given were that cheviot wool being of a coarse quality, and little other kinds having ever been made, the machinery in the town is adapted for coarse wool only; and of course we cannot work fine [wool] to advantage. And another thing the above named articles, Stocking-Yarn in particular has been, and can be made here as well as anywhere else, and all the other [articles] also excepting Cloth and even it too if we keep to the low qualities.

19 February. Received from R. & S. Henderson Glasgow a chest of Indigo:

	Gross	462 lb.
	Tare	117 lb.
		345

Weight charged 344 [lbs.] at 5s. 4d. Over weight 1 [lb]. 6 months.

List of pieces finished and to be finished in March:

8	pieces Dk. Blue of	1s.	10d.	sec piece	Dyed
39	,, ,, ,, ,,	2s.	0d.	sec sc ,,	,,
34	,, ,, ,, ,,	2s.	2d.	sc ,,	,,
31	,, ,, ,, ,,	2s.	4d.	sc nd ,,	,,
21	,, ,, ,, ,,	2s.	6d.	nd ,,	,,
15	,, ,, ,, ,,	2s.	9d.	nd on ,,	,,
9	,, ,, ,, ,,	3s.	0d.	on ,,	,,
3	,, ,, ,, ,,	4s.	0d.	sh wool died [sic]	
5	,, ,, ,, ,,	4s.	3d.	,, ,,	,,
5	,, ,, ,, ,,	4s.	6d.	,, ,,	,,
1	,, ,, ,, ,,	5s.	0d.	,, ,,	,,
2	,, ,, ,, ,,	5s.	6d.	,, ,,	,,
1	,, ,, ,, ,,	7s.	0d.	,, ,,	,,
2	,, Light Blue ,,	1s.	10d.	sc	
5	,, Grays ,,	1s.	7d.	sec	
1	,, Drab ,,	2s.	8d.	er	
2	,, ,, ,,	2s.	0d.	nd	
1	,, ,, ,,	2s.	0d.	sc	

[1] Flannel manufacture appears to have been growing considerably at this time. Exports from Scottish ports in 1827 were valued at almost four times the sum for 1825: *cf.* Public Record Office, Customs 14, vols. 37, 39. The Board of Trustees for Manufactures also offered premiums for imitation Welsh flannel.

2	pieces Drab	of 1s. 10d.	sec sc
6	,, ,,	,, 1s. 6d.	sec
2	,, Olives	,, 2s. 9d.	er
12	,, Dk. Blue	,, 2s. 8d.	on wool died
5	,, ,, ,,	,, 2s. 6d.	nd on
2	,, ,, ,,	,, 2s. 4d.	nd
4	,, Blue Duffels	1s. 6d.	
218[1]			

Wool laid to our Machines this week	17 Stones sec
	30 Stones sc
	47

24 February. It appears by our present experience that to mix different parcels of wool together is a bad plan, they do not mill right together and stands only about 24 yds. instead of 28, that is, warp made of one kind and weft made of another.

28 February. Milled this week 40 pieces.

11 March. From James Isaac, Melrose, for drawback on soap[2] £15
To P. & C. Wood, Leith for oil, £20 10s. 6d.

Cash received at Journey	£287	14s.	6d.
To Robt. & John Henderson	91	0s.	0d.
	£196	14s.	6d.

12 March. Lodged in the Leith Bank, £100.

14 March. To the Machines 2 weeks, 88 pieces.
Milled this week 34 pieces.
Cost of one set of Robt. Sanderson's cards from Stead & Paterson, Leith Walk, £125.

[1] Only about 13% of this stock is in any sense quality cloth, *i.e.* priced at 3s. per yard and above (*cf.* p. 89, n. 1).

[2] Soap carried a considerable excise duty at this time, and was much used by woollen manufacturers for scouring purposes. They could claim a rebate or drawback on the soap thus used. The duty was repealed in 1853.

19 March. Mr Gandy says he makes and sells to the carpet Manufacturers three ply black yarn as low as 6d. and 7d. the lb. which is most astonishingly low; the yarn is perfectly clean, they scour it in the Mill with fullers earth.

21 March. Instead of webs being charged 4d. each to be charged 3d. after this date.[1]

23 March. We have frequently been short of low priced piece dyed Dark Blues. The understated is our present stock lying finished in the shelves:

sec	4 pcs	nd	9 pcs
sec sc	11 pcs	nd on	4 pcs
sc	21 pcs	on	1 pcs
sc nd	15 pcs		55

All orders of the March Journey are executed.
To Thos. Richardson for carriage of tazels,[2] £2 1s. 0d.

24 March. To John Thomson for 4 Doz. of deals at 1s. 9d. per Doz. 7 in. broad, 7s.

28 March. To William Brown balance of Rent	£4	17s.	0d.
James Brown's flesh		15s.	0d.
	£5	12s.	0d.

Weight of a pack of tazels $1\frac{3}{4}$ cwt. N[umber] of tazels 13,500.

Discounted in G. Craig's John Galbraith's Bill	£22	8s.	0d.
Dis[coun]t		7s.	9d.
	£22	0s.	3d.

To John Thomson for 4 Doz. deals 7 in. broad at 1s. 9d., 7s.

30 March. Milled last week 32 pieces.

[1] This probably refers to the payment received by a hand-loom weaver for each yard of cloth woven: *cf. Statistical Account of Scotland*, vol. ii, 311.

[2] *i.e.* teazels.

Sent to Robt. Sanderson's Machines	10 St.		on
3 March d[itto]	5 St.	3 lb.	er
3 March ditto	14 St.	8 lb.	on
	29[st.]	11[lb.]	

To Geo. Fairgrieve for carriage of Indigo, 3s.

It is not a little extraordinary to see the changes of trade. I recollect since I began business of almost refusing orders for Dk. blues at 3s. 6d. per yd. being thought to low a price; now 2s. 6d. is thought a good price and from that to 2s. od. the greater proportion of our Cloths are sold at.[1]

31 March. From H. Balantine[2] and R. Imket[?] for Carriage of Indigo, 3s. To H. Balanetine and R. Imket for 100 lbs. of Indigo at 5s., £25.

James Richardson 1 pc Drab 1s. 6d.
1 pc Gray 19d.
1 Dk. Blue 2s. 2d. and 2s. 6d.

To be sent 16 April.

3 April. To bran, 1s. od. To P. Scott for reeling, 2s. od. To Listing, 3s. 6d.

8 April. 120 pieces in the shelves. Mostly Dark Blues at and below 2s. 6d., and only like 20 pieces we call not so very saleable.

Those taking Cloths to the Glasgow market just now are meeting with very bad encouragement; the accounts from the manufacturing districts of England are very bad too and by the Newspaper reports a general dullness prevails throughout Britain at the present time.

Low as the raw material is there is evidently a smaller profit upon our Cloth than at any former period which cause may be traced to the low-priced English Blues that comes in competition with ours, and which has partly thrown ours out of the Market.

[1] *Cf.* entry for 17 June 1828, above, p. 72.

[2] Henry Ballantyne, who though listed by Brown as having 'failed' in Galashiels in the crisis of 1829 (see entry for 25 May 1829, below, p. 103), later founded Henry Ballantyne & Sons at Walkerburn, near Galashiels. His family came to dominate the woollen trade of the Tweed valley.

The making of Stocking yarn appears to us a better trade than the Galashiels Blues, or Grays either.

9 April. To Machine boys[1] for by-hours, 1s. 8d.

10 April. Whatever we purchase or whatever we do the necessity of making every inquiry beforehand and having as perfect a knowledge as possible of what we are about is in every transaction of ours more and more evident, which the two following instances will partly show.

Robt. Usher, Newcastle, sells his fullers-earth at 3s. 9d. the Cwt. and of which we lately ordered a tun, but immediately countermanded it thinking we would get it cheaper somewhere else. After inquiry we find we can get it from Sanderson & Paterson at 3s. 3d. [cwt.] and without being at the expense of the cask; now a tun of earth for which we will pay to Sanderson & Paterson £3 5s. would have cost us from Robt. Usher £4.

The other instance is a charge made by Thos. Henderson for the carriage of a pack of Teazels from Edinr. He charged 5s. and was paid for it and when seeing properly into it he ought to have charged only 2s. 7½d.

Another instanced may be added which was John Hislop's charge for teazel rods, he actually took 3s. when he made them first and after inquiry has been made it is found they can be made from 1s. to 1s. 6d. each the very same article.

13 April. Bot. of Robt. Usher from James Rutherford

2 cwt. 2 qr. Logwood [at] 16s.	2	0s.	0d.
1 cwt. 1 qr. Camwood[2] [at] 23s.	1	8s.	9d.
3 bags		3s.	0d.
	£3	11s.	9d.
Cam[wood] returned	1	8s.	9d.
	£2	2s.	0d.

[1] Probably 'billy-boys', who were employed by the slubbers to join the short slivers of wool together as they came from the carding engine, to prepare them for slubbing. This was an irksome and sometimes dangerous task later replaced by the invention of the piecing machine, reputedly by John Melrose, an engineer in Hawick.

[2] A wood from West Africa used for dyeing red.

14 April. To Buckholmside Machines 8 St. 7 lbs. of nd. To Robt. Sanderson's Machines 9 St. 10 lb. of on.

Milled last week 32 pieces.

To our own machines 24 St. of sc.
24 St. of sec.
—
48

To John Dun for 2 cwt. of Copperas at 7s. 6d., 15s. od.

18 April. The Club meeting was held last night but nothing transpired except that Robt. Paterson's and Archd. Cochrane's trip to Ireland to sell cloth did not turn out well; the reasons given are that our Cloths are not known there, and scarcely a piece [of] narrow Cloth even of English make is to be seen, all broads. A[rchibald] C[ochrane] had some plaiding with him and he thinks Belfast not a bad market for that article. Robt. Lees was twice at Belfast within this short time past and he gives the same account of the Cloth trade; he even tryed some broads[1] but he found the English to beat him.

22 April. Valuing the Hi[ghlan]d wool at 6s. od. [stone of 24 lbs.] the yarn will cost 8d. lb.

27 April. Improvement of the last month: New cash book for inserting cash received and paid out only and which lets us see exactly to what amount we do every day, week, month and year seperately.

Dying black wool with 7 lbs. of logwood to the Stone of copperas instead of 5 lb. of logwood as formerly. Burning ashes mixed with small coals and well wet with water which is a great saving.

State of Trade. The last month has been looking gloomy. Newspaper accounts bad; rather looking better now, and hopes of better still before Whitsunday.

To our Machines last week 27 St. of sc; 13 St. of nd. Milled last week 34 pieces.

[1] A reference to broadcloths. Most Galashiels cloths were 'narrow', that is 36 inches wide in the loom to give a finished width of about 29 inches.

28 April. To Comslie[1] wool, £11 11s. 0d. To Jas. Sime junr. for a pack of tazels, £5 2s. 6d. To a stamp 2s. 6½d. To a letter 11½d.

30 April. Payments to be made before the middle of July:

Wages, coals etc.	£90
To Sanderson & Paterson for earth	£9
P. & C. Wood for oil	£20
J. Blaikie's Bill	£226
Henderson, Glasgow	£23
for wool in July	£90
sundries	£22
	£480

11 May. Milled last week 22 pieces. To the Machines last week 36 st. of on; 7 St. sc Gray.

13 May. We have just about 500 pieces booked of this years make.

14 May. When to buy coals as we need them, and when to lay in 10 or 12 cart loads:

From 1st. of June to the first of Sep[tembe]r the price is low and equal; in Sep. (for they remain generally as low in that month as they do through the summer), as many ought to be laid in as will serve in Octr., Novr., Decr., Jany.; and in Feby. when they are again lower than through the winter we ought to buy to serve us March, April and May. The reasons given for these variations in price are, in the summer months the Carters who supply Edin-[burgh] with coals throughout the winter is obliged to drive to the country and of course makes them plentyer here and when they return to drive to Edinr. in winter grow rarer and of course dearer. The coarseness of the weather and the badness of the roads in winter helps in making them dearer in that season, so when the roads grow better which is generally in Feby. which is before seed time of the land is in proper order for working, makes them cheaper in that month than for the three following, when the coal drivers are

[1] Situated about three miles N.E. of Galashiels.

less or more engaged with their pieces of land, in driving limes, sowing their corn and setting their potatoes etc.

It will take £50 a year to keep us in coals and were we to follow the above plan it would save us at least £5 yearly which would pay us well for a few extra poun[d]s being laid out three months or four.

15 May. To bran, 1s. To letter, 9d.

21 May. School books, 1s. 4d.

23 May. To wages, £23 14s. 7d. Lass' wages, £4 4s. 0d.

25 May. To Sanderson & Paterson 45 cwt. earth at 3s. 6d.,

	£7	17s.	6d.
Dis[coun]t		11s.	4d.
	£7	6s.	0d.

To school wages, 16s. 6d. To subscription for school, 4s. 0d.

State of Trade. Trade still dull, accounts had and few sales are making of Cloths.

The way things has turned out now we would perhaps have been better of wanting the 500 St. of wool we Bot. from J. Blaikie in the month of Jany.; although we thought at that time that the demand would keep good, the surest data to walk upon is never to buy an article untill we are in want, which is no easy matter to judge rightly upon.

List of the Manufac[ture]rs.

Robt. Sanderson, slubs, etc.	£1,200
Geo. Paterson	1,100
Jas. Roberts, failed Oct., 1829	900
Robt. Walker, failed Oct., 1829	1,000
John Fairgrieve, failed Oct., 1829	900
James Bathgate	1,300
J. & H. Brown	1,600[1]
J. & W. Cochrane	1,000

[1] Brown sees himself as the biggest manufacturer in the town.

Robt. Gill & Son	1,200
Thos. Gill, failed Oct., 1831	300
James Hunter, failed Oct., 1829	900
William Roberts	600
Robt. Paterson	600
John Lees, failed Dec., 1829	600
Arch. Cochrane	800
James Sime & Son	1,200
Henry Sanderson	1,000
Thomas Clapperton, failed Oct., 1829	300
Alexr. Clapperton, failed Oct., 1829	300
James Rutherford, failed Oct., 1829	600
Thomas Davidson, plaiding	200
William Thomson, yarn	1,000
Thos. Mercer, slubs	600
Rich. Lees & Sons, slubs, failed Nov., 1829	400
John Gledhill, failed July, 1829	400
Christofer Gledhill, flannel	200
Francis Ingels & Son	300
Joshua Wood, yarn	400
Henry Balantine, plaiding, failed	300
George Roberts junr., yarn	1,200
James Sanderson, yarn	600
W. & A. Hislop, stockings	600
James Watson, ditto	400
James Berry, failed Oct., 1829, Wm. Dobson d[itt]o, [and] a number of smaller ones say	1,000
	£26,000

The quantity of business done by each is only supposed, and is likely to be very incorrect in some instances. There is 15 sets of Machines in the town which will manufac[ture] about 22,000 Stones a year, value about £12,000.[1]

The half of the Machinery goes upon clothing wool, the other half upon Stocking yarn, flannels, plaiding, etc., etc. There will have been about 20,000 lbs. of Foreign wool used last year in the twon, the largest quantity ever known to be made use of in any

[1] *Cf.* the entry for 24 July 1828, above, p. 76.

year before; the other kind of wool used is laid white cheviot. Light goods is like[ly] to supersede the Cloths. The English is beating us in Cloths.

26th May. The water is light, it can scarcely drive the two mills at proper speed.[1]

27 May. To the library 4s. 0d.

28 May. What we intend making next for four months:

June – Blue baizes
July – 1 turn Grays, 1 D[itt]o Drabs
August – Grays
Sepr. – 1 turn Baizes and 1 Grays

Although we gave the last black wool 7 lbs. of Logwood to the stone yet the colour is not good, but we ascribe it to the wool not being clean and now thinks it should all be scoured to make a right colour.

£11 11s. 0d. settled by contra acct. with Jas. Bathgate on the 19th which ought to have been stated in the Cash book as received and paid out to keep it correct.

1 June. To Robt. Sanderson's Machines	10 St.	10 lbs.	black sec
		22	white Mix
	11	8	
Weight of sheet		12	
	10	20	
Off for Willying[2]		20	
	St. 10	0	

To boys for by-hours, 1s. 10d.

[1] This could lead to uneven yarn and thus a poor quality of cloth.

[2] An operation carried out on dirty wool to facilitate scouring and to save soap. It was originally done by flailing the wool with willow rods (hence the name), but by the 1820s was doubtless performed by a rotary machine operated either by hand or water. It was also a process used to open out and blend wool.

3 June. To lamp subscription 5s.

5 June. Milled last milling time 32 pieces [Dk. Blues and Mixtures].

To the Machines last turn 120 lbs. of Cheviot er D. Blue
240 lbs of Spainish Blue
24)360(15 stones.

Milled this week 10 pieces.

5 June. To a school book, 1s. 3d. To stamp, 4s. 7d.
List of Cloths on hand:

3	pieces	Blue Baize	sc
5	,,	L. Blues	sc
4	,,	L. Blue	sec sc
1	,,	Olive	er
1	,,	Drab	na
2	,,	,,	nd
2	,,	,,	sc nd
2	,,	,,	sc
3	,,	,,	sec
10	,,	wool Dyed D. Blues	on
2	,,	,, ,, ,,	nd on
1	,,	,, ,, ,,	nd
3	,,	Grays	sec
5	,,	D. Blue piece Dyed	sec
60	,,	,, ,, ,,	sec sc
35	,,	,, ,, ,,	sc
28	,,	,, ,, ,,	sc nd
42	,,	,, ,, ,,	nd
10	,,	,, ,, ,,	nd on
33	,,	,, ,, ,,	on
1	,,	,, ,, ,,	on er
2	,,	,, ,, ,,	er
1	,,	Wool Dyed Blue	sh
260			

There are 158 of these finished for sending off and 46 dressed ready to press; the other 56 are all milled and nearly ready for shearing. In comparing the above list with the one in May last year we find we have 75 pieces more on hand, but the above are of a better assortment than last year's list.

6 June. We have long been wishing to get into a stock of Cloths similar to the present, that is the greatest quantity to be low priced D. Blues; and now when we have them they are not like[ly] to sell, but this spring business has been very dull. When the reason does come, having such a stock of coarse goods will enable us to judge whether or not we have been correct in our views.

Borrowed from James Watson,	£125		
Borrowed from Geo Craig at 3 mos.	£100		
	£225	0s.	0d.
Dis[coun]t of Bill	1	0s.	10d.
	£223	19s.	2d.

To John Blaikie's Bill, £225 14s. 0d.[1]

9 June. From Geo. Paterson for Cloth sold him 9 March, £10 5s. 0d. Out for triffles, 4d.

One cannot meet with manufacturers just now without hearing from them dismal accounts of the badness of trade, dull sales, low prices, and little or nothing doing.

Calculation of 1 St. of wool made into nitting yarn, 3¼ ozs to the Cut:[2]

[1] This, and the entries immediately preceding, seem to indicate liquidity problems. Stock was high, goods were not selling and money had to be borrowed in order to meet Blaikie's bill. Note, once more, the very low rate of discount charged by Craig.

[2] The Galashiels 'cut' was equal to a 300 yard hank, so that this entry means that the knitting yarn weighed 3¼ ounces per 300 yds. This would indicate the diameter, or 'grist' of the yarn and thus its fineness. Note that there were 24 ounces in the pound at this time.

Wool		18s.	0d.
Slubing		4s.	0d.
oil		1s.	0d.
Spinning and twining		2s.	8d.
reeling			4d.
scouring			4d.
	£1	6s.	4d.
25 per cent profit and expences		6s.	8d.
	£1	13s.	0d.

8 sl[ips][1] 3 C[uts] at 4s. 0d. 4s. 0d. the slip is the price Geo. Roberts says (or rather has said here this day) he gets for his yarn at 3¼ oz. the Cut. That weight he says too is the kind that most is sold at.

Having as much wool on hand as will serve us to the 1st Octr., and intending to work 12 pack a month in Octr., Novr., and Decr., 7 pack a month in Jany., Feby., March and April, and to be out of wool 1st May so as to turn our hand (if necessary) to the making of anything else. Upon that view, and on consideration we have resolved to buy just 64 packs of Cheviot wool and that light laid border wool which we consider a great deal better value than the heavy laid coarse wool in this quarter. We have had a trial of all the kinds now.

12 June. On the month of Jany. last, we used some very false reasoning to induce us to purchase wool at that time; for to make a larger quantity of Cloth than usual by 8 or 9 pieces a week, which has the effect of producing a larger stock than we could reasonably expect to have sold to our ordinary customers; for we never thought of seeking new ones although we should have reasoned thus that when we or any other manufacturer else was going to begin to make the double of the Cloths we used to do, we should have required the double of the customers.

Let this statement be a warning to future theorys; things never [ought] to be depended upon unless built upon substantial reasoning. We imagined because that we were selling at the rate of 20 pieces

[1] A slip was equal to 12 cuts (hanks) of 300 yds. Thus the length of yarn on a slip was 3,600 yards.

a week that it would continue instead of considering that what caused the demand was principly the season, and not that another season was fast approaching when very few was likely to be needed and of course our reasoning was bad and ill founded.

13 June. Instead of the views we took [i.e. on 9 June concerning wool usage] we think the following more correct. As we shall sell more goods in Octr., Novr., and Decr. we ought to be prepared with a stock suitable to demand; therefore to manuf[acture] 5 or 6 pieces a month more in the months of Aug., Sepr. and Octr. would be better than refering it to the time we wunded[?] the goods – an error we have committed this year which has had the effect we would wish to steer clear of, viz. a too heavy stock. So being overstocked at present there will be no occasion for doing more than our usual (unless trade be very brisk) this year, so instead of needing 64 packs 50 will be quite sufficient to keep us going to the month of May when we wish to be out [of wool] to have it in our power to turn our hand to anything else if need require.

We have frequently had to regret making our Cloths too thin this last year, it is a great error and perhaps a greater one to make them too strong, but we should rather incline to that side as the other, for the generality of our merchants likes them stout and were we to persist in making them thin there is no doubts but it would hurt our trade very much. Neither too thin nor too stout is the only article to please and pay at the same time. Too thin does not please. Too stout does not pay.[1]

20 June. To wages, £18 12s. 1½d.

The report of Inverness fair is that laid cheviot wool is selling at last year's price, which was from 8s. to 11s. [Stone of 24 lbs.], the greater part about 9s. Offers of 8s. and 8s. 6d. is given for the double st[one] of Highland wool. None sold.

24 June. We were spunging yesterday and the air (and of course the water) was very warm and soft which had the effect of taking

[1] This is not so much a comment as to whether cloth should be made of fine or coarse wool but how many weft courses ('shots per inch') it should contain. The higher the number of courses per inch of cloth the stouter the cloth, if one assumes a yarn of equal grist.

the pressing to quick and unequal off. The air in summer should be cold and frosty to suit spunging.

To Journey for expenses, £4. Milled last week 18 pieces.

28 June. From Henry Balantine No. 501 34 yds. Plaiding at 11½d., £1 12s. 7d.

6 July. Milled last week 26 pieces.

8 July. To apprentice 6d.

8 July. Cash brought from Journey				£321	17s.	0d.
Rec'd. for Geo. Roberts	£13	12s.	0d.			
Rec'd. for Thos. Davidson	£ 1	3s.	0d.			
Rec'd. for Jas. Watson	£26	19s.	0d.	£ 41	14s.	0d.
				£280	3s.	0d.
2 Bills	£53	7s.	6d.			
Inter[est?]		12s.	5d.			
				52	15s.	1d.
				£332	18s.	1d.
Paid when on journey to I[nver]ness:						
Robt. & John Henderson				£ 22	2s.	6d.
Jas. Richardson				1	10s.	0d.
expenses at d[itt]o 14 days				10	11s.	0d.
				£ 34	3s.	6d.
[Plus]				£332	18s.	1d.
				£367	1s.	7d.

10 July. To Wm. Brown for balance of rent up to Whitsunday 1829, £9 4s. 6d. From Geo. Roberts for collecting money, 7s. 0d.

Calculation of Blue Flannels:

sc – 1s. 6d. 36 [inches?]
sc – 1s. 7d. 38
sc – 1s. 8d. 40

nd or sc nd, 1d. more on each kind.

11 July. The Blue flannel trade is a new one with us and I dont know how it may succeed but in trying them last journey farely has found that a great quantity may be sold if we can make them as good and as cheap as the English, and I see no reason why we should not equal if not excel them in that article; both our wool and our Machinery is adapted for making *them*. (So is theirs query. Wool Dyed blues quite different.)

13 July. William Riddock, Alloa Shipowner, there informed me when out last that he could bring in fullers earth from London for 27s. the ton, cost price at London £1, freight 7s. and by laying it down at Fisherow we would save some dues.

This is another lesson showing us that we ought never to be at rest until we have tryed every quarter whether or not an article cannot be bought cheaper or not. For this spring we was near givin £4 the ton but got it at £3 5s. 0d. and now see we might have had it at £2 10s. 0d. laid down at our door by takin 20 ton as above.

14 July. *Stripes*. For our ordinary piece Dyed Cheviot wool Cloths:

10	threads	Blue
2	,,	Red
6	,,	Yellow
2	,,	Red
10	,,	Blue
2	,,	Red
6	,,	Yellow
2	,,	Red
10	,,	Blue
2	,,	Red
6	,,	Yellow
2	,,	Red
10	,,	Blue
—		
70	,,	all Listing yarn

For Wool dyed Blues:

10 threads		Yellow for tearing off	
20	,,	Blue	same as the weft of the web
2	,,	Yellow	
4	,,	Blue	,, ,, ,, ,, ,, ,, ,,
12	,,	Yellow	
4	,,	Blue	,, ,, ,, ,, ,, ,, ,,
2	,,	Yellow	
20	,,	Blue	,, ,, ,, ,, ,, ,, ,,
2	,,	Yellow	
4	,,	Blue	,, ,, ,, ,, ,, ,, ,,
12	,,	Yellow	
4	,,	Blue	,, ,, ,, ,, ,, ,, ,,
2	,,	Yellow	
20	,,	Blue	,, ,, ,, ,, ,, ,, ,,
2	,,	Yellow	
4	,,	Blue	,, ,, ,, ,, ,, ,, ,,
12	,,	Yellow	
4	,,	Blue	,, ,, ,, ,, ,, ,, ,,
2	,,	Yellow	
142	,,	the yellow listing yarn	

This stripe would look better with a cut but not too bare.

14 July. Wool dyed:

10 threads		Yellow for tearing off
12	,,	Blue same as weft
6	,,	Yellow
10	,,	Blue
6	,,	Red
6	,,	Yellow
10	,,	White
6	,,	Yellow
6	,,	Red
10	,,	Blue
6	,,	Yellow

88 Blue same as weft, the rest listing yarn

Wool Dyed and striped with Mohair:

10	threads	Yellow for tearing off, common listing yarn
24	,,	Blue same as weft
12	,,	Yellow hair or white
24	,,	Blue
12	,,	Yellow
24	,,	Blue
12	,,	Yellow
118		

the upermost of these two would either do with or without a cut, but the undermost must be left rough.

To the Machines	150 lbs. sec
Weight of two sheets	8 lbs.
	142 lbs.

Rink Fair. Little or nothing done, white wool expected to be 1s. 0d. or 1s. 6d. lower than last year. Laid [wool] at last year's price. There is very little laid wool in the Country this year, the farmers got such a small price for it last year, which has made them keep it all white, at least a greater part of them. The accounts from Inverness since the fair is that most of the laid cheviot is sold at about last years prices or rather better.

List of our customers:

Porteous & Smith, Edinburgh
John Syme, Edinburgh
J. & W. Campbell & Co., Glasgow
William Gilmour & Co., Glasgow
John Shield, failed, Glasgow
A. & J. McKeand, Glasgow
John Frazer, failed, Glasgow
John Galbraith, failed, Glasgow
*Chalmers & Kilgour & Co., Glasgow
John McIntyre & Co., Glasgow
James Richardson, Falkirk
*Robt. Smith, Falkirk
*Thos. Hardie, Falkirk
*Wm. Heeming, Falkirk
James Stuart, Alloa
Andrew Robb, Alloa
John McEwan, Crieff
John Richardson, Crieff
*Alexr. McRosty, Crieff
Thos. McEwan, Crieff
William Miller, Methven (failed)
Thos. Robertson, Perth
Robt. Robertson, Perth
Hood & Jackson, Perth
*Thos & John Forsyth, Perth
Andrew Ireland, Perth
*Colon Golon, Perth

★Wm. D. Campbell, Perth
★Alex. Cameron, Perth
Roderick McKenzie, Perth
George Bruce, Erroll
William Archbald, Alloa
★John Archbald, Menstry
John Douglas, Dundee
★Helen Heeming, Dundee
★Robt. Moyes, Dundee
★Colon Golon, Dundee
★G. L. Baxter, Dundee
William Barker, Aberdeen
William Elmslie & Son, Aberdeen
James Johnston Senr., Aberdeen
★James Rae, failed, Aberdeen
James Connan, failed, Aberdeen
Samuel Johnston, failed, Aberdeen
A. & L. Jeans[?], failed, Aberdeen
★James Mitchell, Aberdeen
★Durno & Michell, failed, Aberdeen
★Brown & Carr, Aberdeen
Harvey Hall & Co., Aberdeen
Robt. Richardson, Selkirk
John Robertson & Co., Selkirk
Andrew Glen, Selkirk
★William Brockie, Selkirk
John Hislop & Co., Hawick
James Isaac, Melrose

We have done more or less business with upwards of 200 houses since 1818 There is only about 12 of these we call good customers. There is perhaps [an]other twenty we call upon and does less or more with, and about twenty of the above we do very little with marked★.

15 July. Adding 25 pieces each [of] coarse Grays and Drabs to our present stock of Cloths, we will then have about 280 pieces after executing the present orders, and if our sales be in proportion to last season, it will take us to the Middle of Decr. before we can expect to have them all sold. From the middle of Decr. last till the first of April we sold 200 p[iece]s and in Ap[ril], May and June 60 p[ieces] – therefore we ought to take up our time with making these 50 p[iece] of Drabs and Grays and the rest with Blue Flannels until the middle of Octr. when we should begin to make 50 p[iece]s a month for four months, that is to the middle of Feby. and from that time to the first of June we should do considerably less, as that is by far the slackest time of the whole year. I at present see no reason to do more than we sold last year but think I see reason to do rather less, for it appears to me that the English low-priced wool Dyed Cloths, and even their same listed piece-dyed ones is gaining ground in the Scotch market, and will I think cut us out altogether by and by. There is no reason why we should make exactly the same quantity as we made last year; by looking into our day book if we see we are selling more let us make more, if fewer make fewer.

To the Machines	836 lbs. sc
7 hand sheets	42 lbs.
	794 lbs.

33 St. 2 lb. Called 31 St. Willyed wool.

16 July. To expences at Rink, £1 10s. 0d. Expences at Club, 1s. 0d.

From Geo. Hall, Bellshill[1]	£12	15s.	6d.
From Simon Dodd, Catcleuch	8	0s.	6d.
	£20	16s.	0d.

Bot the following lots of Cheviot wool in Reed water:

Mark Robson, Dykehead, about 60 St. at 10s. 0d. and 3d. more refer'd to him.

Stuartsheil[2] herds, about 24 St. at 9s. 6d.

Mr Paterson, Yatesfield,[3] about 130 St. [at] 10s. 0d. 6d. more refer'd to us and 6d. less refer'd to Mr Paterson.[4]

Mr Matthew Reed Oldtown, about 200 St. at 9s. 0d.

Mr Clark, Highgreen, about 50 St. at 10s. 0d.

—— herds about 15 St. at 9s. 0d.

Jas. Sime & Son has the half of the above.

To Simon Dodd for wool	£35	4s.
,, ,, ,, butter[5]	6	6s.
To Matthew Reed for wool	24	10s.
	£66	0s.

18 July. To wages, £21 10s. 0d. To expences at Boswell fair, 10s. 6d.

[1] Probably, 'Bellshiel', near Rochester, Northumberland.

[2] Situated east of the main road between Rochester and Otterburn, Northumberland. [3] Similarly situated between Rochester and Otterburn.

[4] When manufacturers purchased a farmer's wool they agreed on a rough price which would be finalised when local fair prices were known (see 18 July, below, p. 115). Thus this batch of wool, with 6d. referred both ways would cost between 9s. 6d. and 10s. 6d. the stone. In this case the wool was actually purchased at 10s. (see entry for 18 Aug., below, p. 118).

[5] The butter may have been for personal consumption but it was sometimes used instead of olive oil in the willeying process (see p. 104, n. 2).

Bou[gh]t of Matthew Young, Burdenside,[1] about 130 St. of wool at 10s. Luckpenny £3.

Boswell Fair. Price of Border Laid wool from 9s. to 11s.; White from 14s. to 16s. Little done except by Gala[shiel]s folk. White 3s. 0d. lower nearly, laid 6d.

Robt. Richardson Selkirk, 1 p[iece] Drab at 2s. 6d.
James Isaac, Melrose 1 ,, D. Blue at 2s. 9d.

20 July. To twine for packing Wetherly[2] wool, 1s. 8d. For Wetherly wool Pd., £31 15s. 0d.

23 July. What we would reckon a fair stock of Cloths:

sh	Blues	4	to	8	pieces	
er	,,	2	,,	4	,,	
on er	,,	2	,,	4	,,	
on	,,	6	,,	10	,,	
nd on	,,	6	,,	12	,,	
nd	,,	6	,,	16	,,	
sc	,,	12	,,	20	,,	
sec sc	,,	6	,,	16	,,	
on	Drab	1	,,	2	,,	
nd	,,	2	,,	4	,,	
sc nd	,,	2	,,	4	,,	
sc	,,	2	,,	4	,,	
sec	,,	2	,,	6	,,	
sec	Gray	2	,,	10	,,	
sc nd	L. Blue	2	,,	4	,,	
sc	,,	2	,,	4	,,	
sec sc	,,	2	,,	4	,,	
sc nd	36 & 38 in	2	,,	6	,,	Blue flan[nel]
sc	,, ,, ,, & 40 [in]	4	,,	10	,,	,, ,,
		73		164		

[1] Most likely Burdonside, which lies about ten miles west of Otterburn, Northumberland.

[2] Wetherly was probably located south-east of Otterburn in the vicinity of Wether Hill.

The first of these [columns] may be considered a good stock in the Spring and the other a good one in the back end of the year before going to the journeys; the one half less may do when the journey's orders is executed.

28 July. Prices of G. Roberts Nitting Yarn for last year, when the white wool was selling at 18s. and 19s. and the laid for dying at 9s. and 10s. the stone:

4	lbs. per Spinnel at	14s. 6d.
5¼	,, ,, ,, ,,	14s. 6d.
6¾	,, ,, ,, ,,	14s. 6d.
9	,, ,, ,, ,,	15s. 6d.
9¼	,, ,, ,, ,,	16s. 0d.
10½	,, ,, ,, ,,	18s. 0d.
12	,, ,, ,, ,,	20s. 0d.
3 shades Blue		20s. 0d.

5 per cent dis[coun]t first journey. A Blue Gray, and Black Gray about 9¼ lbs. weight per Spinnel is the kinds that is most in request. Perhaps we may in the course of time turn our attention to the yarn trade when the above may assist us.

30 July. Stock:

sec	6	pieces value	1s. 5d. nett
sec sc	55	,, ,,	1s. 8d. ,,
sc	65	,, ,,	1s. 10d. ,,
sc nd	26	,, ,,	2s. 0d. ,,
nd	47	,, ,,	2s. 0d. ,,
nd on	10	,, ,,	2s. 6d. ,,
on	47	,, ,,	2s. 8d. ,,
on er	6	,, ,,	2s. 10d. ,,
er	3	,, ,,	3s. 0d. ,,
sh	8	,, ,,	3s. 10d. ,,
	273		

176 of these is papered up ready for sale, the half of the other 97 is nearly finished for pressing; the others among hands.

31 July. 1 Cwt. of Copperas, 7s. 6d.

5 August. To Coffee Room, 8s. Milled last week 24 pieces.
To the Machines last week: 21 St. of sec
19 St. of sc
—
40 St.

Galawater was very large yesterday, it took away the caul at the dam head and Robt. Sanderson's caul and the banks of Gala at different places. Damage £100 to £150.

7 August. Price of Cards given by Morffie Lime, Card Maker, Kendal.:

36 by 5 In.	80 Coton Crown[1]	6s. 1d.	Sheet
,, ,, ,, ,,	90 Fine Coton Crown	6s.11d.	
,, ,, ,, ,,	100 ,, ,, ,,	7s. 4s.	
,, ,, ,, ,,	100 Fine Super Crown	7s. 10d.	
,, ,, ,, ,,	110 ,, ,, ,,	8s. 3d.	
,, ,, ,, ,,	120 ,, ,, ,,	8s. 8d.	
26 by 5 In.	100 Fine Coton Crown	5s. 3d.	
,, ,, ,, ,,	100 Fine Super Crown	5s. 8d.	
,, ,, ,, ,,	110 ,, ,, ,,	6s. 1d.	
,, ,, ,, ,,	120 ,, ,, ,,	6s. 5d.	

Fine Coton Crown is 8 Crowns upon the In[ch]. Fine Super Crown is 9 Crowns upon the In. Cleaner plates 3s. per yd. These plates is one half cheaper than Stead & Paterson's and their cards in some instances 1s. 1d. the sheet higher charged than the above.

8 August. Manufactured 700 pieces this last year, the greatest quantity ever we made in one year before, but we should have made fewer as we have too heavy a stock.

[1] That is, the number of teeth or metal tacks per square inch. The rollers of the carding engine were covered with these teeth set into leather. The greater the number of teeth in a given area the finer the sliver of wool produced.

13 August. To expences at Melrose fair, 2s. 6d. The white wool was considered 1s. lower yesterday than it was at St Boswells.

15 August. Paid for wages, £19 6s. 7d.
Expences for packing wool between

J. Sime & Son & us:	£1	11s.	0d.
2 lb. twine		2s.	6d.
Stamps, 2 at 4s. 7d., 1 at 3s. 7d.		12s.	9d.
Settled	£2	6s.	3d.

Paid for wool, £50 3s. 6d.
Our share of expences and stamps as above £1 1s. 10½d.

17 August. To school wages, £1 3s. 6d.

18 August. Wool packed last week:

Mark Robson, Dykehead, at 10s. 3d.	46	St.
C. Headly, Rochester, at 9s. 0d.	12	St.
J. Paterson, Yatesfield, at 10s. 0d.	122	St.
Wm. Smith, Dudleys,[1] at 9s. 0d.	34	St.
Stuartshield herds, at 9s. 0d.	24¼	St.
M. Reed, Oldtown, at 9s. 0d.	240	St.
Herds, Oldtown, at 9s. 0d.	4¾	St.
Mr. Clark, Highgreen, at 10s. 0d.	51	St.
Gibshiel[2] herds, at 9s. 0d.	13¼	St.
M. Young, Burdenside, at 9s. 6d.	130	St.
	677¼	

Bought at same time and left unpacked:

Thos Ord, Lumsden, at 10s.	82
B. English, Woodhouse,[3] at 9s.	112
Jas. Sime & Son the half	)871¼
	435½

[1] Or Dudlees, located deep in the Northumberland fells, east of Rochester.
[2] A remote farm just off the Pennine Way, about five miles south-west of Rochester.
[3] Located to the west of the Roman Dere Street, about ten miles south of Rochester.

Jas. Hogg, Nethershiel,[1] at 9s.	72½
Jas. Hogg, Torpentine[?][2] at 9s. 9d.	29
Comslie Highland	39
Wm. Robertson Wetherly at 10s.	61
Old wool value at 10s.	240
12)	877 St.
	73.1 Packs.

877 St. average about 9s. 6d.	£416	11s.	6d.
Paid	170	0s.	0d.
	£246	11s.	6d.

We never had cheaper wool and we may say Indigo too as we have just got in 330 lbs., average price 3s. 8d. per lb. from Messrs. Downie's Glasgow which looks remarkably well at the money.

19 August. Bot from Henry Sanderson 16 yds. Broad Blue at 10s. 6d., £8 8s. 0d. 5 per cent at 4 months.

Thos. Stanford's order–1 p[ie]ce Drab at 2s. 2d.
1 ,, Dk. Blue at 3s. 0d. and 3s. 6d.

24 August. Rent:	Machine House	£1	0s.	0d.
	Tenters		11s.	9d.
	Garden		14s.	0d.
	Caul		6s.	9d.
		£2	12s.	6d.

25 August. To 39¾ cwt. of coals at 9d., £1 9s. 9d. This Coalman was for cheating me out of a cwt. and ¼; he called the carts that much lighter than they were.

State of Trade. We have been selling very few Cloths and believes very few have been selling in the twon this four months past; from reports business has been more than ordinary dull this

[1] Nethershiels is situated at the head of Lugate Water west of Stow, a few miles north of Galashiels.

[2] Possibly Torquhan, near Nethershiels, which could, therefore, have been farmed by Hogg as well. But the original entry appears to read 'Torpentine'.

last Spring and Summer throughout England and Scotland. Our future prospects depends on how the crop is got secured; it looks well at present and if it is got well in we will have a brisk back end. If otherwise we will have but a very so and so trade this year.

27 August. I have often thought about this season of the year after our wool was bought in, and the prices that was likely to be got for goods; [so] that I formed very correct opinions how trade would pay throughout the year.

My opinion is this year that our trade will not pay us above 7½ per cent profit on the money turned if even it reaches that high.

31 August. To our share of expences for Nethershiel wool, 4s. od.

Price of weaving Plaiding on a 12 quarter loom[1] 3 plaidings wide, and all below.

12 – 3 [is] 3d. per yd.
12 – 3 [is] 3½d. per yd.
13 – 3 [is] 4d. and then rises ¼[d] on each set till a 20 – 3.

1 September. It is our opinion at present that we have for the last two or three years past been spinning too round, especially the weft which we think now ought to be no rounder than the warp; the warp should be one set if not two smaller than formerly and weft the same, the weight made up by adding breadth. This we think will be an improvement upon our present system.

3 September. Calculation of a fortnights Blue Duffles:

48 St. of wool at 10s. od.	£24	os.	od.
Machine House wages	2	os.	od.
Machine House rent	2	os.	od.
Machine House Cards, etc.	1	os.	od.
Wages for Drying and Dressing	6	os.	od.
Indigo	7	os.	od.

[1] Twelve quarters refers to $\frac{12}{4}$ times the 37″ yard (ell) and would thus measure 111 inches.

Redwood and Coals	1	0s.	0d.
Other rents and Teazels	1	0s.	0d.
Oil	2	10s.	0d.
Weaving	7	0s.	0d.
Spinning	2	10s.	0d.
	£56	0s.	0d.
30 pieces at £2 2s. 0d. nett	63	0s.	0d.
Profit	£7	0s.	0d.

8 September. It is said that experience is the best teacher. In the year 1825 when things fell dull and our cloth would not sell we began and made our fine Cheviot wool into wool-dyed Drabs instead of dark blues, but found that would not do either. Then we dyed it into wool dyed Blues and that would not do; we next tryed fine foreigne wools and that failed too, and latterly we have been making a quantity of low priced cheviot Blues and they have been stucking too, and presently we are engaged [in] making Blue Duffles and is going to make Blue and White Plaidings. How these will do we know not, but we have found by our experience that the others will not do.

10 September. Paid for Wm. Brown Subscription school, 9s. 1d. Paid for share of pig to W[illiam] B[rown], 8s. 0d.

From Jas. Sime & Son, £7 11s. 9d. which we paid for them in the border.

11 September. To William Thomson's Mill:

weight of first sheet	237 lbs.
weight of second sheet	198 lbs.
	435 lbs.
weight of two sheets	14
	24)411(17.3 [Stones]
	2.3 [St.] Allowance
	15.0 St.

12 September. To wages, £18 0s. 5d.

The prices fixed upon for weaving Plaiding: 12 – 3, 2½d.; 12 – 4, 3d.; 14 – 3, 3d.; 14 – 4,[1] 3½d. Weaver pay the warping. All things else upheld.

14 September. Debts due by us about	£560	0s.	0d.
Cash debts due about	£360	0s.	0d.
	£200	0s.	0d.
Sums to pay this month:			
Bill, 20 Sep.	£11	0s.	0d.
R.R.Ed'n[burgh]	9	0s.	0d.
12 Sep. Last [?]	1	8s.	0d.
Henderson, Edin[burgh]	3	6s.	0d.
Wages, Coals etc.	33	6s.	0d.
	£58	0s.	0d.

15 September. The following are the result of calculations made this day: 36 English lbs. of our tar[r]ed[2] cheviot wool gives 21 lbs. of finished Cloths Duffles or Plaidings. Valuing this sc wool that we make Duffles and Plaidings of at 10s. 0d. per Stone and allowing 10 per cent profit we would be enabled to sell White Plaiding at 18d. per lb. or 10d. per yd., ¾ Blue Plaiding at 21d. per lb. or 1s. per yd., Blue Duffles at 21d. per lb. and price per yd. according to their breadth, and for sec Grays and Drabs at 17d. per lb. or 16¼d. per yd. Sc Grays and Drabs at 21¼d. per lb. or 20½d. per yd.

Dark Blues: sec sc at 21d. per lb. or 20d. per yd.
sc at 22d. per lb. or 21d. per yd.
nd at 2s. 3d. per lb. or 2s. 1d. per yd.
on at 2s. 6d. per lb. or 2s. 4d. per yd.

all nett money. Average value of the wool 10s. stone.

19 September. To carriage of reeds, 6d.

Drawn £50 at 4 mo[nths] from Geo. Craigs for James Stewart, Alloa. Dis[coun]t and Com[mission] £1 2s. 2d. Paid Jas. Stewart £48 17s. 10d.

[1] The reference means 12 and 14 quarter looms (see p. 120, n. 1), 3 and 4 plaidings wide.
[2] *i.e.* 'laid' wool (see p. 72, n. 2).

24 September. Kind and quantity of goods to make at present:

12	p[iece]s	40	in[ch]	Duffles
30	,,	36	,,	,,
30	,,	38	,,	,,
8	,,	27	,,	,,
4	,,	27	,,	Camlets[1]
24	,,	27	,,	white Plaidings
18	,,	27	,,	,, ,,
2	,,	38	,,	,, ,,
6	,,	36	,,	,, ,,

134 pieces which includes those on hand and in making.

[We] has sold 70 pieces of Duffle since we began to make them in July.

25 September. Stock of Cloth on hand of which 185 are finished, 51 are ready for pressing, 16 among hands finishing.

55	pieces	D. Blue	sec sc
30	,,	,, ,,	sc
2	,,	,, ,,	sc nd
45	,,	,, ,,	nd
9	,,	,, ,,	nd on
39	,,	,, ,,	on wool dyed
5	,,	,, ,,	on er
2	,,	,, ,,	er
6	,,	,, ,,	sh er wool dyed[2]
1	,,	,, ,,	sh
2	,,	L. Blue	sec sc
2	,,	,, ,,	sc
8	,,	Drab	sec
4	,,	,,	sec sc
3	,,	,,	sc
2	,,	,,	nd
1	,,	,,	on
9	,,	Common Grays	sec

[1] A cloth designed to imitate camel hair.

[2] These pieces Brown has made from a mixture of Spanish and fine Cheviot wool.

	6 ,,	Baize	sec
	2 ,,	,,	sc
	252		
[Plus]	134		
	386 Value about 50s. each £965.		

It is said that want of care does no more damage than want of knowledge. I think we should be careful to have all the above goods sold ere the first of Jany.

Lengths, weight of warp, and weight of a single piece out of the loom for:

12. 13. 14. Reed[1]		56 yds.	31 lbs.	33 lbs.
15. 16. ,,		60 ,,	29 ,,	33 ,,
17. 18. ,,		62 ,,	30 ,,	35 ,,
Duffles	36 in.	56 ,,	29 ,,	33 ,,
,,	38 ,,	56 ,,	30 ,,	34 ,,
,,	40 ,,	56 ,,	31 ,,	35 ,,[2]

This will scarcely be altogether correct but it is better to have a rule with a few faults than no rule at all and the above will do untill such time as a better one can be thought of.

26 September. To carriage of Cards, 1s. 4d. To James Hutton for 3 times using his smoking house, 6d.[3] To brimstone, 4½d.

28 September. Interest from money lying in the L[eith] Bank, £1 19s. 4d.[4]

[1] For 'reed' see p. 61, n. 6. A 12 reed has 240 'splits' in a loom width of 37 inches since there are 40 threads in a 'porter' and each split has two threads. A split is the gap between the teeth of the reed. A 14 reed would therefore be calculated thus: $\frac{14 \times 40}{2} = 280$ splits each with two threads.

[2] Notice that the addition of the weft makes only a small difference to the weight of the finished piece.

[3] At that time plaiding made from white wool was sometimes smoked over a peat fire, or with sulphur to tone down the colour: '. . . this man's trousers [were] . . . well smoked . . . with an age of peat reek, which by no means improved the appearance' ('Reminiscences of the Tweed Trade', *Border Advertiser*, 9 Dec., 1874). As Brimstone is mentioned here Brown was probably using the sulphur method.

[4] Brown's cash assets seem to have been very small at this date which accords with his heavy stock and the slump in sales.

Out for sundries since March and not marked down, 4s. 9½d. (errors).

The following is what we had out of 17 St. of rather heavy laid wool. It was all spun warp the wei[ght] of which was 344 lbs.

short of weight	64 ,,
	408 lbs. or 17 St.

Number of slips 197 or rather better than 11 slips 6 cuts the stone so we cannot calculate less than 9d. the stone for spinning.

We find we have just as near as maybe 14 lbs. of finished goods out of 24 lbs. of our laid wool; if the wool is light laid and clean it will yield a little more and if dirty rather less. 14 lbs. may be considered an average.

30 September. To B. Hislop for whisky to the Machine house, 1s. 11d. To brimstone, 4d.

1 October. To William Thomson's machines:

weight of 1st sheet	237 [lbs]		
weight of 2nd sheet	231		
	468		
weight of 2 sheets	24		
24)444(	18 [st.]	12 [lbs]	
	2	8	allowance
	16	4	

5 October. Prices that R. Gill pays for weaving on 12 qu[arter] looms:

16 Reed and under	3d.
17 and 18 Reed	3¼d.
19 and 20 ,,	3½d.
21 and 22 ,,	4d.
23 and 24 ,,	4½d.
25 and 26 ,,	5d.
27 and 28 ,,	5½d. wool dyed 6d.

The weavers pay nothing for warping,[1] nor loom rent[2] but pays 1s. each loomful for Pirns[3] and pays for popin [?bobins].

To Jas. Sime [piece number] 2289 – 25 yds. Drab sec.

To a Broad-loom, £6 10s. 6d.[4]

7 October. To tenter hooks, 1s. for 200. To expences at Journey, £4.

10 October. To wages, £21 8s. 4d.

12 October. To Jas Hutton for three times using his smooking house, 6d.

14 October. To Wm. Johnston for sorting teazels, 6d. Ordered from Eagle & Henderson ½ cwt. of brimstone sold at 18s. 0d. per cwt.

19 October. To Horsburgh for sitting up in the churchyard, 3s.

22 October. From Robt. Richardson, Selkirk:

Wool including sheet	88 lbs.
suppose sheet	8
	80 lbs. of wool

23 October. Cash from journey, £209 14s. 6d. Bills from journey, £144 4s. 0d.

[1] Warping is the act of feeding the warp threads through the 'splits' in the reed of the loom and attaching the ends to rollers, which revolve to turn on the cloth as the weft threads were woven in. On a fine cloth there could be as many as 1,300 warp threads while a coarse cloth had about 600. It was thus a time-consuming process which could waste the weaver a lot of time and therefore earnings. Here Brown pays for the warping to be done.

[2] The mention of loom-rent suggests that the weavers did not own their own looms but rented them from Henry and James Brown. The renting of manufacturing equipment from the masters was a common practice at this time which only gradually died out in the course of the nineteenth century in handicraft trades such as hand-loom weaving and stocking knitting.

[3] Spools on which weft yarn was wound. The weavers thus paid for the winding of their yarn.

[4] The price suggests that this was a second-hand loom.

Expences for 15 days at journey £9 17s. 6d. which is at the rate of 13s. 0d. a day and upwards of 2½ per cent on money collected.

From James Richardson, Falkirk, to Thos Davidson	£7	2s.	0d.
Di[tt]o J. Stewart	4	4s.	0d.
Paid T. D[avidson]	£11	6s.	0d.

To Thos. Davidson for goods 20 July, £1 9s. 0d.

To Henry Sanderson for goods 19 Aug., £7 12s. 0d. Lent Henry Sanderson £12 11s. 0d. (Nov. 23, pd. £4 2s. 0d.; Nov. 27, pd. £8 9s. 0d.)

27 October. To candle, 8d. To school wages, 9s. 6d.

31 October. To John Fairgrieve for Potatoes, £2 0s. 0d.[1]

To Archd. Elliot's acct.	£3	5s.	0d.
Geo. Brown		8s.	6d.
	£3	13s.	6d.
a/c by Cloth		9s.	2d.
	£3	4s.	4d.
Disc[oun]t			4d.
By Cash	£3	4s.	0d.

(To receive deals to the amount of full 5 per cent Dis[coun]t.)

2 November.

To Wm. Thomson's Machines	236 [lbs]		
sheet	12		
	24)224	9 St. 5 lb.	
		18 lb.	for Willying
		8 St. 3 lb.	

To Robt. Sanderson's about 6 St. on.

State of Trade. Goods selling but at very low prices. Since we

[1] This represents a considerable amount of potatoes and it is possible that Brown intended them to help fermentation. *Cf.* Fairlie, *op. cit.*, 495 note 1; 501.

began the Blue Duffle trade in July we have sold one hundred pieces and upwards, and 50 to 60 white and blue Plaidings. We expect to make a trade of these things. Galashiels Cloths has still the appearance of going out of use.[1]

5 November. To Jackson, Langholm, 5 gross weft pirns, £1 10s. 0d.

7 November. To wages, £23 2s. 3½d.

Drab:

Shumac	1 lb.	0 oz.
Mulmadder	2	0
Logwood		4
Yellowood		12
Copperas	1	0

For two p[iece]s of stout tweeled Cloth:

Bright Madder	2 lb.	0 oz.
Mul Madder		12
Yellowood		8
Copperas		8

11 November. Bot. of A. J. Downie a chest of Indigo at 3s. 6d. per lb. delivered at Leith by Bill at 9 months or if paid in Feby. 5 per cent dis[coun]t.

12 November. Cash and Bills on hand and debts due us £723

due by us about	385
Balance in our favour	338

Sums to pay in a month:

14 Nov.	£30
4 Dec.	25
6 Dec.	16
Wages, etc.	31
	92

(14 Dec. £30 15s. 0d.)

Prices Robt. Gill pays for weaving on 12 quarter looms:

Plaidings.		Camlets.	
10 – 4 and all below,	3d.	16 and all below	3¼d.
11 – 4 and 12 – 4,	3½d.	17 and 18	3½d.

[1] He was correct in his surmise. See p. 54 above.

12 – 3 and all below, 3d.		19 and 20	$3\frac{3}{4}$d.
14 – 3	$3\frac{1}{2}$d.	2s. off 90 to 105 yds. for Pirns.	
16 – 3	$3\frac{1}{2}$d.		
2s. off 90 to 105 yds. for pirns.[1]			

Lodged with G. Craig a bill of Wm. Biggar to Robt. Scott endorsed to us by Porteous & Smith, Edinr. of £15 15s. od. dated 12 Oct. 4 Mo[nths].

To Insurance, £3 10s. 3d.

Names of individuals who have failed here in Oct. 1829.

Name		Amount			
Thos. Clapperton	in about	[£]4,000	Pay about 4s.	per £.	
Alexr. Clapperton	,, ,,	500	,, ,, 6s.	,, ,,	(4s.)[2]
James Hunter	,, ,,	700	,, ,, 6s.	,, ,,	(4s.)
Robt. Walker	,, ,,	3,300	,, ,, 6s. 6d.	,, ,,	(4s. 6d.)
John Fairgrieve	,, ,,	2,500	,, ,, 9s.	,, ,,	(7s.)
James Roberts	,, ,,	1,800	,, ,, 5s.	,, ,,	
James Rutherford	,, ,,	2,300	,, ,, 7s.	,, ,,	(4s. 6d.)
James Verry	,, ,,	500	,, ,, 5s.	,, ,,	
Wm. Dobson	,, ,,	500	,, ,, 11s.	,, ,,	(7s.)
		£16,100			

One third of this sum is occasioned by additional rankings, the whole loss to the country will be from 6 to £7,000, the half of which will be lost by people in Galashiels. The principal cause of these failers has been the want of management.

13 November. To Bill in National [Bank], Jedburgh, £30.

16 November. To lime,[3] 2s. 3d. Soap, 6d.

19 November. To Wm. Gill for 33 yds. Flannel, £2 9s. od.

24 November. To H[enry] B[rown] for servant's wage, £2.

[1] See p. 126, n. 3.
[2] The figures in parentheses were probably added later and represent the amount in the £ actually paid to creditors. [3] Used to increase alkalinity in the indigo vat.

27 November. Goods to be gotten ready for March journey:

Cloths

8	pieces	D. Blue	from	21d. to 2s. 2d.
8	,,	,, ,,	,,	2s. 2d. to 2s. 6d.
8	,,	,, ,,	,,	2s. 6d. to 3s. 0d.
4	,,	,, ,,	,,	3s. 0d. to 3s. 4d.
4	,,	L. Blue	,,	19d. to 22s.
4	,,	Drabs	,,	18d. to 2s. 0d.

Duffles

4	,,	27 in[ch]
8	,,	36 ,,
8	,,	38 ,,
6	,,	40 ,,

Plaiding

6	p[ieces]	Blue	27 in.	
6	,,	,,	36 ,,	
6	,,	,,	38 or 39 in.	
50	,,	White	,, ,, ,, ,,	10d. to 11d.
18	,,	,,	,, ,, ,, ,,	9½d.
6	,,	,,	,, ,, ,, ,,	8½d.

Camlets

2 p[ieces] 14d.

158[1]

28 November. To Mill next week:

2	p[ieces]	Cloth Lt. Blue	sc
2	,,	Drab	sec sc
2	,,	,,	sec sec
2	,,	Lt. Blue	,, ,,
4	,,	Drab	sec
2	,,	Duffle	36 in.
6	,,	Tweeled Gray	sec
18	,,	White plaiding	

38

[1] The column in fact amounts to 156 pieces.

Among weavers:

12 [pieces]	White Plaidings		
4 ,,	Blue	,,	36 in.
4 ,,	Duffles	,,	38 ,,
2 ,,	Cloths		sec sc
2 ,,	,,	,,	sec

To lay to the Machines:

20 St. for White plaiding
7 St for Cloth er
23 St for Duffles and Blue Plaidings

To a cart of peats, 6s. 6d.

30 November. To Jas. Bathgate for slubing at Buckholmside, £15.

Received in small sums, 8s. 2d. From A. Elliott, 6 deals of 5 in.[1] From N. Wood for flannel, 3s. 6d.

1 December. To tenter hooks, 2s.

5 December. To wages, £25 18s. 6½d.

7 December. To John Fairgrieve 16 lbs. of our 3s. 11d. Indigo.

9 December. To John Fairgrieve's[2] Mill, 15 St. 10 lbs. on. (3 Dec.).

Robt. Sanderson, 9 St. 2 lbs. er.

11 December. Mr John Aitchison, 11, West Register St., Stationer, Edinr.

Gray paper 4¾d. per lb. at 3 mo[nths].
Coppy paper 6¼d. per quire.

12 December. To James Robert's mill 24 St. 13 lb. of sc nd for plaiding.

[1] See entry for 31 Oct. 1829, above, p. 127.

[2] This man is listed as having failed in business in the crisis of 1829 (see entry under 12 Nov., 1829, above, p. 129). He is undertaking commission work here but is back buying indigo.

To mill next week:

9 white Plaidings	4 Duffles 36 in.
4 Blue Plaidings 36 in.	8 Blue Cloth sec sc
8 Tweeled Grays sec	2 Drab sec
	35

Wool to the Machines next fortnight:

10 St of on er	14 St of sc Duffles
14 ,, ,, sec sc	14 ,, ,, nd

Among the weavers:

21 White Plaidings	10 sc
6 er	2 sec sc
8 nd on	

My opinion is that our cheviot wool should be brocken to answer all the purposes of making Cloths, Duffles and Plaidings, viz 6 kinds, sec, fine sec, sc, nd, on, and er and all broken fine, say:

1	St. sec	out of a pack	3	St. nd	out of a pack
1½	,, sec sec	,, ,, ,, ,,	1½	,, on	,, ,, ,, ,,
4	,, sc	,, ,, ,, ,,	1	,, er	,, ,, ,, ,,
			12	St.	

I believe there will be too much er at that proportion, the proportion of course would vary with the quality of the parcel of wool.

12 December. Stock of finished goods on hand which includes all that is milled:

6	p[ieces] er sh wool Dyed Blue	1	p[ieces] Plaiding
15	on piece Dyed Blue	2	Raised Grays
3	nd piece Dyed Blue	2	L. Blues
2	sc nd piece Dyed Blue	5	Coarse Drabs
2	on Drab	6	Duffles
1	Camlet	2	Blue Plaiding
		47	

15 December. Stock of goods on hand at different times:

1828:	March 26	157 pieces	1829:	Feb. 19	218 pieces
	May 14	185		June 5	260
	Augt. 30	142		Sep. 25	386
	Dec. 3	152		Dec. 12	47

17 December. To James Bowman, Langholm,

indigo at 3s. 9d.,	£3 15s. 6d.
bag	6d.
	£3 15s. 6d.

21 December. To Cotton wick for the Mill, 1s.

22 December. To Rutherford's Roup,[1] £10 14s.

23 December. Sent to Robt. Robertson, Selkirk, 2 spindles of Yarn cost £1 5s. 8d. Pd.

24 December. Sent the above today a pair of blankets at 9s.

25 December. Wool laid to the machines last week:

4 St.	Black	for listing
15	nd	for Cloth
15	sec sc	,, ,,
13½	sc	for Blue Plaidings
47½		

Our stock is very low at present, we have only in our warehouse and presshop together 40 pieces including Cloths, Duffles and Plaidings, and has almost none finishing.

This town is in a most disastrous state, at present no less a number than 20 individuals have failed in business since this time twelvemonth, whose engagements will reach near £30,000; years hence

[1] *I.e.* the public sale of Rutherford's equipment.

it will [be] asked what were the causes of such a downfall; within this last five years trade has not been paying well, that, with the facility of getting credit both with the banks and the country (for the Banks were too liberal especially the National); for instance there are individuals whose names are upon 40, 50, 60 and some 70 Bills. J. Rutherford is said to have had £500 of accomodation from the Banks.

Add to these two reasons another and that perhaps not the least of the causes, Bad Management or the want of Abilities in the Individuals to carry on business.

Names of the failers:

1. William Aimers
2. John Gledhill
3. Thos. Clapperton
4. Alexr. Clapperton
5. Robt. Walker
6. John Fairgrieve
7. James Roberts
8. James Hunter
9. James Stirling
10. James Rutherford
11. Richd. Lees
12. John Lees
13. Robt. Brown
14. John Davidson
15. James Berry
16. Farquhar McDonald
17. Adam Sanderson
18. Stewart Dryden
19. A. & J. Rutherford
20. Henry Balantine

26 December. To Mill next week:

4	p[iece]s	er B. Cloth
6	,,	nd Blue Cloth
2	,,	sc nd ,, ,,
6	,,	sc ,, ,,
4	p[iece]s	sec sc Blue Cloth
2	,,	sec sc L. Blue
4	,,	White Plaiding
30		

At the weavers:

18	white Plaidings		
8	[pieces]	nd for Cloth	
8	,,	sec sc ,, ,,	
3	,,	Blue Plaiding	38 [inch]
3	,,	,, ,,	36 ,,
2	,,	Duffles	38 ,,
42			

Wool to lay to the Mill:

for	6	p[ieces]	on er	Blue Cloth	$10\frac{1}{2}$	St.	
,,	8	,,	nd on	,, ,,	14	,,	
,,	4	,,		Duffle	36	[inch]	$21\frac{1}{2}$ St.
,,	2	,,		,,	38	,,	
,,	3	,,		,,	27	,,	
,,	6	,,		Blue Plaid	27	,,	
	29						

[Total] 101 [pieces], 46 St. supposed to be got ready about the middle of Feby.

28 December. To Henry Balantine for 33 yds. Plaiding, £1 9s.

29 December. To John Fairgrieve, 12 lbs. of our 3s. 11d. Indigo.

THE NORTH BRITISH RAILWAY INQUIRY OF 1866

edited by W. Vamplew, PHD

★

INTRODUCTION. In the decade following the great railway mania of the 1840s the North British Railway Company became a favourite clay pigeon of the financial press. Built in a hurry, several of its bridges and embankments collapsed and the clifftop section north of Berwick fell into the sea; a cheese-paring maintenance programme put 29 of the company's 71 locomotives simultaneously out of commission; and inefficient operating practice led to the Post Office advertising for a carter to carry the mail between Edinburgh and Berwick.[1] Decrepit equipment, negligible dividends, [2]and mounting debts were all symptoms of 'the hopeless atrophy' into which the company had fallen.[3] In contrast, the next decade brought prosperity. Under a new chairman, Richard Hodgson, the railway became the largest company in Scotland; dividends and the shareholders became more than passing acquaintances; and the same journals which had previously criticised the company now proclaimed that 'the growth and increased stability of the North British . . . has been altogether marvellous'.[4]

So marvellous in fact that it was too good to be true, as was discovered by John Walker, a new company secretary, when he began to investigate the company's books after coming across an irregularity in the surplus property account. His scrutiny revealed

[1] An entertaining but well-researched account of the early days of the North British can be found in J. Thomas, *The North British Railway*, i (Newton Abbot, 1969).

[2] The promoters of the railway had talked of dividends in the order of 8%. Actual disbursements on ordinary stock were 1847 (half year) – 2½%, 1848 – 5%, 1849 – 3½%, 1850 – 1%, 1851 – Nil, 1852 – Nil, 1853 – Nil, 1854 – ⅜%, 1855 – Nil, 1856 – 1¼%.

[3] *Railway Times*, 13 December 1851.

[4] *Ibid.*, 17 March 1866.

that, far from being prosperous, the company was in dire financial straits with revenue inadequate to cover the dividends which were actually being paid out of capital. When, against his advice, Hodgson insisted that a 3% dividend would be declared in September 1866, Walker informed two directors, John Ronald and John Beaumont, of his suspicions as to the company's true financial position. The board investigated the allegations, but Hodgson was able to convince his colleagues that, given breathing space, the company could weather the storm.

Unfortunately for Hodgson, James White of Overtoun, a leading shareholder, had heard rumours of the company's troubles and had determined to 'request' a shareholders' inquiry. White, the proprietor of a Rutherglen chemical firm, knew about railway finances as he had been the chairman of the Glasgow and South Western, another major Scottish railway company. If that was not enough to worry Hodgson, White was also the chairman of the National Bible Society of Scotland and, as a strict Sabbatarian,[1] not disposed to look with favour on a man who willingly operated the North British on a Sunday. Hodgson tried to tempt White with a promise of the next available seat on the board, but White was not to be bought and persisted with his demand for a full investigation of the company's affairs. Sufficient other shareholders agreed with him – perhaps because the proposed 3% dividend had been cut to 1% – to force the issue through at the statutory half-yearly meetings.

White virtually nominated the investigation committee which comprised Sir G. Graham Mongomerie, Bart., M.P., Robert Young and Peter Clouston, Glasgow merchants, George Harrison and John Irving, respectively merchants from Edinburgh and Carlisle, Dr Alex Mathew of Aberdeen, and George Robertson, an Edinburgh solicitor. Their report – reprinted below – did little to relieve the anxieties of the shareholders, for it revealed that 'a careful and most ingenious fabrication of imaginary accounts' had

[1] The Sabbatarians were vociferous in their opposition to Sunday railway operations. At almost every shareholders' meeting the issue of working on the Sabbath was raised. The Tay Bridge disaster was even attributed to Sunday travelling (*Herapath's Railway Journal*, 27 March 1880). Initially they frequently succeeded in obtaining the suspension or limitation of Sunday operations, but over the century, as companies grew in size, their efforts were less successful.

been perpetrated in order to disguise the illiquid position of the company. Far from being able to pay the dividends which had been declared on the ordinary stock, the North British could not genuinely meet some of its guaranteed and preference share obligations. By charging over £300,000 to the capital account which should have been met out of revenue, the annual accounts for at least three and a half years had been 'systematically cooked . . . to exhibit an ability to pay the particular dividend desired by Mr. Hodgson'.

★

The importance attached by Hodgson to the maintenance of dividends stemmed from the lumpy nature of railway capital expenditure. That it occurred at discrete intervals rather than being spread evenly over time hampered the utilisation of ploughed-back profits, the prevalent method of financing industrial expansion, since it would have necessitated the creation of substantial reserves for future investment; and reserves were anathema to railway shareholders. They argued that it was unfair to a fluctuating body of shareholders to retain current profits in the hope of obtaining future returns.[1] They would not accept that using undistributed profits to create capital assets might increase the value of their stock and raise the possibility of capital gains. And who can blame them? Although the concept of transferable shares with limited liability was not new, it had certainly been popularised by the railways,[2] so there was relatively little long-term experience by which shareholders could be guided. Furthermore, the experience that there had been in railway shareholding had tended to encourage a demand for dividends rather than a tolerance of ploughing back, for when the profits anticipated in the railway mania had failed to materialise, the market price of shares fell so far below par as to negate any possibility of capital gain for the original shareholders.[3]

[1] W. Chambers, *About Railways* (Edinburgh, 1865), 19.

[2] On this see H. A. Shannon, 'The Coming of General Limited Liability' in E. M. Carus-Wilson (ed.), *Essays in Economic History*, i (London, 1954).

[3] In October 1845 Caledonian £100 Ordinary Stock was selling at a 22% premium, in October 1847 at a 34% discount, in October 1848 at a 68% discount, in December 1849 at an 80% discount, and in April 1850 it reached its nadir of 86% discount. *Herapath's Railway Journal*, passim. North British stock fell to a low of £29. E. D. Chattaway, *Railways: Their Capital and Dividends* (Edinburgh, 1855), 26.

In any case the railway companies were expanding too rapidly for profits to have fully financed the growth even if they had been available. It was therefore essential to attract fresh capital into the enterprises and the obvious way to encourage this was to maintain reasonable dividends. Moreover, such a policy would also have served to maintain the market value of the shares and thus facilitate the flotation of new issues without a discount.

Where ordinary stock was at a low standing companies might have to turn to preference and guaranteed shares.[1] There was, of course, less likelihood of a share falling in value if a dividend was either guaranteed or at least promised first claim on the profits. The new shares also attracted a new type of investor into the railway capital market, the seeker of a reasonably stable income who was relatively unconcerned with the liquidity of his assets. The North British was one of the first railways in Scotland to introduce preference shares when in 1849 the board deemed it 'absolutely necessary to complete the works' and thought 'no better, more economical or more equitable mode of raising the requisite funds could be devised'.[2] Other companies were less enthusiastic, believing such issues to be 'an act of gross injustice to the original shareholders as it was never contemplated by them', though they were prepared to admit that 'there may be cases in which they cannot be done without'.[3] In addition some companies feared that in certain circumstances too high a return would have to be offered to induce the taking up of preference and guaranteed stock and this would have to be borne in perpetuity.[4]

As far as the investing public was concerned, preference shares had value only if there was an expectation of profits on which the right of preference could be exercised. Similarly, guaranteed shares were attractive only if it was believed that the company could make good its guarantee. This was not always apparent. The

[1] Theoretically the issue of preference shares could be due to a desire of the ordinary shareholders to expand the company without impairing their own powers of control (preference shares carried less voting rights), or to the railway companies taking advantage of a period of easy money to raise capital at low fixed interest rates. A detailed search of company reports and minute books failed to reveal any instances of this in practice.

[2] *Report of Committee of Inquiry*, 26 July 1849, 6. Scottish Record Office (SRO), RAC(S) 1/1A.

[3] *Herapath's Railway Journal*, 23 September 1848.

[4] See *e.g.* remarks of the Aberdeen chairman in 1848. SRO, RAC(S) 1/36.

chairman of the Aberdeen railway criticised his shareholders for taking up only £6,000 of the company's £30,000 issue of 5% preference stock, but he really could not expect any more, as this issue ranked behind a previous one of 6% preference stock which was still waiting for its dividend to be paid.[1] During a later period of financial distress some companies went so far as to attempt to establish pre-preference stocks, but the patience of existing shareholders was too exhausted and the public's belief in guarantees too shaken for this expedient to be adopted.[2] Nevertheless, as a rule guaranteed and preference stock were more enthusiastically received than ordinary stock which had to participate in the general fortunes of the companies: indeed the growth of Scottish railway share capital in the 1850s and 1860s was dominated by such shares.[3]

The maintenance of dividends was seen as a major plank in the North British financial policy both to encourage re-investment and also to attract fresh funds by giving investors confidence in the company's performance and prospects. This was not unusual; where the North British differed from other railway companies was in going to the extreme of paying them out of capital.[4] However, had Hodgson not stooped to false representation, it is feasible that confidence in North British stock would have slumped so low as to force the cessation of part, or even of all, operations because of an inability to raise funds.

*

The North British had been caught between the scissor blades of excessive capital expenditure and insufficient revenue. There is no doubting that capital was seriously misallocated in the construction

1 *Herapath's Railway Journal*, 30 November 1850.

2 *Ibid.*, 10 April 1867; 8 June 1867; 16 November 1867.

3 The proportion of all shares bearing preferential and guaranteed dividends rose from 16% in 1849 to 28% in 1854, 32% in 1859, 42% in 1864 and 51% in 1869. (calculated from the *Railway Returns* of the Board of Trade, corrected for omissions.) The proportions of net new issues bearing such dividends was 63% between 1849 and 1859 and 84% between 1859 and 1869.

4 Perhaps the least subtle legal move to maintain dividends was the unnamed English company which altered the dates of its financial half-year, as it was entitled to, so that its declared half-yearly dividends would be reasonably uniform (*Railway Times*, 9 September 1843).

of the railway. The Report emphasises the amount spent on preliminary and parliamentary expenses. To this should be added land: estimated to cost £218,000, land for the original main line and branches soared to over £571,000. One reason for this was 'the number of noblemen's and gentlemen's residences which . . . were interfered with', the proprietors of which naturally demanded compensation for the inconvenience and loss of amenity.[1] Opposition to the railways on aesthetic or amenity grounds was not uncommon, though most of it proved susceptible to financial persuasion; so much so that it was alleged that objections were being raised deliberately to procure cash from the railway companies.[2] One contemporary railway journal justifiably hit out at the Scottish landlords of the mania era:

> The greatest difficulty railway interests have to contend with in Scotland is the unreasonable demands, – nay, the avaricious cupidity of the owners of the soil. The most sterile patch of the Ochills, the bleakest moor in Nithsdale, the craggiest acre within the shade of the Grampians, touch it but by a railway, and you will hear of land valued at £3 an acre that never yielded as much grass as would suffice for a week's summer keep to a Shetland pony. Spoiling the view from the hall, 'laying open the privacy' (a favourite phrase) of a gentlemen's residence, coming too close to a rabbit warren or smoking the gude wife's washing, are but a few of the items manufactured in 'railway claims shops'.[3]

Clearly the market position was in favour of the seller since the railways needed the land as an essential prerequisite to constructing the way and works. A narrow strip of land would have little agricultural value in its own right and thus the price paid by the railway companies must have included a fair proportion of economic rent. The Scottish Central, for one, found that 'claims were pressed, not merely on the ground of the value of the land, or the

1 *Report of Committee of Inquiry*, 26 July 1849, 4. SRO, RAC(S) 1/1A.

2 As far as can be ascertained this was first suggested for Scottish railways in 1838 (*Railway Times*, 7 April 1838).

3 *Herapath's Railway Journal*, 22 January 1848.

injury it would suffer, but on the ground that the company could not do without it'.[1] Thus, although land costs certainly contributed to the North British financial problems, it was not unusual in being exploited by the landowners: between 1840 and 1868 at least 25% of Scottish railway construction costs were expended on land and compensation.[2]

Another factor making for an inflated capital account was the number of railway companies taken over by the North British. A full list can be found in the Report. Frequently nominal stock had to be created to induce shareholders in the other companies to exchange their shares for those of the North British. Moreover, much of this paper capital bore preferential or guaranteed dividends, thus contributing to the North British distinction of having more of its capital bearing such dividends than any other Scottish railway.

In addition the spate of amalgamations, particularly those of the 1860s, left the North British with large numbers of inferior rolling stock which had to be rebuilt or replaced. This, coupled with the company's financial difficulties, was the reason why the North British involved itself in purchasing wagons on hire purchase. Although a £62 vehicle would eventually cost £75, instalments eased the pressure on immediate outgoings and were thus popular with Hodgson. Such a move was not unusual: indeed at times the giving of favourable terms seems to have been more important in securing a contract than the efficiency of the stock concerned.[3] This led to the development of 'wagon companies' who built or bought wagons and then hired them out or sold them to the railways on deferred terms. Such finance companies were slower to develop in Scotland than in England, but two were finally projected, both having close ties with the railway companies. The board of the Glasgow Wagon Company included directors of the Edinburgh and Glasgow, the Glasgow and South Western, the Forth and Clyde Junction, the Scottish Central, and the Scottish North Eastern railways, whilst, as the Report shows, the Scottish Wagon Company was organised by officials of the North British.[4]

[1] *Ibid.*, 17 March 1849.

[2] Calculated from company accounts. SRO.

[3] See *e.g.* SRO GNS 1/1, 345; EPD 1/3, 381; *Herapath's Railway Journal*, 19 September 1857.

[4] *Herapath's Railway Journal*, 16 July 1864; 28 January 1865.

Little is known about the Glasgow company, but the Scottish Wagon Company originally operated on the principle of purchasing wagons and then selling them, though later they may have hired them out. The prospect of spreading out payments must have appealed to the railways for the wagon companies prospered; in 1874, for example, when the Scottish Wagon Company was the least successful in Britain, it still paid a dividend of 8%, a return which most railway shareholders would have envied.[1]

It can also be suggested that some North British branches could never have yielded a reasonable rate of return even if costs had been minimal. To claim that 'more than half the North British is made up of branches to mouldering old towns and cross lines over hills sacred to sheep and wandering botanists'[2] was an exaggeration, but an ex-official of the company could justifiably state that several branches were built 'which it was thought would be valuable feeders to the main line. They have proved to be the very opposite, and have sucked it financially dry'.[3]

Both amalgamation and overconstruction can be attributed to the same cause – intercompany rivalry, and, more especially, rivalry with the Caledonian. This dated back to the origins of the two companies, for both were conceived in the late 1830s to meet the demand for a railway to link Scotland with England. At that time it was generally considered that only one transborder line could be profitable so eventually the competing promoters agreed to let the government decide which railway should be built. The decision went in favour of the Caledonian's Annandale route, but financial difficulties delayed its building and the east-coast North British was authorised to proceed instead. However, with the nation moving towards railway mania, the supporters of the other transborder scheme reiterated their proposals and succeeded in having the Caledonian sanctioned once again. Unfortunately they had overestimated the volume of potential traffic and intense price and service competition developed in an effort to secure what traffic was available. By 1850 the loss of revenue from this competition led the companies involved to accept the provisions of an English and Scotch [*sic*] Traffic Agreement as to the apportioning of re-

[1] *Ibid.*, 23 January 1875. [2] *The Rialto*, 30 March 1889.
[3] Chattaway, *op. cit.*, 26.

ceipts from through traffic. This did not end the rivalry as both the North British and the Caledonian, burdened as they were by fixed debts, were still anxious to obtain as much of the transborder traffic as possible. By 1863 the agreement had been so strained that £50,000 a month was being held undistributed by the Railway Clearing House because of disputes. The debate over the construction of the Forth and Tay bridges was, in part, associated with this competiton for the Anglo-Scottish traffic, for bridging the great eastern estuaries would shorten the route to the north and thus possibly attract traffic to the North British.

There was also fierce competition for internal Scottish traffic. Although every company seemed to accept the idea of having an exclusive privilege to occupy certain territories, they could not agree in whom the divine right had been invested. The North British, for example, claimed that they were entitled to construct the Hawick to Carlisle line as this was a logical extension of its Edinburgh to Hawick cul-de-sac; the Caledonian, on the other hand, claimed that, as it already possessed a major station at Carlisle, any railway approaching Carlisle was naturally its. Indeed throughout the nineteenth century the practice was for one of these companies to pursue the other wherever it went. Almost all the 147 miles of North British line under construction in 1866 was aimed at competing with existing or potential Caledonian operations. The battle was not merely between these two companies: the net result of the ubiquitous and universal competiton was that at the turn of the century only Oban and Ayr of the Scottish towns of any economic importance were served by a single railway company. The prevailing attitude appeared to be that attack was the best form of defence: a company should get in first and occupy a territory, either by construction or take-over, and then battle in parliament to prevent the introduction of hostile lines. Such debates over territorial demarcation were one reason why the North British had spent over one million pounds on parliamentary expenses.

Inter-company rivalry may also partially explain the investment made by the North British in steamboats. Rather than wait for the Irish traffic to come to them instead of to other companies operating on the west coast, the North British board decided to run boats in conjunction with their railway services. This came about when the railway company had leased the Port Carlisle Railway, the Silloth Railway, and Silloth Harbour in 1861, and at the same time had purchased the vessels of the Silloth Bay Navigation Company in order to make use of what they had earlier termed 'the great facilities for the shipment of coals, minerals, and passengers to Ireland and the west ports of England.'[1] However, after John Burns, a steamboat owner, obtained an interdict against the company, they were given parliamentary permission for railway-owned steamers to ply only between Belfast and Silloth. This led to several of the railway directors making the offer to run a packet company on the guarantee that personal losses would be made up from the railway funds. The company was not directly profitable but, like much other ancilliary investment, served to attract custom to the railway.[2]

*

It remains to be explained how Hodgson was able to wield practically independent control of a concern as large as the North British. Limited liability[3] had enabled the company to raise some £15 million of share capital, yet, although the railway was the property of many, its operating and construction policies were decided by only a few individuals. Twice a year, at the statutory general meetings, it was possible for the shareholders to challenge the directors' policies, but generally they remained sleeping partners, content until they became aware that something was wrong. Then, however, they could be roused from their lethargy. In the post

[1] SRO, HRP(S) 35.

[2] It is impossible to prove that the ancilliary enterprises were direct loss-makers as the railways were not required to publish separate accounts for these concerns. However, the very fact that separate accounts were not forthcoming coupled with the evasive replies often given by directors to shareholders' questions points to this being likely. We certainly know that the North British Steam Packet Company was 'an unfortunate and unremunerative undertaking' in itself (*Report*, 10). For more on Scottish railway ventures into shipping see W. Vamplew, 'Railways and the Scottish Transport System in the Nineteenth Century', *Journal of Transport History*, N.S. i, (1972).

[3] Great emphasis was laid by railway promoters upon the fact that shareholders in their enterprises did not risk unlimited liability. The prospectus of the North British proclaimed in block capitals that 'no subscriber [was] liable beyond the amount of his subscription'.

railway mania hangover almost every company in Scotland, including the North British, was subjected to a shareholders' inquiry and in some instances the boards were overthrown.[1] But first the attention of shareholders had to be drawn to any trouble and perhaps the most obvious sign of this was low dividends, so if regular and reasonable dividends were paid, as was Hodgson's policy, there was less likelihood of an uprising. Moreover, the shareholders could only judge from what they were allowed to see. Not all companies were like the General Terminus and Glasgow Harbour Railway whose shareholders were told that 'you will all see the necessity of our not stating at present, what profit we may have made from the sales of land which we have already affected. To do so might expose the affairs of the company too much.'[2] However, even without such overtly blatant restriction the North British investigation showed how imperfect was the flow of information from the directors to the shareholders. Yet why should the shareholders question the company's reports and accounts when a leading financial journal could lavish such praise on the North British as:

> We have frequently had to characterise the reports issued by the directors of this company as having in them much of the quality and force of state papers . . . we look in vain, indeed, to the half yearly or special missives of any other company for explanations so full, so convincing and so efficient in aim . . . the board have deemed it their duty invariably to put the shareholders in possession of the grounds and objects of every important step taken on behalf of the company . . . nothing has been withheld or disguised.[3]

It was the standard of accounting techniques and practice that enabled Hodgson to hide what he was doing not only from the shareholders but also from fellow-members of the board, though, of course, many of the latter were mere figureheads and thus unlikely ever to question Hodgson's statements. Well into the nineteenth century railway accountancy was scarcely a formal science,

[1] SRO RAC(S) 1/1A, 1/3; *Herapath's Railway Journal*, 9 March 1850; 11 May 1850; 18 May 1850. [2] *Herapath's Railway Journal*, 10 April 1847.
[3] *Railway Times*, 17 March 1866.

either in doctrine or technique. The keeping of accounts was obligatory but personal judgement so often decided their format that there was little uniformity between companies or even, over time, within the same company. Items in one set of accounts could find no parallel elsewhere. In the case of the North British the accounts were so distorted as to be understood only by those who set them out. The company was not alone in its deception. The accounts of the Caledonian were once described by *The Times* as being in 'just such a tangle as one might dream of after supping on lobster salad and champagne'.[1] By careful camouflage a profit of less than £4,000 was shown in the published accounts as being nearly £32,000.[2] Further north, the Great North of Scotland's apparent prosperity in 1865 turned out to be because interest on the cost of its branch lines had been debited to the wrong account.[3]

That, until 1868, each company was 'at liberty to adopt the form [of accounts] it considers most convenient, and to vary that form from time to time'[4] obviously made it difficult for the auditors to perform their task effectively, especially when their duties were ill-defined. The auditors of the Scottish Central were not alone in their complaint that it would 'have been a great satisfaction to them had the nature and extent of their duties been more specifically defined than they are by the existing Acts of Parliament'.[5] Nevertheless, it is arguable that to trust to 'the honour and honesty of the officials of the company', as was done in the North British case, was scarcely an auditor's prerogative.

Confusion and perplexity faced the scrutineer of railway company accounts. In July 1841, early in the Railway Age, the *Railway Times*, a leading financial journal for investors, criticised the present state of chaos and complained that 'for want of system, and of correlative facts, their utility is sadly limited'.[6] A series of articles followed which examined the principles on which a uniform system of keeping railway accounts ought to be constructed, but nobody heeded their advice. Parliamentary legislation set minimal requirements in that each railway had to produce a half-yearly

1 *The Times*, 30 September 1850.

2 *Herapath's Railway Journal*, 24 January 1852.

3 *Ibid.*, 1 April 1865.

4 *Royal Commission on Railways* 1867, XXXVIII, xxiii.

5 SRO RAC(S) 1/34, July 1849.

6 *Railway Times*, 13 July 1841.

balance sheet, but a substantial degree of latitude was given in the calculation of profit and loss.[1] Each company went its own way. How could voluntary standardisation of accounts be expected when there was no consensus about what constituted depreciation or even capital expenditure?

Writing on the distinction between the capital and revenue accounts, William Chambers, the chairman of the Peebles line, declared that they must be kept entirely separate, even though this 'introduces a great complexity into the financial affairs of railways'.[2] Too great it would seem for most Scottish railway companies, nearly all of which, deliberately or accidentally, exhibited a decided confusion between capital and revenue in their accounts. Even in its pre-Hodgson days the North British was not immune from switching items at will from one account to another: in 1849 a shareholders' inquiry found that 'the distribution of charges between capital and revenue has been correctly made', but only three years later another investigation revealed that almost £34,000 'had been charged to capital instead of revenue under the heads of interest discounts, salaries and general charges'.[3]

Expenditure on improvements and better replacements raised further problems. Some companies were aware that betterment should be distinguished in the accounts. George Graham, resident engineer on the Caledonian, tried to convince his directors that improvement of the permanent way could be justified as capital expenditure.[4] At one stage the North British classified the 'improvement value on rebuilt waggons' separately in the capital account, and the Great North of Scotland did likewise with the cost of the additional weight of rails after relaying portions of their track.[5] Generally, however, companies took the line of least resistance and charged *all* replacement costs to capital. It was much easier to do that than to deduct anything from revenue. William Chambers summed up the position: 'were the shareholders to look to ultimate advantages, they would sanction the payment for

[1] A brief survey of the legislation can be found in H. Pollins, 'Aspects of Railway Accounting before 1868' in A. C. Littleton and B. S. Yamey, *Studies in the History of Accounting* (London, 1956).

[2] Chambers, *op. cit.*, 19.

[3] *Report of Committee of Inquiry*, 26 July 1849, 6. SRO, RAC(S) 1/1A.

[4] National Library of Scotland, MS. 6356, f. 16, 18 September 1855.

[5] SRO RAC(S) 1/1, July 1856; *Herapath's Railway Journal*, 10 October 1865.

permanent improvements out of the current revenue; but . . . shareholders for the most part care nothing for the remote and contingent prosperity of the undertaking, and will not, or cannot, make a corresponding sacrifice'.[1]

This attitude of the shareholders was directly responsible for overcapitalisation of all Scottish railway companies. Closing the capital account was a major pre-occupation of most boards. In September 1852 the North British directors announced that they were 'deeply impressed with the great importance of having the capital account closed, as they are quite aware how much, in the case of this company as of others, this would add to the confidence of the shareholders and the public . . . and the directors will make it a leading object of attention to do so on the earliest possible day'. The Caledonian board too felt that 'the only way to give confidence in railway accounts is to prevent the possibility of further capital expenditure'; the Peebles board elected to pay for new rolling stock out of revenue so as to prevent 'original cost remaining a perpetual charge against the company'; and by 1858 the Edinburgh and Glasgow reported that it was nearly at the 'desirable position' of closing its capital account.[2] All these plans proved fruitless in face of the shareholders' views. As one authority pointed out, 'in remarkably few cases [before 1865] have railway companies been able, or been disposed to close their capital account'.[3]

Depreciation was another major topic for discussion. Was it fair, it was asked, to 'the shareholders of a railway [who] are not associated together like a common partnership, always the same parties, but [who] are a fluctuating body – in one half and out the next. To tax, therefore, one half year for the wants of another is unjust, and the injustice is heightened when the tax is not for a certain want, but an undefined one.'[4] Most companies, however, made some provision but generally these were of an experimental nature. The North British, for example, decided that no depreciation fund was required for rolling stock since the locomotives,

[1] Chambers, *op. cit.*, 19–20.
[2] *Herapath's Railway Journal*, 29 September 1855; 20 October 1855; Chambers, *op. cit.*, 20.
[3] *Herapath's Railway Journal*, 20 March 1858.
[4] *Ibid.*, 2 September 1848.

carriages and wagons could be kept in an efficient state by 'ordinary' replacements and repairs. They did, however, establish a fund for the permanent way and buildings. In any case depreciation was *the* variable item in the accounts. What Pollins' study pointed out for south of the border was no less true for Scotland: depreciation would frequently be forgotten when the maintenance of the dividend required such a sacrifice.[1]

That the accounts were really only intelligible to the persons setting them out raises the question of the culpability of Lythgoe, the company accountant in charge of the North British books since July 1862. He might have been unwilling to risk losing a relatively attractive railway career and thus maintained a silence about Hodgson's manipulations. Yet if he had felt uneasy to whom could be have turned? His immediate superior, Rowbotham, the general manager, was a Hodgson man and, as for the directors,

> I have no access to the Board whatever, nor to any of the Directors, or Committee or Directors.
> In short you were not an independent officer? – No I was not.[2]

Hodgson ruled as absolute monarch, at least until Walker entered the palace.

★

Railway frauds were not rarities, but the North British affair was possibly unique in that it was not done for personal gain. At one stage of his career, Hodgson is alleged to have stated that 'I have not served the Company for money; it has been a matter of love with me'.[3] It may have been love of power rather than mere affection for the North British, but there is much to justify a later statement made to the Committee of Investigation 'that any irregularities which have occurred in the accounts, have been solely with the view of maintaining the status of the company in a lengthened period of trial, and of promoting its ultimate prosperity'.[4]

[1] Pollins, *op. cit.*, 343–349.
[2] *Minutes of Evidence to Committee of Investigation*, 21.
[3] *Herapath's Railway Journal*, 1 October 1864.
[4] *Minutes of Evidence*, 30.

Dedication was not enough. The shareholders were adamant that he should go in order that confidence in North British stock could be restored. He did not leave alone. Out went eleven of the fifteen directors, Rowbotham, Lythgoe, and the auditors. White himself refused a directorship because of ill-health, but four members of the investigation committee joined the board and the accountants who had assisted the inquiry became the new auditors. The problems of the North British were not solved simply by removing the old board, but the new directors' decisions to reduce financial and constructional commitments eased the path to recovery, though preferential dividends were not fully paid until 1872.

By this time railway accounts had become standardised by law. Following the report of a Royal Commission in 1867 the Regulation of Railways Act was passed in 1868. This, for the first time, told the railway companies in some detail what they were expected to show in their accounts. Perhaps the most important requirement was that the published balance sheet should distinguish fixed and circulating capital. Henceforth, though not eliminated, deception of railway shareholders was less easy, and fraud on the scale practised by Hodgson was not witnessed again.

W. V.

THE REPORT BY THE COMMITTEE OF INVESTIGATION TO THE SHAREHOLDERS OF THE NORTH BRITISH RAILWAY COMPANY[1]

Introduction

The Committee of Investigation appointed at the General Meeting of Shareholders on the 28th September, lost no time in entering on the enquiries embraced in the Resolution of the Meeting. As these related chiefly to Books and Accounts, they at once obtained the professional services of Messrs. WALTER MACKENZIE and JAMES WYLLIE GUILD, Accountants in Glasgow, in prosecuting the investigation. These gentlemen have been indefatigable in their application to the duties assigned to them.

The Committee have anxiously considered the varied information now presented to the Shareholders, in fulfilment of the duty imposed by the remit, of verifying the Revenue Account as at 31st July last; of rectifying the Statements of Revenue and Capital; and of presenting a view of the Company's Liabilities.

The Committee desire to make some general remarks on the matters dealt with in the Accountants' Report; and they will find it convenient to do so by taking up – I. Capital; II. Revenue; III. Liabilities and Obligations; and, IV. Remedial Measures.

I. CAPITAL

Original Undertaking

The North British Railway Company, as now constituted, is a combination of numerous independent undertakings. Incorporated in the year 1844, with a main line fifty-eight miles in length, and an authorized Share and Loan Capital of £1,000,066 13s. 4d.; it now comprehends within its system 781 miles open to traffic; 147 miles authorized by Parliament, and partly under construction; an authorized Share and Loan Capital of £22,210,712 15s. 10d.; and a gross Annual Revenue exceeding £1,250,000.

[1] A surviving copy of this report, together with the minutes of evidence taken by the investigation committee can be found in the Scottish historical records of the British Transport Commission, filed under RAC(S) 1/1B. Originally housed at 23 Waterloo Place, Edinburgh, onetime headquarters of the North British, these records are now in the possession of the Scottish Record Office.

The Capital hitherto created amounts to £15,414,625 8s. 4d.; the borrowing powers amount to £5,799,507 7s. 6d.; the ordinary Share Capital is £4,771,230 8s. 4d.; the Participating Preference (Edinburgh and Glasgow Ordinary) Capital, entitled to a minimum dividend of 4½% is £2,422,485, and the other Preference Stocks of the Company, represent the large amount of £8,220,910, the priorities of which Preference and Participating Preference Stocks are determined by the Amalgamation Act of 1865. The order of preference is correctly set forth in the published Reports to the Shareholders.

The following Tabular Statement exhibits the description, amount, and date of creation of the several Preference Stocks, with the rates of dividend payable thereon, distinguishing those which have a lien upon the Revenue of their respective lines, and those where the dividends are – 1st, cumulative; 2d, contingent on one year's profits; and 3d, contingent on half-year's profits.

The lines leased by the Company are – the Peebles, Port-Carlisle, Carlisle and Silloth, and Edinburgh and Bathgate; and those worked by the Company for payment of a percentage on their gross traffic receipts, are – the St. Andrews, Leslie, Devon Valley, Berwickshire, and Milngavie Railways.

Borrowing Powers

The Committee have satisfaction in repeating the assurance given by their professional Assistants, that the borrowing powers of the Company have not been exceeded, but were at 31st July last still available to the extent of £95,550 18s.[1]

Share Capital

They are also satisfied that the nominal Share Capital of the Company, so far as issued, is not in excess of the amount authorized and received by the Company in respect of it.

[1] The authorisation Acts of railway companies required a proportion – usually half – of share capital to be paid up before borrowing powers could be exercised; and borrowing was statutorily limited to a fixed percentage of total authorised capital. However, several companies appear to have evaded both provisions thus incurring excessive short-term liabilities. *Select Committee on Railway Companies' Borrowing Powers*, 1864, XI.

Date of Creation	Description of Stock	Amount of Stock	Rate of Dividend			
			Lien	*Cumulative*	Contingent on One Year's *Profits.*	Contingent on Half-Year's *Profits.*
Sept. 1, 1846	Stirlingshire Midland Preference Stock	£150,000	5½	...	...	...
July 22, 1847	E., P., & D. Granton Preference Stock	97,720	...	...	4	...
Sept. 6, 1848	Monkland 6 per cent. Guaranteed Stock	55,000	...	6	...	...
Sept. 6, 1848	Monkland 5 per cent. Guaranteed Stock	90,000	...	5	...	...
Sept. 6, 1848	Monkland 4½ per cent. Guaranteed Stock	2,950	...	4½	...	...
March 8, 1849	N. B. No. 1 Guaranteed Stock	780,200	...	5	...	...
July 25, 1849	E., P., & D. Second Preference Stock	550,000	...	...	4	...
Dec. 4, 1850	Stirling and Dunfermline Stock	450,000	4	...	...	...
Oct. 24, 1855	E. & G. No. 1 Preference Stock	275,000	...	5	...	...
July 15, 1856	N. B. No. 2 Guaranteed Stock	223,272	...	5	...	...
Sept. 6, 1859	Border Union Stock	394,240	...	...	5½	...
July 21, 1859	Selkirk Preference Stock	2,880	5	...	...	...
July 3, 1860	Jedburgh Preference Stock	80,580	4	...	...	...
Aug. 1, 1861	E., P., & D. Kinross-shire Preference Stock	53,000	5	...	...	...
Aug. 9, 1861	N. B. £10 Guaranteed (1861) Stock	296,820	...	...	5	...
Sept. 27, 1861	E., P., & D. F. & K. Preference Stock	53,850	...	...	4½	...
Aug. 11, 1862	E. & G. No. 2 Preference Stock	404,209	...	...	...	5
Aug. 30, 1862	West of Fife Preference Stock	136,000	5	...	...	...
Aug. 30, 1862	N. B. £5 Preference (1862) Stock	350,000	...	...	5	...
Oct. 15, 1863	N. B. £12, 10s. Preference (1863) Stock	990,000	...	...	5	...
July 20, 1864	Wansbeck Preference Stock	70,000	3¾ &4	...	...	...
No. 29, 1864	E. & G. No. 3 Preference Stock	557,000	...	...	...	5
Aug. 31, 1865	Monkland Preference, (Ordinary) Stock	563,379	...	...	...	6
Aug. 31, 1865	E. & G. Preference (Ordinary) Stock	2,422,485	...	...	4½	...
Oct. 12, 1865	N. B. £10 Preference (1865) Stock	1,614,810	...	...	...	5

Debenture and Share Registers

The Debenture and Stock and Share Registers of the Company appear to contain a correct record of the transactions to which they relate.

Summary

The Capital Account has been unduly increased by carrying to it directly, as well as indirectly, sums of large amount on various Accounts. The apparent means of the Company have also been increased by treating as assets various Suspense Accounts not available to meet the liabilities of the Company. It having been found impossible, within the limited time available for their examination, to classify or separate these, the Committee instructed their professional Assistants to ascertain the position of the Company by a particular examination of the Revenue Statement specially remitted to the Committee for verification, and by a general examination of so many of the Statements of previous half-years as should be necessary to trace the origin and progress of the Suspense Accounts, brought to the knowledge of the Shareholders for the first time in the Directors' Supplementary Report of September last, and previously concealed under the general entry of 'sums due to the Company less sums due by the Company'. The farther remarks of the Committee on Capital expenditure will therefore be more fitly made when dealing with the Revenue Accounts.

II. REVENUE

The Revenue Account remitted to the Committee for verification is the third balance that appears in the Balance Book of the Company applicable to the half-year ending 31st July last.

The first balance in the Book brought out a free revenue of £268,265 5s. available for dividends. This balance having been previously examined was, on 5th September, certified as correct by the Auditors. On 10th September they gave in a Report with reference to that audit.

The second balance was not audited or certified, and is a general balance only.

The third balance which forms the subject of remit was prepared under a special direction from the Board, that it should be made out 'strictly relative to the receipts and expenditure for the half-year'. The audit of it was followed up by a Report from the Auditors, who, when certifying its correctness, deleted their signatures to the previously certified balance-sheet.

The Accountants have prepared an Adjusted Revenue Account for the half-year ending 31st July last, exhibiting, so far as they have had the means of ascertaining, the charges that, according to correct practice and the usage of other Railway Companies, should be placed against Revenue. The result is, that after paying Debenture Interest due at Whitsunday last, a free Revenue of only £113,591 2s. 7d. appears available for the payment of the Preferential Dividends, according to their priority, amounting to £208,441 5s. 5d.

The additions to the expenditure entered in the Adjusted Revenue statement consist of the following items:

Rolling Stock	£17,752	0	0
Fortnight's Wages, etc., for the period from 18th to 31st July 1866. . . .	23,557	10	8
Boilers to Ferry Steamer . . .	5,072	14	8
Citadel Station at Carlisle . . .	1,000	0	0
Parliamentary Expenses	16,300	0	0
Interest on unproductive Works and Bank Balances, etc.	22,758	1	6
	£86,440	6	10

Line Renewal

The Accountants specify, but do not include in the expenditure, £39,022 8s. 8d. on account of Line Renewals. The Committee are not in possession of sufficient information to deal with this question in all its details, or to state what portion of this sum should be carried against Revenue. The practice of other Companies in dealing with such expenditure is so varied that no definite rule can be laid down; but the Committee have no hesitation in expressing their opinion that the large, and, in the case of two half-years, improper accumulation to 'Suspense' of relaying expenditure, cannot be justified, more particularly when it is noticed that from 1858 to 1864, the ordinary requirements of the Line had either been imprudently overlooked, or, at all events, had not been sufficiently attended to. During these years the total sum expended was:

Amount accumulated, up to 31st July 1862,	£9,569	0	6
Additional to 31st January 1863, . .	861	14	8
,, 31st July 1863, ...	3,435	9	8
,, 31st January 1864, . .	2,123	5	4
,, 31st July 1864, ...	2,135	15	10
	£18,125	6	0

of which there was charged against Revenue, during these five half-years, only £6,000.

At July 1864, the relaying could evidently no longer be postponed, and the subsequent Accounts shew the following amounts *actually* expended, although in July 1865 and January 1866 much more was *debited* to the Renewal Account, viz.:

1865, Jan. 31, ...	£19,594	7	8
1865, July 31, ...	22,582	6	1
1866, Jan. 31, ...	45,226	16	3
„ July 31, ...	49,314	8	8
	£136,717	18	8

During these half-years there was charged to Revenue only	£64,500	0	0
but it practically included £17,417, 13s. 11d. and £29,255, 18s. 5d. over-debited, which was in reality ordinary maintenance, . . .	46,673	12	4
So that only	£17,826	7	8

or less than £4,500 each half-year, has been actually *paid* out of Revenue.

The improper and unwarranted augmentation of the Renewal Account by charges reported by the Company's Engineers as belonging to Ordinary Maintenance, appears to the Committee to be one of the most unjustifiable operations which has come under their notice during the Investigation.

At the General Meeting of Shareholders in March 1865, it was arranged that £15,000 should be charged to Revenue half-yearly towards the Line Renewals then in progress. At that time, the system embraced 485 miles of railway, while it now extends to 781 miles. A corresponding additional provision should therefore have been made for relaying, especially as a considerable portion of the Line is stated in last Report to be in a defective condition.

Rolling Stock

The Rolling Stock Account has also been unwarrantably relieved of £17,752. The amount brought back from Capital to

Rolling Stock is the result of a calculation made of the extra cost of the mileage working of engines and other Rolling Stock on the western section, as compared with the mileage run by the Rolling Stock over the other portions of the Company's system. That excess is taken to be the cost of renewing and restoring the plant taken over with the western section at 1st August 1865, and is charged to Capital as if that expense had actually been incurred, and the value of the Rolling Stock to that extent actually increased, which is not the case.

Interest Account

The Directors charged to Capital £16,213, credited to Interest Account, as interest on unproductive works; but the Accountants have transferred it to the Adjusted Revenue Account as a proper charge against the half-year. The Committee concur with the Accountants in the opinion, that in no view should interest of such a character be added to Capital Account.

The Accountants have also prepared a statement of the sums placed to Capital or Suspense Accounts, instead of to Revenue, in the seven half-years ending 31st January last.

	£	s.	d.
These consist of amount carried to surplus property, etc., ...	£269,285	12	5
And to Capital and other Accounts, .	80,048	6	9
	£349,333	19	2
Deduct balances prior to 31st July 1862, .	45,197	15	2
Making the total amount short charged,	£304,136	4	0

This large accumulation of Revenue expenditure, not provided for, and now disclosed for the first time, forms one of the chief sources of the financial difficulties in which the Company is placed. This expenditure has either been charged direct to Capital Account, or disguised in the books of the Company, under the Accounts of 'Surplus Property' and 'Suspense'.

The amounts thus kept out of Revenue Expenditure have been paid away in Dividends not earned, and the deficiency thus occasioned has necessarily been provided for by advances from bankers and other temporary loans, which swell the present pressing obligations of the Company.

Parliamentary Expenses

An important item of the Company's obligations consists of Preliminary and Parliamentary Expenses incurred in consequence of the rival aggressions, undue competition, and too rapid extention, that have characterized the policy of this and other Railway Companies, and which, during the last four years, amount to the large sum of £260,026 12s. Part of this outlay was doubtless necessary, and might at the time it was entered upon have been considered justifiable; but the Committee are satisfied that a very large portion of it has been unnecessarily incurred, and produced no corresponding beneficial results to the Company. Of this amount it appears that there has been paid and charged against

Capital, ...	£133,713	10	11
That a part paid, but left in open balance, and made to appear as an asset of the Company, amounts to	47,313	1	1
And that there is still unpaid, ...	79,000	0	0
	£260,026	12	0

Of the £133,713 10s. 11d. charged to Capital, £69,642 18s. 5d. is carried to Preliminary and Parliamentary Expenses, and £64,070 12s. 6d. to Construction – obviously for the purpose of concealing from the Shareholders the real cost to the Company of their Parliamentary contests. The amount incurred during the last Session of Parliament is about £64,000, of which £32,600 is stated as the cost of promoting unsuccessful and opposing rival schemes.

Of the latter amount, the Accountants, in their Adjusted Revenue Account for the last half-year, have placed one-half (£16,300) against Revenue.

Having regard to the whole circumstances, the Committee approve of this allocation, although difference of opinion may exist as to the correct charging of Parliamentary expenses, the practice of Railway Companies not being uniform. It might be considered hard, under existing circumstances, to apply to the Account of 31st

July last, a more stringent rule than the practice of some other Companies; and it may be argued that, when Parliamentary expenses are exceptionally forced on a Company, there is a propriety in spreading such exceptional expenditure over more than one half-year's Revenue, as the circumstances may determine, provided the Shareholders are duly informed of the amount which has been incurred.

Waggons

In considering the Rolling-Stock Account, the attention of the Committee has been directed to the vague and uninstructive returns relating to this property in the recent half-yearly Reports. An examination of these does not show whether the waggons destroyed or otherwise rendered useless, have been regularly replaced in addition to the stated accumulations. They have not had time to inquire minutely into this property, but they have reason to believe, from what has come under their observation in the examination of the officials, that a considerable difference exists between the actual and reported stocks. A portion of this discrepancy is stated to have been found in the Edinburgh and Glasgow and Monklands Stock Accounts when taken over, but it will be necessary to obtain an exact return of the whole Stock of the Company before the real deficiency can be ascertained.

The system of purchasing waggons from public companies on deferred payments, has been inquired into and considered by the Committee and they are satisfied, that although it may be a great convenience at the time to Companies not having command of money, yet it is in the end a most expensive arrangement for the Shareholders. In addition to this objection, it improperly augments the real cost of Rolling-stock, and to the extent of such erroneous augmentation relieves Revenue at the expense of Capital. The mode in which these accounts are dealt with in the North British Company's books results in the interest, which is clearly a charge against Revenue, being debited to Capital.

North British Steam-Packet Company

The agreement between the Railway Company and the North British Steam-Packet Company has satisfied the Committee that the Steam-Packet Company was *de facto* an integral part of the Railway Company, and was originated to avoid the prohibitory provisions of Parliament.[1] Its directors were members of the Railway Board, and it will doubtless be insisted that the Railway Company are bound to relieve the Packet Company of all loss arising on its operations. That it has hitherto been *per se* an unfortunate and unremunerative undertaking is undoubted, but whether it may not indirectly have benefited the Railway, the Committee have not had the means of ascertaining. This is a matter which will require the careful consideration of the Executive – who will be able to judge whether it is for the interest of the Company that such Steamboat arrangements should be continued.

Suspense Accounts

In dealing with the successive Revenue Accounts and other half-yearly Statements, which have been laid before the Shareholders, the Committee cannot disguise from them, that, apart from carrying to Capital, sums which should properly have been put to Revenue, complicated and elaborated exertions have been made to conceal a large amount of expenditure under the head of Suspense Accounts, consisting of 'Line Renewals', 'Line Suspense', 'Surplus Property', otherwise 'Postponed Expenditure', 'Locomotive Suspense', 'Suspense Account, No. 2', 'Suspense Account, 1863', and 'Contingent Account'. All these Accounts were in a greater or lesser degree nothing more than ready and convenient outlets created to provide for charges which should properly have been carried against Revenue.

III. LIABILITIES AND OBLIGATIONS

The Abstract of the Financial position of the Company, as at 31st July last, prepared by the Accountants, shewing the present and

[1] Most, if not all, railway companies did not obtain rights to operate sea-going vessels in their original Acts. This could only be rectified by obtaining new powers but a strong parliamentary lobby of steamboat owners generally succeeded in preventing this. Their argument was that the railways would run vessels at a loss in order to attract customers for through journeys by sea and rail. The boat owners' action therefore rendered it necessary to establish steam packet companies as separate enterprises. *Select Committee on Railway Companies' Powers*, 1864, XI.

future obligations, as well as available and contingent assets, demands the serious consideration of the Shareholders. The true position of the Company, as there disclosed, exhibits a large amount of present indebtedness, postponed contracted liability, and future obligations, partly undertaken and partly contingent, to meet which there is really nothing but unissued Stock and Debentures. The present and postponed liabilities of the Company, according to that Report, amount to £1,875,625 19s. 11d., to meet which, there are the unexercised borrowing powers of the Company – £95,550 18s., and the power to issue Preference Stock and Share Capital, which it has not been found possible to make available.

To enable the Company, therefore, to meet these obligations which cannot be postponed, will require a sum largely in excess of any amount which can be raised under their present statutory powers, and it is therefore necessary immediately to consider and determine what steps should be taken to extricate the Company from their present embarrassed position, so as to prevent the sacrifice of their property.

The Committee hoped that the present Board would have been in a position to afford them some aid in considering this important and pressing matter; but they regret to report that they have been disappointed in this expectation.

The large and increasing working expenses will require the instant attention of the Directors, otherwise any *increase of traffic* will be more than absorbed by the *increase of expenditure*. The results shew that stringent measures of an economical character are indispensably necessary, otherwise all benefit from the development of the resources of the Company will be lost to the Shareholders.

Responsibility of the Executive

Such is the unfortunate result presented by the Report of your Committee's Accountants. But while the Report contains many important matters for the consideration of the Shareholders, this Committee, as a Committee of *Investigation*, felt that one subject particularly called for their immediate and most careful inquiry. The system which the Accountants trace in the Company's Books is not merely one of general deception of the Shareholders and misrepresentation of the Company's affairs: it is not merely deliberate falsification of the Accounts from year to year, so as to shew to the Shareholders and divide among them a Revenue which was not in existence, and was known not to have been earned: but it was a careful and most ingenious fabrication of imaginary accounts, begun and carried on from time to time, for the purpose of supporting the falsified Half-yearly Statements of Revenue, and the general misrepresentation of affairs. It thus became the immediate duty of the Committee of Investigation to inquire as to the responsibility for operations so discreditable, and leading to such disastrous results.

In the Chairman's circular letter of 14th September last, he expressed himself as 'unwilling to cast upon others responsibility which attaches almost exclusively to' himself. But the question remained, how far the other Directors were cognizant of the matter? Eleven of the Directors had anticipated the inquiries of the Committee – ten of them, by a joint-statement, expressing their entire ignorance of any irregularities in the Accounts, and their non-participation in such mis-statements, if any.

Auditors

The Committee afforded the Auditors an opportunity of making explanations, and required the various officials of the Company to produce all reports, letters, memoranda, or other instructions received by them, or in their custody, relating to the position of the Capital and Revenue Accounts during any of the financial half-years since 31st July 1862. The Auditors have satisfied the Committee that the duties discharged by them have been laborious – that, from time to time, they transmitted to the Board Memoranda or Reports applicable to the half-yearly audit, which they understood, to be qualifications upon the certificates that they signed, and that from time to time, these reports had been partially given effect to by corrections made during the ensuing half-year. These Reports do not appear to have been laid before the Board, but to have been handed to the Chairman to deal with. They also stated that the mass of entries and number of books necessary to be examined within the space of one, two, or at most three days, allowed them for verifying the balance-sheets required for publication, and the general nature of the Journal entries, precluded the possibility of such a minute examination as they would *now* consider necessary, and that in asking for information they trusted to the honour and honesty of the officers of the Company, not only that the explanations given were correct, but that they fully exhausted the subject on which explanation was sought.

The Committee have examined the various Reports above alluded to for several years prior to 31st July last, and while these exhibit evidence of anxiety and care in the interest of the Company, they do not shew that the Auditors had discovered or pointed out the deceptive nature of the Journal entries. The attention of the Auditors seems to have been directed more to checking the vouchers with the entries in the Cash-Book than to examining and following out the Journal entries by means of which the operations were effected, and upon which the adjustment of the Half-yearly Accounts so materially depends.

The Committee think that in future a more efficient audit is absolutely necessary, and that the result of each audit ought to be reported specially to the Shareholders, as well as to the Board of Directors.

The Committee had under examination other Officials of the Company, and in particular the Secretary, Manager, and Accountant.

Secretary

Mr. Walker, the Secretary, who previous to 12th April last held the office of Treasurer, has given the Committee important evidence. In February last, finding that the Preference Shares (1865) had not been taken up, and impressed with the perilous position of the Company, he addressed to the Chairman the following letter:

RICHARD HODGSON, Esq.,
Carham Hall. *Edinburgh, 21st February* 1866.

DEAR SIR – Since I learned that the Caledonian were for peace, had made up my mind that the North British and they would come to terms. I hope I may not be disappointed. No one can estimate better than yourself the advantages of an arrangement between the Companies; and whatever may be your views, you will no doubt seize the opportunity, when they can best be expressed and carried out for North British interests. At this time, which I hope is the turning-point of the North British, I cannot remain silent and be faithful to my duty to yourself as the Chairman of the Company, and the exponent of its policy.

The financial position of the Company is far from being satisfactory, and I do most sincerely believe that the prosecution of further new lines will cause embarrassments which may overpower us. Before matters come to such a state that it would be impossible for the Directors to deal with them, I would most respectfully but earnestly impress on you the imperative necessity that exists for rest.

The Capital Account of the Company is increasing at a rate which it is clear to me the increase on Revenue, if it make no greater stride than it has for some time, will be inadequate to meet the additional interest or dividend; and the prospective calls on Capital Account are so serious that the greatest difficulty will be experienced in providing for them. I believe we may be able to tide over till the autumn, but unless we are in a position to move off the 1865 Shares before then, I do not see now we are to be able to meet our engagements. We cannot make a Call on those Shares, as the number of them subscribed is so small that our nakedness would be too plainly published in our next half-yearly accounts. Now, from what other source can we expect means to carry on the contract-works and pay for plant, etc.? We will shortly have some Debenture powers available, but I am looking to these to meet the Whitsunday interest. Money may, it is true, be borrowed on the Shares from Financial Companies, but this would be at rates so onerous that I hope the alternative will not be forced upon the Company.

Then our Revenue Account is, as you know, in the most unsatisfactory state that it can possibly be. The interest and expenditure on unopened lines is practically not charged to Revenue; and at 31st July last there stood against the account to be met at a future day the following claims, viz:

Rail. Renewal Account, ...	£29,377	16	4
Locomotive Suspense Account, . .	740	5	3
Line Suspense Account, ...	24,341	17	4
Wages Account, ...	14,575	1	6
Suspense Account 1863, . . .	15,996	0	0
Surplus Property, ...	84,400	0	0
	£169,431	0	5
Add E. and G. Renewal Account, . .	22,341	12	1
	£191,772	12	6

The suspension of this large amount of Revenue Expenditure, with the Traffic Receipts retained by the Clearing-house under the English and Scotch Traffic Agreement, and the heavy outstanding accounts by station agents and others, sufficiently explain the difficulties of our position. The liquidation of £191,000 – and I fear the amount may be increased as at 31st January last – will of itself eat up the surplus receipts for the next four years, although these should increase at the rate of 7¼ per cent, the rate of progress last half year.

Our difficulties must, therefore, be looked in the face and met, otherwise the consequences will be most disastrous to all concerned. I am afraid the Members of the Finance Committee are not sufficiently alive to our position. I have not ceased to urge on them to refrain from incurring fresh liabilities, and to point out the difficulties I experience in negotiating loans; but I would be going out of my place were I, without your express authority, to make a statement to them which might affect the policy of the Board. As, however, the Members of the Finance Committee are charged with the duty of providing the ways and means for the Company, I beg respectfully to suggest to you that you should take an opportunity of explaining to them the actual position of matters.

The only way by which, in my humble opinion, we can rapidly and easily improve our position, is to come to terms with the Caledonian. We are competitors with them at Dundee, Perth, Stirling, Glasgow, Edinburgh, Peebles, and Carlisle, and at all places beyond these important stations, so that a traffic arrangement could be entered into with great advantage to both Companies. I would urge the relinquishment of all the great schemes of this year, and the acceptance of the facilities which I understand the Caledonian are ready to give; and the mere fact of their admitting us to the Wishaw District, would, if the running powers were found unsuitable, prove the preamble of any Bill we might at a future period apply for. The Scottish North-Eastern Railway should be held in property jointly, and this relationship would save us and the Caledonian from hereafter paying more for the Great North and Highland Railways than they were actually worth. The agreement that would follow would practically supersede the English and Scottish Traffic Agreement; and as the Caledonian are, I understand, the only Company that holds out against its modification now, they might give way on this, to us, most important point.

The construction of new lines will fan the flame of competiton between the two Companies, while an arrangement such as is indicated would promote the interests of both. The Caledonian find the North British equally strong with themselves in traffic powers, and therefore not at all likely to succumb to them as the Edinburgh and Glasgow did. They, like us, will lose by war, but gain by peace. A single sentence as to the Forth Bridge. This Bridge and connecting Railway will cost not less than a million and a half, and the interest, for a number of years, would hang like a dead-weight on us. To make this expenditure pay, additional gross traffic, to the extent of £3,000 a week, would require to flow over it. Where is this traffic to come from? It is little less than a third of the whole revenue earned north of Perth.

I beg you will receive this communication in the same spirit in which I make it, and that you will give it your serious consideration.

Yours faithfully, J. WALKER

P.S. – The enclosed statement will, I think, prove that the Caledonian have not paid too high for the S.N.E.R.

Mr. Hodgson replied to Mr. Walker as follows, but as the letter was marked 'Private', Mr. Walker declined to produce it, and a copy of it was sent to the Committee by Mr. Hodgson:

DEAR SIR, – I have read more than once the whole of your statement, and there is much of it that I am working hard to effect. Nothing renders this more difficult than the slightest encouragement to those with whom we have to deal, to think that we are wavering, or can be influenced by such appeals as are made by Mr. White and his coadjutors. It is this that makes the Cal., when pretending to seek peace, seek to cheat.

I do not admit your estimate of the cost of the Bridge of Forth, unless you join to it the Tay Bridge and Glenfarg line, as well as other approaches. If it were to cost 1½ millions, I would not make it; but the fact is that, without the Bridge, the wealth of Fife never can be developed, and the existing traffic is no criterion whatever.

As to the *knowledge* of the Finance Committee, a little knowledge is a dangerous thing, and in some cases much knowledge would be much more dangerous. I think they know quite enough, and will not readily provoke expenditure. I will, till money is cheaper, keep from new contracts, except for rolling stock; and even yet, if no faltering become visible, I hope to set aside a very large proportion of this session's prospective expenditure. – I am, yours,

RD. HODGSON.

I am studying and consulting Mr. Rowbotham as to the value of the S.N.E., with your statistics in hand.

February 24, 1866.

In August last the Secretary, when informing the Accountant of the amount of Dividend accruing on Preference Stock, to be charged against that half-year, inquired how the Accounts were likely to stand, and was informed by him that the Chairman looked for a dividend of 'three per cent., with £15,000 over'. From his knowledge of the financial position of the Company in his own department, and of the increased expenditure in the Locomotive Department, into which he had examined and reported on to the Board, Mr. Walker was convinced that such a result was impossible, and sought an interview with the Chairman; and as he believed that no Dividend could honestly be paid on the Ordinary Stock, he pressed the Chairman to abandon his intention of declaring such a Dividend, and to submit the matter to the Board. The Chairman having declined to do this, the Secretary thereupon procured the Abstracts of Expenditure for Maintenance of Way, and, having made what he considered a fair estimate in that and other departments, he came to the conclusion that the decrease in the Net Revenue, as compared with the corresponding half-year of 1865, amounted to £89,782, or about £40,000 short of what was required to meet the Preference Dividends.

On arriving at this result, the Secretary wrote to the Chairman the following letter:

RICHARD HODGSON, Esq., *Chairman*,
North British Railway Company. Edinburgh, *4th September* 1866.

DEAR SIR, – With reference to our interview on Thursday afternoon on the subject of the Half-Yearly Accounts now being made up, I saw Mr. Lythgoe the following day, when he informed me that it is not your intention to liquidate the Suspended Revenue Expenditure standing in the Company's Books under the head of 'Surplus Property', but, from time to time, as the property is sold, to credit the Account with the proceeds. This, in my opinion, aggravates the unfortunate state of matters, and amounts to neither more nor less than deliberately paying dividend out of Capital. That a *bona fide* dividend can be paid now, or in March next, is simply an impossibility, and to delay the explanations which the Board are entitled to must be at the risk of being charged with criminal concealment.

I have most anxiously weighed your arguments in favour of delay, but I fail to perceive their force. The former manipulation of the Surplus Property was effected without my knowledge, or I certainly should have urged you to refrain from such a step; and eleven months ago, when I pointed out to you the irregularity, you replied that everything should thereafter be fair and above board in the accounts. The farther and larger operation now proposed plainly proves that we are in a most hopeless position, and if your intentions are carried out, and a 3 per cent. Dividend declared, we shall, as at 31st July 1866, stand burdened with upwards of £200,000 of Suspended Revenue Expenditure, in addition to a Permanent Way Suspense Account of about £150,000. These enormous amounts would even have been very much larger, but from the circumstance of Capital having been, it appears, half-year after half-year, saddled with a large portion of the Revenue Expenditure. With these stern facts before one, there can be no doubt the payment of a dividend to the ordinary Shareholders is a thing not to be dreamt of for many years.

In these circumstances, it appears to me that not a day should be lost in making the Board aware of our position. Painful as it is for me to differ with you, I must, if you decline to acquaint the Board, do so myself. – Yours faithfully, J. WALKER.

The Secretary received no answer to this letter, but was informed by the Chairman that he was coming to Edinburgh two days thereafter.

On the following day, seeing the necessity of immediate action, the Secretary shewed a copy of this letter to two of the Directors, who met on the Company's business.

The Statement of the ten Directors, already referred to, shews that no time was lost in acting on the information thus communicated.

The documents which have been laid before the Committee bear internal evidence that early in the present year the Secretary anticipated, with great exactitude, that the affairs of the Company would be in the position which has now been realized, and that he has, during the past eight months, repeatedly brought the financial complications, and their inevitable results, before the Chairman and the Board. The Committee find that in a statement prepared by Mr. Walker, exhibiting the estimated receipts and payments, from 1st June to 30th November 1866, submitted to the Finance Committee on 30th May last, and considered and referred to the Board on 16th June thereafter, the following Memorandum occurs: 'Assuming the whole of the Debenture Loans to be secured, and the Preference Stocks to realize par, both very unlikely to be obtained, there will remain a deficiency of £128,000. The only other asset of importance that the Company have at present to fall back on, is the 1865 Preference Stock, and it is hopeless to expect at this time, to float it. This state of matters requires the serious attention of the Directors, and unless measures are at once devised and carried out to obtain funds, the time will very soon arrive when it will be impossible for the Company to meet its engagements'.

General Manager

As the Secretary's evidence related more to the discovery of the mis-statements than to their origination, the Committee continued their inquiries farther back into the department of Accounts and Audit, which is conducted under the charge of the General Manager, by the Accountant with assistants and clerks.

The General Manager, Mr. Rowbotham, informed the Committee that he was cognizant of the irregulatities in the Accounts, and that Dividends were declared and paid which had not been earned; but that he did not order or instruct the operations by which the Balance-sheets were made to show results unwarranted by the position of the Company, and that the instructions given on that subject emanated directly from the Chairman to the Accountant. He also stated that, although he is the recognised medium of communication between the Board and the department of Accounts and Audit, he did not convey to any member of the Board his knowledge of the irregularities.

Accountant

The Accountant was then specially examined, and his evidence before the Committee confirmed in detail the general statements made by Mr. Rowbotham, but with important additions. It appears from his evidence that not only were the mis-statements of the half-yearly accounts made by direction of the Chairman to him, but that these were made deliberately and advisedly, generally upon a preliminary draft prepared by the Accountant shewing the *true* state of affairs, which, after being inspected by the Chairman, was altered by the Accountant into such a form as to carry out the wishes of the Chairman, and shew the desired dividend. The Accountant handed to the Committee two of the documents referred to, one of which is as follows:

Estimate for January 1865

I. If *all the Expenditure* be charged, the Balance of Revenue will fall short of paying Preferential Dividend, by the sum of

			~~£53,420~~ (*sic*)
viz:–	232411	= Col. 5	38,971
	6340	= 11	
	238751		Less Brt. Forward
Less Capital Col. 4	3028		2013
	235723	Working Exps.	36,958
	63747	Interest.	
	299470	Wor. Exps. & Interest.	
	352890	Revenue.	
	53420	Balance for Dividend.	
	92391	Dividends (Prefce.)	
	38971		

Wages, 21st December to January 31st, to be entered in Books, and then transferred ~~changed~~ (*sic*) to Rolling Stock Susp.	£18,520
Stores to stand as they are already charged . .	19,345
Relaying to be put to Renewal Susp., . . .	19,000
Newcastle Station Terminus, ...	1,100
Poor's Rates, carry forward to next half-year, . .	1,700
Reduce Interest, say for Interest on advances to sundry undertakings, ...	3,500
Do. p. Interest on Plashetts Branch, . . .	400
Do. p. Interest due City of Glasgow Bank, . .	1,000
	64,565
	27,607

Edinburgh, 15th October 1866. – Produced by me in my examination to-day before the Committee of Investigation of the North British Railway Company. (Signed) J. P. LYTHGOE.

The Accountant being shewn the original, in his own handwriting, the following evidence was given by him:

Is that a calculation of yours at January 1865 shewing what the state of matters would be if all the maintenance, etc., were correctly charged as compared with what was intended to be charged? – Yes.

Did you each half-year submit a similar statement to Mr. Rowbotham, to the Chairman, or to the Directors? – I had no access to the Directors at all. I usually went to Mr. Rowbotham, and he got Mr. Hodgson to fix a time to come in and see what was to be done, and the ways and means were adopted to pay a certain dividend. In fact, good account-keeping has been sacrificed to the payment of dividends.

You have stated that from your examination of the Revenue accounts of January 1865, you found that the revenue was some £36,000 deficient to pay your Preference Dividends? – Yes.

Did you report that to Mr. Hodgson, or Mr. Rowbotham, or any of the Directors? – Yes, I took it to Mr. Hodgson when he was in Mr. Rowbotham's office. I mentioned it also to Mr. Rowbotham.

Before the January accounts were published? – Yes, I required instructions what to do.

What were the instructions you got? – It was arranged what I should do. The Dividend must be paid under any circumstances.

Were these the words used? – I would not like to bind myself to the words. Mr. Hodgson and Mr. Rowbotham and I were present; and I will not be sure whether Mr. Hodgson gave me instructions that day or a day or two afterwards, but I was told to bring out a dividend of 2¼ per cent. that half-year.

Can you not give us a little more specifically what actually took place, the explanations you made, and the statements that Mr. Hodgson made? – No. He was a long time mute, and so was Mr. Rowbotham. I remained there in the hopes of getting some instructions, but I don't think I got any instructions that day.

Were the instructions given you by Mr. Hodgson, specifically that you must bring out the accounts so as to pay a dividend of 2¼ per cent? – Certainly.

How did you do that? By making these cross-entries? – Yes.

I should like you to make up a statement shewing where the money has been got for the dividend since January 1865.

Then we were at the conference which you had with Mr. Hodgson when the state of matters was brought under his notice and he desired you to make the entries in the books so as to pay the $2\frac{1}{4}$ per cent. dividend. Were the entries which I have gone over in detail made by you under his instructions? – Yes; or with his approval, – particularly the Line Renewals. That was certainly a novelty of his.

You specially mention that as done under his instructions? – Yes; he was very anxious that I should properly understand that. The other entries were just left to my book-keeper.

In July 1865, January 1866, and July 1866, there was a continuation of the same system. In each of these half years was there a similar conference between you and Mr. Hodgson, showing the difficulties of your position, and that the accounts must be cooked to bring out the dividend wanted? – That was always the case.

Was that done on the same principle that had been adopted in January 1865, and always under his specific instructions? – Yes.

Did you receive specific notice to make in each half-year a specific dividend? – Yes.

All the four half-years? – Yes.

And this half-year your orders were to make a three per cent. dividend as before? – Yes.

At any of these half-years, were any of the other Directors, or Mr. Rowbotham, specially made cognizant of the state of your accounts, or with the changes that had been made, or was it brought under the notice of the Auditors by you or any of your subordinates? – No. I never brought anything under the notice of the Auditors in the books. The books were there to speak for themselves; and as regards any of the other Directors being informed of the state of matters, I am not in a position to speak to that.

Have the Annual Accounts as laid before the Shareholders been systematically cooked, so as to mislead them as to the true position of the Revenue and Expenditure of the Company, and simply to exhibit an ability to pay the particular Dividend desired by Mr. Hodgson, regardless of the free revenue of the

Company being adequate for that purpose? – Yes; that has been the plan.

From your knowledge of the accounts of the Company, do you consider the Surplus Property Account anything more than a double charge of Capital, it having been already paid for in the Capital Account, so that opening this account is just making capital pay twice over for the same thing? – I think it virtually amounts to that.

Tell us honestly – was the object of making these cross-entries not for the purpose of confusing the Auditors, to prevent the sums from being followed easily? – Well, there is a good deal in that. I daresay that was an important element in the matter. You see I was working for the Directors, and they were supposed to be working for the Shareholders.

Do you hold yourself responsible for the correct statement of the accounts in the Books of the Company? – No; I do not.

Then who is? – Well, my superior officer, I believe, Mr. Rowbotham.

You mean that you make entries in them according as he desires you? – Either him or Mr. Hodgson, one or other. Of course, nothing is done without Mr. Rowbotham's concurrence.

Among the documents handed to the Committee, under the same call, a press copy of the following statement, prepared by the Accountant and handed to the Chairman, explaining the adjustment of the first prepared half-yearly Account for July 1866, is very important. The proposed adjustment is in it carefully tabulated.

IV. REMEDIAL MEASURES

The systematic concealment thus practised on the Shareholders, and the crisis which has ensued, renders it absolutely necessary that the management of the affairs of the Company should, without delay, be placed in the hands of a Board possessing the confidence of the Shareholders and the Public, so that such measures may be devised and carried out as shall restore the character and position of the Company, and ensure that its affairs shall in future be conducted with integrity.

HALF-YEAR

	Expenditure			Deductions, viz.—					
	Arrears at 31st January 1866	Current Expenditure, Feb. 1st to July 18th, 1866	Total	On account of Surplus Property	Charged to Capital—Arrears of Repairs on E. & G. and M. R.	Charged to Suspense Accounts	Total Deductions from Expenditure	Expenditure to Report, as at 31st July 1866	Expenditure as reported 31st July 1865
	£ s. d.	£ s. d.	£ s. d.	£ s. d.	£ s. d.	£ s. d.	£ s. d.	£ s. d.	£ s. d.
Locomotive	24,120 14 10	103,613 3 3	127,733 18 1	40,677 14 10	7,683 0 0	...	48,360 14 10	79,373 3 3	72,087 0 0
Carriages and Waggons	7,688 15 9	30,637 15 5	38,326 11 2	8,596 15 9	10,069 0 0	...	18,665 15 9	19,660 15 5	24,247 0 0
Line	15,834 0 5	99,906 12 7	115,740 13 0	23,034 0 5	...	34,314 8 8	57,348 9 1	58,392 3 11	52,581 0 0
Tunnel Inclines	587 17 8	3,245 14 0	3,833 11 8	1,307 17 8	...	...	1,307 17 8	2,525 14 0	2,787 0 0
Ferries	3,660 18 3	13,378 9 9	17,039 8 0	4,442 18 3	...	5,072 14 8	9,515 12 11	7,523 15 1	7,160 0 0
Traffic	19,750 8 8	96,625 19 0	116,376 7 8	37,215 8 8	...	...	37,215 8 8	79,160 19 0	75,544 0 0
General	896 14 4	8,917 18 4	9,814 12 8	1,246 14 4	...	...	1,246 14 4	8,567 18 4	10,939 0 0
Canal	223 12 4	902 10 9	1,126 3 1	293 12 4	...	...	293 12 4	832 10 9	1,081 0 0
	72,763 2 3	357,228 3 1	429,991 5 4	116,815 2 3	17,752 0 0	39,387 3 4	173,954 5 7	256,036 19 9	246,526 0 0
Other Expenditure	...	36,753 6 5	36,753 6 5	...	...	...	...	36,753 6 5	33,561 0 0
Interest	...	110,732 15 2	110,732 15 2	...	16,000 0 0	...	16,000 0 0	94,732 15 2	91,587 0 0
Preference Dividends	...	220,857 15 7	220,857 15 7	...	...	...	...	220,857 15 7	201,759 0 0
	72,763 2 3	725,572 0 3	798,335 2 6	116,815 2 3	33,752 0 0	39,387 3 4	189,954 5 7	608,380 16 11	573,433 0 0

Revenue.—*Cr.*	By Receipts from Traffic, less cartages		£638,738 3 1
	,, Do. from other sources,		16,259 11 6
	,, Balance brot. from 31st January		4,782 14 10
	,, Balance from R. C. H.		15,000 0 0
			£674,780 9 5
Dr.	To Expend. as above	£608,380 16 11	
	To Ordy. Dividends at 3%	49,772 0 8	
			658,152 17 7
	Balance to carry forward,		£16,627 11 10

As it has been officially communicated to the Committee that the Board, at a meeting held on 23rd October, resolved to place their seats individually in the hands of the Shareholders, for the purpose of a new Board being elected at the meeting to be held at Edinburgh, on Wednesday, the 14th of November, at Twelve o'clock noon, for considering this Report, the Shareholders will then have an opportunity of nominating the parties into whose hands they are prepared to commit their property and the future management of the Company.

The Committee have anxiously considered the best means of restoring the credit of the Company, and promoting its future success, but the subject is so beset with delicate and important questions, that it appears to them that the consideration of this subject should be left to the reconstituted Board of Directors, and as Parliamentary powers for accomplishing this may be necessary, they recommend that the requisite notices should at once be given, the terms of which should be so comprehensive as to embrace any scheme that may be devised and approved of by the Shareholders.

The Committee, while they cannot but attach blame to the Board for the present position of the Company's affairs, have no hesitation in expressing their conviction that the conduct of the Chairman has been so unjustifiable as to preclude the possibility of his being allowed to retain any official position in the Company. They, however, are of opinion that the services of some of the present Directors may, with advantage, be made available to the Company, should they be willing to act in the present emergency.

The Committee consider that the Manager and Accountant ought to have communicated to the Board the irregularities carried out in their department, and ought not to have been parties to the improper entries made in the Books, and that they should at once have taken care that all the Directors were made cognizant of the irregularities suggested by the Chairman.

They feel it due to Mr. Walker, the Secretary, to say that the Shareholders are greatly indebted to him for the straightforward and independent manner in which he has acted throughout for the interest of the Company.

In conclusion, the Committee desire to express their sincere sympathy with the Shareholders, many of whom, they are aware, must be greatly inconvenienced at not receiving their usual Dividends, and disappointed at the results brought out in this Report. Bearing in mind, however, that the present exceptional and untoward state of matters is attributable to gross mismanagement, which it is hoped may never again occur, and not to any normal condition of the Railway property, the Committee feel assured that, – relieved from the promotion and construction of new Lines and Works under which the Company has laboured for the last few years; exercising strict economy in the expenses of maintenance and management in all departments; a watchful care over the cultivation of traffic at remunerative rates; and with unanimity of action on the part of the Shareholders and Executive, – the large and valuable property of the Company will be so fostered, and its inherent powers developed, as to prove that, although some of the Shareholders may for a time be deprived of the return which they calculated upon from their investment, they are possessed of a property of great and increasing value, which will ultimately surmount the difficulties with which it is at present unfortunately surrounded.

The Committee cannot conclude without expressing the obligations they are under to Messrs. Mackenzie and Guild, the Accountants employed in the Investigation, without whose valuable assistance, given at much personal inconvenience, they could not, within so limited a period, have presented to the Shareholders so complete an exposition of the Company's affairs.

JAMES WHITE, *Chairman.*
G. GRAHAM MONTGOMERY.
PETER CLOUSTON.
GEORGE HARRISON.
JOHN IRVING.
ALEX. C. MATTHEW.
GEO. ROBERTSON.
ROBERT YOUNG.

EDINBURGH, 30*th October* 1866.

THE BEGINING AND THE END OF THE LEWIS CHEMICAL WORKS, 1857–1874, by D. Morison

edited by T. I. Rae, PH D

★

INTRODUCTION. This brief history of the Lewis Chemical Works was written in 1895 by D. Morison, who, as becomes apparent during the course of the narrative, was production foreman at the Works. The idea of distilling oil and tar from the peat of the bogs of Lewis was conceived by Henry Caunter, apparently a servant or agent of Sir James Matheson, the proprietor of the Lewis estate at the time. Sir James, envisaging the scheme as a source of employment for the people of the island, encouraged Caunter, who, in association with Dr. B. Hariot Paul, an industrial chemist, set up a distillation plant just outside Stornoway. Morison narrates the story of the trials and errors these men made, and the accidents which occurred, before an effective plant was set up. In 1861 it was operational; but unfortunately, just when his abilities as a chemist were most needed to develop the by-products of the distillation, Dr Paul left Lewis. The failure to appoint an efficient chemist in his place, who could have exploited effectively the chemical processes, was, in Morison's opinion, the main reason for the subsequent decline of the Works, to Sir James Matheson's financial loss. A not immodest man, he is quite emphatic that the decline could in no way be attributed to D. Morison.

Morison shows himself as a man of forthright judgment, a stern critic of ineptitude, and of an independent turn of mind. He respected those whom he regarded as his social superiors only if they merited that respect – and he had very little for Henry

Caunter, the manager of the project. Undoubtedly he kept his place in a fitting and proper manner; but when the opportunity occurred he was not slow to let Caunter, or any other, know what he was thinking. He was probably self-educated. He was lent books, probably not all technical (for he had clearly read some of the works of Thomas Carlyle), both by Dr Paul and by Sir James Matheson; and his practical knowledge came by experience – he 'had bit by bit understood the requirements of the Work and the Nature of the Dangerous Gases'. Clearly he was a capable and intelligent man, but his character would scarcely have endeared him to his immediate superior.

The manuscript, written in a small quarto exercise-book containing 61 leaves, was acquired by the National Library of Scotland in 1967 from a descendant of Morison, and its present reference number is MS. 9586. Most of the text is written on one side of the page only, and Morison used the blank sides to add notes and further comments; these notes have been inserted in the following text in square brackets in their appropriate places. Morison's original spelling and, to a large extent, punctuation has been retained. Unfortunately it has not been possible to reproduce any of the line drawings and plans also in the manuscript. The text is presented as a straightforward narrative without annotation.

T. I. R.

THE DISTILLATION of Hydrocarbon oil from Peat in the Lewis Island was first conceived by Henry Caunter Esqre a retainor of Sir James Mathison Baronet Propritor of the Lewis Island.

Mr Caunter was a Gentleman of extensive Knowledge and a sanguine temperment, possessed with an ardent desire to Therorise and experiment with the hope of Making a descoverey hitherto unknown to the Arts and Sciences, A gifted speaker able to convince his hearers however sceptical – a first class Portrait painter, a Geoligist and Antiquarian of high standing. [Mr Caunter was always on the lookout for Fossels of which he had a large Colection, representing the Evolution, Coal, Ice, Flint, Stone, Bronze and other Prehistoric periods, on all he could descant with ease. A robust Bodied Gentleman 16½ stone Weight, subject to Gout in his Feet.]

Having great influence with Sir James and Lady Mathison Whoes well Known Generosity, and an unsparing hand, spent Large sums of Money on Works with the aim of benifiting and improving the condition of the overplus unskilled Labour on the Lewis Estate, Which in many cases proved discouraging for further outlay. Nevertheless Sir James did not hesitate in allowing Mr Caunter to proceed with experiments with the hope of Utilising the unproductive Peat Bogs on the Estate.

Mr Caunter associated with him a Tinsmith then residing at Stornoway, Who acted as Gas and Water Manager, Plumber and Fishing-Net Barker and clok repairer. [At that time the Tinsmith (Wilson) was considered in Stornoway and all over the Island, the authority on any Job requiring ingenuity, Would take in hand to improve the completest Steam or other Engine ever invented, a first Class Judge of a Dram whither Foreign or home Manufacture. Over all an agreeable little Man 8½ stone Weight 5′ 6″ high.]

They (Messrs Caunter and Wilson) Comenced operations by fitting up an apparatus for experimenting on the Distillation of Peat at the side of a Fish Pond in the Vicinity of the Lewis Castle, where soon the descovery was made that the Distilation of Peat was *deadley* to Fish in a Pond. (But not till too late that it was equally deadley to Fish in a River.) [The Experimental Work was put up adjoining a Burn, Contributary to the Creed River, Famous for its Salmon Fishing. The Building afterwards Converted into Workmen's Houses, Which is the only relic yet remaining of the L. C. Works Creed. It was rumered that the Exisemen had descovered that somthing else then Peat was distilled. But on examination it was proved that it was only a few Bottles of Glenlevet which Wilson had hid about For his own requirements when fitting up the apparatus.]

The Killing of the Fish in the Pond led to the Experimental Works being removed to the out side of the Lewis Castele Grounds. Where they were fitted up on a larger scale a Kiln built, Complicated Condencers fitted up, a large quantity of Peat Cut and stacked to be brought in to the Works by a Boat on a Canal Cut in the Bog (the Canal fully $\frac{3}{4}$ of a Mile long). It being reported and generally beleived through the Island that the Gentleman at the Castle (Mr Caunter) was to make Candles out of Peat. Which gave the Works the Name of the Candle Works during its existance. [Mr Caunter then resided at the Castle while the Glen House was under repairs.]

For about Two years various changes and alterations from time to time was done on the apparatus, When by patience and perceverance, About half a Ton of Peat Tar (Crude Hydrocarbon) was gathered from the Distilation of the Peat Gases. [Through over boiling and evaporation the Peat Tar Manufactured at the Experimental Works was so dry and Pitchy that dry Bisket Barrels was light enough to hold it.]

Mr Caunter could go no Farther, That is to Distill the Peat Tar into refined oils and Parifine (He laid no claim to Chemical Knowledge). Which in the begining of 1859 led Sir James Mathison to bring Dr B. Hariot Paul, an eminent London Analyst and Chemist to experiment and Analyze the Peat Tar Manufactured by Mr Caunter. [Dr Paul's reputation as an Analyst was of high standing, only lost the high position of the Government Anylist by a few votes less then Dr Angus Smith.]

There was a Laboratory Built and fitted up (adjoining the Glen House where Mr Caunter resided) where Dr Paul conducted the Analysis of the Peat Tar referred to, and also Tar Distilled under his own superentendance after rebuilding and altering the Kiln put up by Mr Caunter and Wilson. [Mr Caunter and Wilson's apparatus was quite upset by Dr Paul to the great greaf of the enventors,

Messrs Caunter and Wilson.] (The writers Personal Knowledge of the Lewis Chemical Works comenced by Building the Laboratory etc. for Dr Paul.)

The results of Dr Paul's Analysis was so promising for the profitable Utilization of the Lewis Peat Bogs, and the employment of the unskilled Labour on the Estate, that with his well known benevolence Sir James Mathison Baronet commissioned Dr Paul to superintend the erection of Large Works for the Distilation of the Hydrocarbon oils etc. from Peats.

No dought Dr Paul realized the Fact that the first operation That is to Erect a Work to extract the Crude Hydrocarbon etc. from Peat was more of a Practical and mechanical then a Chemical operation (and was aware that the want of the Practical Knowledge for the First operation was the rock which wrecked the Irish Peat Co's Work.) [The History and cause of Failure of the Irish Peat Co's Work, see Musprat, Volume 2nd.]

Dr Paul lost no time in begining to alter and operate on Mr Caunter's Kiln and Condencers, and after a series of experiements Dr Paul and Mr Caunter went to Germany to visit the only Peat Works then in existance. All they saw at the German Works was that empty Herring Barrels with the Stornoway Brand did service as Condencers, set and conected like Wolfs bottles with Wooden pipes, the Gases escaping in all directions through the Joints. The rest of the Works was in Keeping. So the trip to Germany at Sir James's expence was a failure as far as Practical information for the Distilation of Peat was Concerned.

In May 1859 Preparation was began to Build a Block Containing 10 Kilns (Five on each side of the Block) on a hight above and within 30 yards or therby of the Experimental Kiln which was kept going for information during the time the New Works was being Built. [The killing of the Fish in the Pond and the dificulty of getting Water was strangly overlooked in chusing a site, when there was such a Field to select from more sutable in many respects.] The Block of Kilns was finished in September and during the following twelve Months a double range of elaborate Condencers was fitted up, and conected by a Brick Flue to an Iron Funnel set on an adjoining Hill to draw the Gases from the Kilns through the Condencers by Natural draught. [The condencers was similar to the Irish Peat Co's Works, but not placed so convenient, Neither with safety Valves provided against explosions.]

A Tramway laid in between the double row of Condencers to admit the Trucks with Peat being brought over the Kiln Mouths, which was closed by Metal Cones hung inside the Kilns, held in position by chains and back weights over a Pulley fixed to the roof above.

The absence of a Definite Plan for the Work from first caused delays and expencive alterations while the Work was being fitted up for first trial. [It was quite evident during the erection of the Works, That the eminant Analyst and Chemist would be more at Home among his Books and in his Laboratory than superintending the erection of the Works.]

In September 1860 All being ready the Kiln Furneces was Kindled for first trial, When soon the unsutableness of the arrangement began to advertize itself in many ways.

First, The Windward side burnt so fierce that the Furnece bars bent down to the Ashpits while the Lee side spewed out Volumes of smoke.

Second, When the Kilns required to be recharged with Peat (every 6 hours) the Gases escaping from the Mouth of the Kilns sickned the Men, the Poisones Gases (Carbonic Oxyde) giving off a disagreeable smell, Felt for miles to the Lee of the Works.

Thirdly, The Condencers Cast Metal Tanks 3′ 0″ × 3′ 0″ × 3′ 0″ Conected by Four rows of Galvenized Pipes 12 Inch Diamr. Would if stritched Horizontal extend 240 Feet each row. Still it was found that the Brick Flew Conecting the Funnel with the Condencers produced More Peat Tar then the whole range of Condencers which produced little more then Brown Water, and during Snow a Brown track of Tar could be seen fully ½ mile to the Lee of the Funnel. [The most of the Water seperated in the Condencers, the Tar held in suspension till after escaping through the Funnel was cooled by the Air then droped on the ground to the lee of the Funnel.]

The result was very disapointing to Dr Paul who at Sir James's expence Planed and superintended the erection of the Work (Mr Caunter only acting as Paymaster).

A Week off and on altering and realtering, but with little improvement. When after 8 days stopage latter end of October 1860 Everything being ready for a fresh start, Dr Paul left the Works in the evening, Giving derections as to how the Kiln Furneces was to be Kindled. The order was: Kindle Two Furneces on one side Then Two on other side and so on till the 10 Kilns was Kindled. This order was strickley carried out till Three Kiln Furnaces on each side was Fired. This six Kilns Furneces supplying Carbonic Oxyde Gas, Four supplying oxygen (Fresh Air) filling the Condencers with an Explosive Gas which a blue hot Iron will Explode.

The result of this Manner of Kindling the Furneces was, that an hour after Dr Paul left the Works a Fearful explosion took place, smashing several of the Cast Metal Tanks to pieces, scattering the Galvenized pipes and crossends in all derections, shaking the Earth, and Causing the Dishes in the nearest House (460 yards distant) to rattle on the Table. In Stornoway it was thought to *Thunder*. Nothing less then a Miracle save the Men on duty. [If Dr Paul had for a moment Consulted his Knowledge of Explosive Gases he would have givin different directions for Kindling the Kiln Furneces and saved the Works. A similar overlook by the Chemist in Charge of the Ammonia apparatus at the Iron Works at Glasgow which by an overlook exploded a few years since with a serious loss of life.]

It may be noticed that none at the Works knew, or pretended to Know, Neither was told the dangerous Nature of the Gases Generated. The absence of a similar Work anywhere made it impossible to get a Man with Practical Knowledge of such a Work to act as Foreman under Dr Paul. In this case Dr Paul and his Foreman was similar, Learning through failures and disapointments.

Dr Paul being recalled to see the Works a *wreck*, as might be expected was much put about. When Firmley told by his Foreman that his orders was strickley being carried out in kindling the Kilns, he ceased to lay the blame on the Men, Admited it was an overlook of his. But would not then say What was the Cause of the Explosion. [Soon after Donald Munro, Sir James's Factor Came to the Works. Expressed the hope that We would attend to Messrs Paul and Caunter's directions in future and not Explode and smash the Works again by not attending to orders. This only shows how Gen[tlemen] make skape Goats of those under them. By Mr

Munro's knowledge of Cross questioning he left the Works with the real Cause of the Explosion etc., or rather the knowledge that the orders for kindling was stricklcy adhered too.]

A squad of tradesmen got who hurriedly patched up the Work. Wooden Tanks put in place of those broken.

In 8 days the Works again ready to be Kindled.

Dr Paul gave different orders this time for Kindling the Kiln Furnaces, which was to Kindle the 10 Furneces similtaniously. Then prepared to leave the Works. When the Foreman demured to proceed till the Dr would explain the Cause of the explosion which wrecked the Works so as to be better able to avoid a repitition. To this reasonable request the Dr reluctantly agreed. [Demured, actually refused to kindle the Kiln Furnaces, Question to be first answered and explained, Knowing that the Gases Generated when the Kilns was Kindled *one by one* Wrecked the Works by Explosion. Is it an unexplosive Gas that will be generated by the Kilns being simultaniously kindled. *If so What Makes it so*. Explain to be understood or stand By yourself and Kindle the Furnaces. Dr Paul soon after the Explosion sent a Book to the Work, all are Explosive Gases.]

The Work was again started. The Gases escaping from the Mouth of the Kilns already refared too, Continued to give Great trouble. Particularly in Calm Weather when charging the Kilns with Peat. A fresh relay of Men in the open Air ready to haul out any that would secumb, take him round by Bukets of Water on his Face and head. [On one occation, Dr Paul being present, Three Men was hauled out to the open Air remained striched on their back in a delirious state for several hours. The after effects disabling them from Work for two days.]

Town and Country Complaining of the sickning and offencive smell from the Works.

By this time Dr Paul was Convinced that the Works as Constructed was a Failure for the Distilation of Peat, Went South in the spring of 1861. Was advised to reconstruct the whole affair.

This was proceeded with. The Condencers elevated 5 Feet above Ground, placed double row each side the Gangway supporting the Tramway. Kiln Furneces fitted up with Ashpit and Fire doors, A Complicated arrangment for Mouth of Kilns to prevent the Gas escaping. A Steam Engene and Boiler to Work an exhaust Fan to draw the Gases through Water, Also a Drum and hauling Gear Conected with the Engene for hauling the Peat Trucks up an incline in to the Works. The Condencers suplemented by Four tall scrubbers (adjoining the Fan) through which a shower of Water was pumped by the Engene to Wash as Dr Paul expected the last trace of Tar from the Gases before entring the Fan. The Gas outlets Conecting the Kilns to the Condencers had a dip of 1½ inch in Water Now in the Main pipe surounding the Works, With a Water joint in Four Cast Metal Tanks, also Four saftey Valves between the Condencers and Hydrolic Main, Constructed so as to releave presshure from within and when required shut of the Hydrolic Main from the Condencers. [Till the Works was reconstructed there was no Water Joints or any obstruction to the Gases through the Condencers.]

The covers of the Scrubbers acted as Safety Valves in Water Joints. The whole range of Condencers From the Fan (at the outer end) to the Kilns Furneces Made Airtight, and sundrie minor details added Calculated to make the Works safe, and also to improve the Works. In short the whole affair was Reconstructed at Great Expence to Sir James Mathison. [The Funell Conected with the Boiler Furnace. Instead as formerly to cause draught in the Condencers and Kilns.] [A Skeleton now Built and fitted up to be By practice covered with skin and Musels bit by bit as it would advertize itself.]

In August 1861 The Works was ready for to be tried, steam got up, the Fan set agoing, The Kiln Furneces Kindled similtaneously soon began to brighten up, the Gases Bubling through the Water joints the Fan going 1600 revolusions per Minute caused a parcel Vacum in the pipes. This caused the Air to enter through the Ashpits to the Fires. The draught in the Furneces depended on the speed of the Fan and not on the Wind as Formarley, Which was a vast Improvement. Dr Paul expressed himself satisfied that after his many disapointments he now got the Works completed for the Distilation of Peat. But was further disapointed, when six hours after the Works was started, the Engene failed to Work the Fan which was found to be full of Tar in the consistancy of Butter preventing the Fan from revolving. [The melted Tar blowen out side by the Fan received in A Box out side.] This at a point where Dr Paul expected the Gases to be washed from all traces of Tar, This showing the great tenacity of Peat Gas, refusing to part with the Tar in suspension while passing through the Condencers and Water Joints untill *churned* by the Wings of the Fan at the extreme end of the long range of Condencers. The Fan was kept clear from choking again by a jet of steam through the Casing, The tar received in a Box placed out side from which the Uncondencible Gas was led by an under Ground Flue to a Funnel into the open Air.

The Works reconstructed as brefly described had still a wide margen for improvements which daly advertisided itself in many ways. The complicated and expencive machenery fitted up to prevent the Gases escaping from the Kilns Mouths was found unworkable and under the new arrangement quite unecessary. It was found that the production of Tar at, and outside the Fan was fulley equal to the production of Tar by the whole range of Elaborate Condencers. [The draught being regulated by the Fan and improved doors to Furneces made the Complicated machenery at top of Kilns unecessary, and in practice unworkable. The whole costing £80 was (after Dr Paul left the Works) removed to the scrap Iron heap which by the many alterations on the Works had grown to large dimentions.] [After Dr Paul left the Works additional Condencers was placed out side the Fan. Which with various improvements as practice would teach led to an increase of Tar produced.]

The uncondencible Gases discharged from the Fan into the open Air was more sickning and more offencive smell than formarly. When the Wind blew it back on the Works the Men on duty stagered about like Excursionists in a steamer Crossing the Minch in a stiff Gale of Wind. Town and Country Complained of the smell. However an accident altho Very alarming led to a complete Cure. On a dark night in December 1861 the Engene Man going about with a naked light accidentaly Catched on the Gas, which Burnt in a Tremendeous Flame as it mixed with the Air, Lightning the surounding Hills, the Fan discharging (at great speed) a Colum of Gas 14 Inches Diamr, Some of the Men on Watch so alarmed that they deserted there posts expecting a repetition of the Explosion already refared too. Fortunately the Wind blew the Flame off from the Works otherwise the result would be sereous.

The Men on duty was so alarmed that Nothing was attempted to put out the Flame. The Foreman (who leaved within 400 yards of the Work) Hurridly arrived and by slowing the Engene and Flooding the Water Joints, the Flame was put out, and with only the Loss of the Wooden Condencers out side the Fan the important discovery was made that the Gas would Burn, and sickning effects done away with.

The Works shut up, a Messenger sent for Dr Paul, who leaved at Garabost, 8½ miles distant.

On his arrival next Morning he appeared rather pleased for the ocurrance, Minutely enquired about the Extent, Colour, etc., of the Flame. [Dr Paul expressed his satisfaction of the discovery that the Gas Burnt and wished he was present to have seen it burning.]

The works was shut up till a gas burner was Built to which the Gas from the Fan was lead by an underground Flue, and several other improvements on the Works. All being again ready, the Works again started First Week of January 1862. When on the Third day to the satisfaction of all concerned, the Gas was Kindled doing away with the Very anoying and sickning effects of enhaling it. [Our worthy Paymaster, Mr Caunter, accompanied Dr Paul to the Works. But not aware that the Gas was to be Kindled, Was greatly alarmed for his Bodly saftey, Earnestly desired the Match witheld till he got to a safe distance, Predicted an Explosion of the Whole affair. He was granted Five Minutes to Escape, Managed up to the Lochs road, before he looked back to see as he expected the Whole show Blown to the Air. Dr Paul greatly amused by Mr Caunter's alarm for his personal saftey.] So far the Lewis Chemical Works was step by step advancing to completion for the Distilation of the Hydrocarbon Oils etc., from Peats.

It may be here Noticed that the Consumption of Peat in the Kilns and Tar made every 24 hours was corectley weighed and Marked in Book for Dr Paul's inspection. Peat used in Kilns from 18 to 20 Tons in 24 hours which give 5 per cent of Tar (Crude hydrocarbon). Peat used for Steam Boiler 3½ Tons.

Preveous to January 1862 the many stopages refared to prevented a corect knowledge of Peat Consumed or Tar made. During the Spring of 1862 the Work was carried on Night and Day untill the latter end of March when a dificulty arose for a supply of Water for the Steam Boiler, Which caused the Work to stop. Preparation made to overcome this dificulty, (The Works being on high Ground made it more so) and also to Extend the Tramways through the Peat Ground etc., etc., [Note. It was very surprising that such a Work would have been place on such a height as to cause dificulty in a supply of Water. This and being near the Fishing river (The Creed) gave trouble during the existance of the Work] and also for the Building of Seats for stills and Evaporating Pans which Dr Paul was preparing (at Garabost where the Works Smithy was) to be set up to Utilise the By products, sulfate of Ammonea etc. [Note. It was to be regreted that the Ammonea Apparatus prepared by Dr Paul was not fitted up before he left. The Acid after being used in purifying the oils at the Refinery, was in a deluted state to be reused to fix the Ammonea at Creed Works, Which afterwards was run in to the Broad Bay with other valuables from the Refinery, Which gave reason for Complaints of the Fish having deserted the Bay. (The deluted Acid which Dr Paul was to reuse for fixing the Ammonea was by his successors run waste in to the Broad Bay.)]

Everything now looked promising for the success of the L.C. Works. Which as Dr Paul said, was not at the stage when he could profitably apply his Chemical Knowledge, and forget his many disapointments in Lewis for the Last 3 years.

On his Visiting the Works First Week of April he (Dr Paul) looked unusually out of Sorts. Remarked it likley that he was soon to leave the Works. (Frankley told the reasons for such a sudden change. Not necessary here to repeat.)

Dr Paul left for London by first Steamer, but not definitively known for 10 days but he would return. But did not, to the great loss of Sir James Mathison, Bt., and all concerned in the Work *Excepting* those *Employed* at the *Refinery* as *will be seen* farther on.

Dr Paul fixed on the extensive sheds at the Brick Works for the refining apparatus, Stills, Pans, Tanks, Hydrolic press and all machenery required for the Distilation and refining of the Tar (Crude Hydrocarbon) distilled from the Peat at Creed L.C.

Works already breafley described. [Note. The Refining apparatus was under cover of the Very Extencive Brick Work sheds. Which with the Machenery served Both purposes, having a large steam Boiler and Pan shed added, and stirring Machenery and Pumps conected with the Engene.]

He had a cottage Built for his residence, Houses fitted up for the various Tradesmen and their Famlies required at the Works. Smitheys, Cooperage, Joiner shop and stables, all supplied with the necessary Matereal and latest improved tools, all fitted up adjoining the Works. He also took charge of the Manufacture of the Brick and Drane Tiles required on the Estate. [Dr Paul soon had reason to regreat having added the Brick and Tile Making to his other responsibilites.]

In addition to the Local Tradesmen [Note. Local Tradesmen at the refinery left at the Refinery by Dr Paul: Two Blacksmiths, Two Carpenters, One Cooper] at the Refinery There was an English Chemest, A Clark, a riveter and Engene Fitter, and there Famlies, and laterley a Brick Maker and his Famley. With the addition of a Squad of Native Labourers etc. All under Dr Paul's direct superentendance.

The Irish Brick Maker and Famley looked as if they were long out of Employment. But soon proved that strong Drink had to do with thir poor appearance. [When the Brick Maker and Famley arrived It would be a dificulty to know what was the origen of their Close. On leaving the Works it took Three carts to remove their Boxes to Stornoway.] Dr Paul was greatly disapointed with him for several other reasons besides intemperance which led Dr Paul to give him his warning to leve the Works in May 1862 (Dr Paul having left in April). [Note. The Brick Maker got his warning to leave the Works 6 weeks before Dr Paul left.] Led to the Brick Maker acting an Important Part at the refinery, as will be seen Farther on.

It was discovered that the Water supply at the Brick Work was deficient. Which led to the Necessity of Building the Stills for First Distilation at a Burn in a Glen (800 yards from the Refinery) Where a cottage was Built for the Workers who was to attend the Stills.

A light Tramway With a Fall of One in Thirty conected the

stills in the Glen with the refinery Where the Carts discharged the Tar from L.C.W. Creed. From thence in Trucks to the Glen. The oils First distilation was in Casks brought up the Encline, all by Manual Labour. [The dificulty and Expense of getting the Tar down and oil up the encline by Manual Labour was found to be about equal to the carting from Creed the whole 8½ miles.]

The Question May arise Why was the Lewis Chemical Works thus seperated in to Three departments and not save Sir James Mathison, Bt. the Enormous Expense incurred by such seperation. When their was such a Field to select a Site where all could be together having plenty of Water, Peat, and also clear from a Fishing River. My answer to this Question is in one Word, *An Enormous Reckless Blunder*. Which the Responsible Parties, Messrs Paul and Caunter called by a More refined Term *An Error of Judgment*.

The Delapited state of the Brick sheds and Machinery (the Engene renewed, Steam Boiler replaced by a New Boiler) and providing a supply of Water for condencing purposes etc. incurred Great expence.

The following was the State of the Refinery when Dr Paul left the Works: a large quantity of Oils and Parifine Wax in the different Stages of Purification; A large store of Chemicals, Acids, Soda, etc. Stills of Various forms, Mixing Pans, Pumps for Oils, and Air exhaust Pumps to be worked by Machinery, Hydrolic Press. In short all required for the Purifying of Crude Hydro-carbon Oils on a large scale was fitted up. [Dr Paul had fitted up at the Refinery A Laboratory fitted up with small coper stills, Pans, and Innumerable Number of Glass Stills and Test tubes also a very complicated Ballance under Glass Cover. Shelfs full of Bottles with Various Chemicals, In short every thing required to conduct Analyzes and Experiments. All too Delicate to be of use to his Successors.]

Smithey had a large quantity of Improved Tools, a stock of Iron and Steel Plates and Rivets for Oil Tanks In course of Construction. Stills and Evaporating Pans prepared to be removed to Creed C. Works for Fixing the Ammonia and Acetic acid. In Cooperage a large stock of Oak Staves and New oil Casks and Coopers Tools. A staff of Tradesmen for the different departments. Two Cart Horses, Spring Cart and Four Wheeled Waggon and two Common Carts.

A large quantity of Peat for Firing Stills, Boilers and Burning Brick.

L.C. Works Creed

As refered too on Page 24th [*i.e.* p. 192] The Lewis Chemical Works at Creed was undergoing repares, having yet a wide Margen for improvements etc as practice would derect. It being known that Dr Paul was not to return to the Lewis, on 22 April Sir James Mathisons Chamberlain accompanied by Mr Caunter came to the Works. The former introducing the Latter as *Future Manager* of the Lewis Chemical Works in place of *Dr Paul.*

Mr Caunter's Fitness for Manager of the L.C. Works may be seen on Page 5th [*i.e.* p. 184], and the relation between Dr Paul and Mr Caunter was not of such a Friendly Nature as to lead to Chemical Knowledge being imparted to his successor (Dr Paul's assistant Chemist having left previously).

Being by appointment at Mr Caunter's residence in the evening after being instaled as Manager of the L.C. Works, He, Mr Caunter read to me an Advertisment for a Chemist to take charge of the refinery at the Brick Works, which was to be *Posted* that evening for publication in the *Glasgow Herald*, also read a Letter to Sir James Mathison Bt then at London, to be provided with a Pony and Trap for driving to and from the Refinery 6½ Miles distant. This looked so far Promising for the success of the L.C. Works.

When enter James Macfaden the Irish Brickmaker from Garabost, Mr Caunter told him that his dismisal would not then be insisted on, as there was Brick required which would keep him Employed till July, and that a Chemist was to be advertised to take charge of the Chemical department.

James Macfaden thanked Mr Caunter for delaying his Dismisal, rising as to leave the Room. Proved that he had a Mind above 'Clay and Brick', Congratulated Mr Caunter on his advancement as Manager, and added with emphasis, *When a Chemist comes to the Works you will be only Manager in Name.* Why get a chemist when I can do it.

Wounderful to relate, Instead of laughing at the Irish Brickmaker for his audacity, Mr Caunter replied by saying. Well James in that case a Chemist need not be Advertised for the Refinery. [What absurdness, A common Brick Maker who scarcely could write his Name to be given the position on which depended the profitable Utelizing of the Products of a Work which Cost so much Money, Risk all and Save My Dignety as Manager. In this Case Mr Caunter had sence But not reason, otherwise was an agreeable Gentleman.]

This on the evening of 22nd April 1862. The runious Failure of the Lewis Chemical Works was pronounced in the Glen House – H. Caunter Esqre and James Macfaden Brickmaker to take the place of Dr B. H. Paul and Mr Whitread his assistant Chemist.

Mr Caunter, Instead of being subordinate to Dr Paul, was now Jubelant. The respect due to him as Manager safer with Macfaden and his Associates *Then with a qualified Chemist.* All the refined oils and Parifine left by Dr Paul was disposed off. The 35 Tons of Tar, on hand at Creed was Carted to the refinery on which they began to operate.

By and By Thirty 30 gallon casks of Lignoline or Parifine oil was sent to the Glasgow Agent. [30 Casks Containing 30 Gallons each Cask Filled warm from the stills, which when cooled in the Casks, thickned.] Which when examined at Glasgow was found so thick that it wuld not come out through the Bung holes. This first *lot* was returned from Glasgow to the refinery, a sufficient proof that a qualified Chemist was required for the Work.

[Soon after Dr B. H. Paul and assistant Chemest left the Works, Complaints made that the oils and Chimical Mixtures which was led to the Broad Bay from the Refinery had killed the Fish. This confirmed by Mr Liddel, Farmer, Grase, The Wind blowing the oil and Tar to oppicite side, lying as a sluck on the shore.]

[Mr George Craig the Works Cooper, was dismissed from the Refinery for daring to take notice of dishonesty at the Refinery.]

I will now leave them Grouping in the Dark to discover the proper manner of Mixing Chemicals and purifing Oils etc. and briefley skitch the proceedings at L.C.W. Creed after Dr Paul left.

The Foreman being in charge at the L.C. Works Creed since the First Brick was laid, also at the Refinery Building, the Boilers, Stills and Pans, Had bit by bit understood the requirements of the Work and the Nature of the Dangerous Gases etc. Steam and Engene, could now apply Practical Knowledge to the improving of the Works, without much interference from our New Manager Who did not pretend any knowledge of the affair, But was for Courtsey sake consulted occationally.

As already referred to, The Works was undergoing improvements after Dr Paul left, among the principal improvements was the Building of a large Vat Containing 2000 Gallons to receive the Tar and Water by Gravity from the Condencers, The exhaust steam from the Engene led in to the Vat through an arrangement of pipes, giving sufficient heat to seperate the Tar and Ammonea Water, this saving labour and Fewal, Instead as before the stuff Carried in bukets to a Boiler to be heated. The Ammonea apparatus Prepared by Dr Paul at the Refinery to be fitted up at Creed (as refared to at Page 30 [*i.e.* p. 194]). The Ammonea apparatus was by Mr Caunter thought rather Complicated and began to simplefy it down to his own Understanding till at last it landed among the scrap Iron. The Tramways was extended through the Peat Ground, Ten additional Trucks (Twenty in all) Which was left full of Peat each evening for the Night Consumption.

Two large Pits dug in the Moss beside the Cart Road, Each Pit to contain 30 Tons of Tar, one Pit filled, cooling to be carted to the Refinery while the other was receiving the Tar distilled daly in a warm state to be in turn cooled for Carting. Additional Condencers was placed between the Fan and Gas Burner, with sundrie other additions and changes to Complete the Works. [The Machinery Built in Mouth of Kilns to prevent escape of Gas was removed to the scrap Iron heap, Which by the various alterations from first had now grown to a large heap.]

There was one improvement Proposed before starting on which Mr Caunter put his Veto. That was to conduct as much Gas to the Boiler Furnece as keep up Steam, however altho the doing was not then insisted on it was not lost sight of as will be seen farther on.

[The large quantity of Peat prepared in 1859–60 and 1861 Not being used owing to the many delays and alteration on the Work, gave better results, owing to the Three summers Drying. A large quantity Estimated at $\frac{1}{3}$ lost in Dross by too much Drying or too long exposed to the Weather.]

On 20 Septr. 1862 The Works was started in a greatley improved state. Our first Weeks work give 7 per cent of Tar (Crude hydrocarbon) or 2 per cent over our Preveous best weeks work. Second Week gave 8½ per Cent of Tar by weight of Peat Consumed in Kilns. Peat as formerly used in Steam Boiler Furnece From 3 to 3½ Tons in 24 hours. Large Ponds dug below the Works to contain the Ammonia Water Condenced (Which averaged 30 per cent of the Peat used). [The quantity of Water depended on the dryness of the Peat and the tempreture of the Air. The Condencers being on the Atmospheric principle gave better results in cold weather.] Which under the overseeing of the Head Gamekeeper the Ponds was emptyed in to a Burn leading to the Creed River When in Flood. But notwithstanding all Precautions, during dry weather it was impossible to prevent injury to the Salmon Fry in the River, by under ground leakage using from the Ponds. Having, In selecting a site for the Works overlooked the Killing of the Fish in the Pond (see Page 3 [*i.e.* pp. 183-4]) Caused Great trouble and expence at the Works, to remedy this as much as possible, by an arrangement of pipes The Ammonea Water was led in to the Ashpits. This dousing the Hot Charcoal droping through the Furnece bars saturating the Charcoal and ashes with Ammonia, which was found Valuable as a Fertilizer, and so used on the improvements going on in the Castle Grounds. In this Manner about ⅓ of the Water was used up.

The uncondencible Gases Burning to Waste. But notwithstanding our Manager prohibition, and without his Knowledge, a Flew was led under Ground, with a rigulating Valve, leading the Gas in to the Steam Boiler Furnece, Air to support Combusion supplied through the Furnece Bars, forming a sheet of Flame below the Boiler etc. This saving 3½ Tons of Peat in 24 hours. Which was added to the Consump of the Kilns with a Coresponding encrease of Tar. The Gas keeping up Steam for 5 days before our Manager visited the Works, his time taken up at the refinery (being supplied with a Poney and Trap by Sir James Mathison).

A sciene at the Works on the Fifth day, or on Mr Caunters first Visit. Descovering the Gas below the Boiler, He entirely lost Temper, quite lost Controll of himself, for as he said, daring to do what he prohibited, and if safe to do Dr Paul would have done it when at the Works, Predicting the blowing up of the Works etc. His Mildest Term was stuborn disabedience. Left the Works in a rage. However a Few lines sent after him With a Months Notice to get another to take Charge at Creed, seing the experience gained by being in Charge from the First Brick laid at Creed was not Valued by him. Next Morning he came to the Work all mildness, and open to reason with him. The same afternoon returned with Sir James Mathison and several Gentlemen, then Visitors at the Castle, and with Hat in hand showed them the Gas keeping up steam, which *he only yesterday completed.* [I made it a rule When Gentlemen visited The Works To give Mr Caunter the Credid for all the Improvements on the Works since Dr Paul left. Always parted with Gentlemen visiting the Works By saying, If Mr Caunter was present he would explain the operation Better then I could. Professor Tyndall and Fairfax and Hexley doughted this, as did others who visited the Works.] [Mr Caunter as well as take credid to himself in my presence told Sir James and the other Gen[tleme]n that Dr Paul would not Venture to use the waste Gases below the Boiler.]

On the Morrow, Mr Caunter came with a paper for me to sign for a years engagement which I then refused. But in a few Days yeilded to the *Noble* and *benevolent Sir James*'s advise, saying I would never have reason to repent staying in his Service. In this way I was engrafted in to the Lewis C. Works. [Mr Caunter was aware that I had at that time Tempting offers to leave the Works and so was Sir James Mathison Baronet, by Mr Caunter.]

The Ammonea Water Still gave trouble. Evaporating Boilers fitted up to consume it by evaporation, Fired by the Gases. By this time its Dangerous Nature understoon to allow it being safley laid by Flews and pipes etc for Fewal where required about the Works. The Water thus concentrated altho proved a Good Fertilizer as top dressing for Grass was not used exepting when *Lady Mathison* was at the Castle. [The large quantity of Uncondencible Gases altho by the least overlook was ready to play Havoc among the Condencers, still, when carefully handled, was as safe as Water in pipes – and when consumed in a proper Furnece, admitting as much (and no more) Air as give Complete Combustion Burns with intence Heat, no smell when Burning.] [The Peat Gas could have been generated in the Vecenity of the vegetable Garden (and out of sight of the Castle and Carriage Drive) lead in a pipe to fire the

Hot water *Boiler* for the *Castle Hot houses*. This dowing away with the smoke blowing about the Castle Windows when the Boiler is Fired. In 1874 an English Gentleman sugested this, But officials objected.]

The Ammonea apparatus prepared by Dr Paul (see Page 36 [*i.e.* p. 197]) which he often said, when fitted up, would take Byproducts out of the Peat Water equal if not more then Pay the Working expence of the Works. The *Brown Acid* after being used at the Refinery was to be reused to fix the Ammonea at Creed, Was by this time allowed to run in to the Broad Bay. About this time A Gentleman Visitor at the Lewis Castle, observing the large quantity of Shells put ashore by the Tides on the South end of the Broad Bay, suggested to gather and Burn them into Lime. Sir James and Lady Mathison being always willing to give employment to the Tennants, ordered the shells to be Gathered, Kilns Built in the Castle Grounds where the Lime was to be used on the Improvements. But on Trial The Kilns found unsutable so in that way proved a Failure and given up. Which lead to a Furnice being Built at Creed Works and the Gases applied to burn the shells during the Existance of the Works, scores of the Crofters in the adjoining Villages, Paid heavy arears of rent by gathering and Carting the shells to Creed Works. [When the Works was undergoing repairs, The Shells was Burnt with Peat Fewal in stead of Gas, a Furnece being added to lower end . . . The flame from the Peat fire acting on the shells similar to the Gas. In this manner all the Lime required for Estate Work could have been Burnt at about half the cost of Irish Lime, The Broad Bay supplying the Shells. All such discouraged by Estate officials. No tips from Lime Agents or Ship owners.] In this Way Generating steam, Evaporating the Peat Water and Burning Shells all the Uncondencible Gases was Utilized. For which our Manager took Credid, as he had an equal right to do as first using the Gas to Generate Steam (See Page 39 [*i.e.* pp. 198–9]).

Every opertunity was taken to farther improve the Works as practice would derect, With the result that our weekley Produce of Tar was from 8½ to 9 Tons. [The Pitch was easely seperated by stirring diluted Acid in the Tar when in a few hours The Pitch was on the Bottom of the Tank. The *Pitch* when Boiled was found equal to Paltic Pitch, and supereour to Coal Tar for Felt Roofing, and Mixed with dry Peat Dross. When cool, Broke up supereour to Coal for Generating Steam.]

The Tar after the Pitch was removed or seperated was found very sutable as a Lubricator for Waggon Axiles and heavy Machenery. [The Lubricative Grease had a percentage of Green oil mixed with it But no water.] [When the Grease was in demand, The Tar was mixed with Green oil *which was unsaleable at the Refinery.*] A demand at a profitable price sprung up, orders increasing till the Demand was equal to the supply. James McFaden and his associates at the Refinery began to Experiment, made Mr Caunter to beleive that $\frac{2}{3}$ by meashure of Water added to the Tar would improve the Grease. He seing our hesitation to make this Mixture, and reminded by him that he was Manager, Stood over the adding of the Water to 3 Tons which was put in Casks. Sent to Glasgow to fulfill an order. All returned by Steamer and no more asked for. [The 3 Tons of Grease Mixed with $\frac{2}{3}$ Water under Mr Caunters Personal superentendance Was ordered to be Carted to Steamer next day. When it was descovered that the Tar and Water had partley seperated and in a crudley state. When appealed to against sending it in that State in Vain, He would have it off. With the result of its return from Glasgow by return of Steamer and no more ordered.] Soon after It was discovered by a ship Captain that the Peat Tar was a superiour Antifouling Grease for Ships Bottoms. Samples sent to several Shipping Ports. In due time Favourable testimonials and orders for Antifouling Grease was received. A Liverpool Ship Chandler, after lenghtned tests Wished to secure all that could be Manufactured, offering a high prise for it. This was again so promising to Get the Tar desposed of from Creed Works Profitably without Chemicals or Chemical operation. However Macfadan and associates began to Experiment, and Convinced Mr Caunter That by parcially distilling the Tar it Would improve the Antifouling Grease. [Pieces of Iron placed under water in the Broad Bay. In a week took up to the Works Made Mr Caunter beleive the Iron lay Coated for 6 Month under water, covered with Tar partly Distilled appeared clean from Fouling. Any Trick to prevent the Tar being sold direct from Creed was the Sole Aim of The Macfadens and associates.] This causing the Tar to be sent to the

Refinery to be Distilled, the resdue, a Tuff Pitch sent south as Anti-fouling Grease which resulted in stoping the orders. After this there was a favourable offer refused for the Peat Tar from Managers of a Shale oil Work to be Distilled with their Crude Oils To Modify the Flash Point of the shale Oil. [Mr Caunter Honestly admited, That his reason for refusing to sell the Peat Tar to the Shale Oil Works was, That it would be an admission of his inability to refine it at Home, and put the Refinery Idle after being fitted up at Great Expense.] [The Flash point of Lewis oil was higher then shale oils.]

It may be here noticed that if the Tar was desposed off direct from Creed Works there would be no Tar for the Refinery, Mr Caunter being under the Influence of Macfaden and his associates, and of such a credulous disposition and without the sagacity to decern his being led by the cleque at the refinery to put a stop to the Tar being profitably desposed off direct on Three occations (see Page 43–44 [*i.e.* p. 201]) For there own interest as will be seen farther on.

Owing to the Failure of the Irish Chemists to Distill the Crude Hydrocarbon oils at the Irish Peat Co's Works (see Page 7 [*i.e.* p. 185]) Led to Chemists and scientific Gentlemen to visit the L.C. Works Creed. [The Lewis Chemical Works was now Famous as being the first successful Work for the Distillation of the Crude Oil (Tar) from Peat on a large scale. The Irish Peat Works having Failed at this Point and The German Peat Works in its Infancy (see Page 7 [*i.e.* p. 185]).] Which by the various alterations and Expencive improvements, was the *Completest*, most *Successful* Work ever put up for the Distillation of the Hydrocarbon oils from Peat. Dr Angus Smith, the eminent Chemist admited as much on a Visit to the Works. A Titled Irish Gentleman on Visiting the Works, said that If the Irish Chemists who erected the Irish Peat Co's Work had known to put up a Work like that, The Peat Bogs would have enriched Ireland. They, he said, Could analyze a *Fly's leg* in a Laboratory, But an Irish Poteen Distiller Could teach them to Distill the Bog (see Page 7 [*i.e.* p. 185]).

Indigo Blue to be Manufactured out [*of*] *Peat Tar.*

In 1865 A German Chemist appeared with Mr Caunter at the

Works, who pretended he was able to Convert the Peat Tar into Real Indigo Blue. Next Day he came alone Minutely examining the Works, expressed admiration for the arrangement of the whole was bluntley asked, If that was not better then Empty Herring Barrels as at the German Peat Works (see Page 7 [*i.e.* p. 185]), appeared startled and give a long answer in German, to which he was replyed to in Gaelic Which put us both on the same level. He departed with more information then Dr Paul and Mr Caunter got at the German Peat Work. [The German Chemist had a written order to examine the Works, otherwise would not be admited. Dr Paul on Visiting the Island as a Tourist believed him a spy from the German Peat Works.] [Dr B. H. Paul spoke about Dyes being one of the By-products of Peat Which he expected to Manufacture, *But not Indigo Blue.*] [After the German left, having occation to Visit the refinery with Mr Caunter, I was shown Experiments going on to Manufacture Indigo Blue. On a table about 15 *pasers* with wisps of Wool, yarn etc steeped in some Mixture, several of the Wisps had a Tint of Blue. All now wanted was the Missing Link, Mr Caunter in *Great Gusto*, a Great discovery to be Made. It *used* out that unknown to him a real Blue was added by the cleque to keep him in Trim.]

The Creed Works was successfully Carried on and improved, Distilling More Peat Tar then could be accounted for after being Carted to the Refinery 8½ miles distant. Could be kept going day and Night (Sunday exepted) for two and three Months before Stoping for repairs. [The Ton of Peat Tar (Crude Hydrocarbon) cost £3 10s. to £3 15s. at L.C. Works Creed. The same quantity at the Shale Works Cost £5.]

Having Plenty of Tar to operate on and not accountable for results, They by *Haphasard* managed through time to make salable oils and Parifine Wax. The oils at first sold for 2s. 9d. to 2s. 6d. and laterly 2s. per gallon. (All By-products run in to the Broad Bay).

A New Work for The Distillation of Peat to be Built within ½ a Mile from the Refinery.

In the spring of 1865 Mr Caunter submited a Plan and detailed Estimate to Sir James Mathison Bt (Then at the Lewis Castle)

For a New Work for the Distillation of Peat. Mr Caunter must have applied his power of Persuading on the *Noble* Sir *James* before he Granted him the sum of £1400 afterwards suplimented to £1600 which to finish would require £2000 This for a Work for which there was no necessity as may be seen from the Foregoing. [Unless on the Faith of the Missing Link for *Indigo Blue* from the Peat Tar being discovered, There was not the Shadow of reason for the New Work, which was the result of Mr Caunters wandering thoughts When confined to his House with Gout for 4 week in the spring of 1866. Its Plan and Condencing apparatus was as Impractable as can be emagined. The Detailed Estimate signed by Sir James amounted to £1400, When spent fully ⅓ the work was yet to be done, £400 was applied for, £200 Granted and spent, requiring £400 More to Finish.]

My Engagment held me bound to superentend all Buildings Conected with the Lewis C. Works. The New work was Commenced on the 21 May 1866, on said Date there was *65 Tons* of Tar on hand at the Creed Works. Had to Close up on the 25th May for want of storage. After £1600 was spent on the New Work, It never was finished. Even to show Its unsutableness, If required for the Distilation of Peats, stood at a sticked Job for several years, Demolished, The Brick sold, Condencers broke up, sold as scrap Iron, The Engene and Boiler brought to the Patent slip saw Mill. Here £1600 of Sir James Mathesons Money flung away. The result of the infatuation and want of decerment of H. Caunter Esqre Manager of the L.C. Works.

It may be Noticed that after Dr Paul left, The Ligoulene (Lamp Oil) was sold at the Refinery to the Vilages Both sides of the Broad Bay, In Bottles, Gallons and Casks. *Cash sales* without any *check* Which will account for what follows.

Mr Caunter altho a Heavey robust Bodied Gentleman, was a Marter to *Gout* in his Feet Had a prolonged attack in Feby 1868 Which Confined him to his House for 10 Days. On calling on him shortly after his return from his first visit to the Refinery after his recovery I found him in Great destress *actually sheding Tears*, Caused as he Confessed by the State he found those in Charge at the Refinery on his (by them) unexpected Visit, all Incapable with *Drink*, a large quantity of Parifine Wax destroyed and unsalable.

The whole Works through other. *Honestly Confessed with Tears*, That he did not Know, or could account for but a small per centage of the Lignoline (Lamp oil) Distilled from all the Tar received at the Refinery for the Last 12 Months. The oil Tanks in *Store* supposed by him to be full of Finished refined Oil, Now descovered Empty. When spoken to, was answered with Insolence By the Macfadens (a small Colony of them having arrived after James got to be Chemist at the Refinery).

The Refinerys Monthly Paysheets was at hand and on examining It was found that 320 Tons of Tar was Certified by J Macfaden to have been received during the Year ending 31 January 1868 Which Cost at Creed Works £1130 add Carting, Chemicals etc at the Refinery. [The Paysheets was made up Monthly for Creed and Refinery, Allocated, Exports and imports shown.] [Mr Caunter acting as Paymaster for which he was most sutable and since Dr Paul left was wholly responsible to Sir James for the whole works.] [Donald Munro, Factor to Sir James to show his displeasure at what he called the Irish Colony of Macfadens and Friends employed on several occations sent their pay in a seperate Bag.] This destressing result as he said in his *over Confidence* in *unworthy Men* and now his suspicion of Foul dealings from first was confirmed. Asked for My Advice to him under this serious State of affairs in which he found himself Which I did in writing next Morning (see next page [*i.e.* below]). Left him late at Night, Pouring out Bolts of excomunication on the Irish Cleque and Confederates, The whole lot was to be Cleared off Bag and Baggage from the refinery. A Chemist was to be got as should at First. This Burst of anger led to a relapse of Gout which Kept him in his room for other 8 Days.

[Creed Gate House, 1st March 1868.

H. Caunter Esqre. Dear Sir, sorry for your distress. The result of misplaced confidence in Men who from first took advantage of the trust you gave them to enrich themselves being by you allowed for 6 years to supply the Villages both sides of the Broad Bay and other places with Parifine *oil*, Cash sales at the Works without check. See how they got you to upset the Lubracating and Antifouling Grease, and again to refuse the sale of Tar direct from Creed to the

Bathgate Shale oil Works and again to spend £1600 on a Work not required. Which stands as an unfinished Monument of imposition on a confining Nature, etc. My advice to you is to confess your discovery yesterday to D. Munro who will sirch in to the affair and dismiss the whole pack, Advertise for a Chemist to take charge in place of those who never should have been in charge of what was so Important To Sir James Mathison Bt., yourself and the whole Estate, and not less to me who gave up promising Situations at my Trade for the L.C. Works at which I got engrafted by the Advice of Sir James Mathison and his Factor after Dr B. H. Paul left the Works.

Yours etc D. Morison
Copy rendered on Date

P.S. You asking my advice last night will I hope excuse my freedom.]

When first able to Drive to the Refinery, The Humbling of the St Edmund Monks to Abbot Samson was acted over again. [*Carlyle Past and Present*] We decide on humbling ourselves before the Abbot, by word and gesture in order to Medicate his Mind. He, replying with much humelety, Yet alleging his own justice turning the blame on us. When he saw us conquered, *became himself Conquered* – swore that he never was greaved so much for anything, First for himself and Cheafley for the *scandal* which had gone abroad – Embraced all of us – *he wept*, We *wept*, What a picture. Behave better ye remiss Monks, and thank Heaven for such an Abbot – or Know that ye must and shall obay.

It might be reasonably expected That after the foregoing descovery a Change would be made at the Rifenery, But a repitition of the Humbling of the St Edmund Monks, Flattery and Blarney, got them into favour again.

Soon after the Cleque began to brake up. First some of James Macfadens relations removed south. Next year James and Famley left for America Where they Bought Farms, and no dought Blissing their Stars for having met with such a Confiding Gentleman as Henry Caunter Esqre Manager of the L.C. Works refinery.

His Brother who with his Famley came to Garabost as Brick, Tile and Flower Pot Maker, succeeded James as Chemist and Oil refiner Till in 1874 The L.C. Works Ceased to exist Both at Creed and refinery. When soon after All the Metal Condencers, Pumps, Stills, Pans, Tanks etc at the Three places, Creed Works, the Refinery and New Works was Broken up and sold as scrap Iron. As was the light Rails (3¾ Miles) laid at Creed Works deverging through the Peat Ground. The Iron rails at the Refinery not sold as may be seen, off the Main Road, Striches of the Iron rails put up as Fences by the Crofters.

And So end the Queens Enemies.

The foregoing will show how the Noble ententions of Sir James and Lady Mathison in spending large sums of Money with the View of benefiting the unskilled Labour on the Estate was frustated by the L.C. Works getting into the hands of uncapable Men, If otherwise would have been a profitable Concern. It maybe seen from the foregoing breaf accont of the Lewis Chemical Works from the beginning of 1859 till end of 1874 That if the Eminant Chemist and Analyst Dr B. H. Paul had the Practical experience in 1859 as he had in 1862, he could have erected the Creed Works in 6 Month in the state he left it at ⅓ the Cost and the Whole Work would be placed together and in a more convenient place, and in many ways more economical in working. This Dr Paul discovered when too Late to remedy. But for all the draw backs, he had no dought of being able to make the affair a profitable Concern, but unfortunatley left when the Works was at a stage when he could put his Chemical Knowledge to profitable use.

After leaving the Lewis Dr Paul read a paper at the meeting of the British Association on the Distillation etc. of Peat by him in Lewis, Considered then the most exhaustive ever wrote on Peat. Tables showing the percentage of the Various Products of Lewis Peat to be supereour to Irish Peat in oils, Parifinc Wax and By-products, when compared to the results found by the Chemists of the Irish Peat Co. It may be remarked that by improvements on the Works after Dr Paul left, the Cost of the Crude Hydrocarbon was fulley ¼ less then when he read his paper, a copy of which I had from him.

On the third year after leving the Works Dr B. Hariot Paul Visited the Island as a Tourist, saw the Works Improved, on leaving

Expressed the opinion That the Creed Works Now was the completest yet erected for the Distillation of the Crude Hydrocarbon Oils from Peat, Predicted its failure For want of a Chemist able to Mix Chemicals and Utilize the Byproducts etc Going to waste.

Being supplied By Sir James Mathison Bt with all Publications refering to the Utilization of Peat at Home and abroad. The Irish Peat Co Work was the most conspicuous. Its History (Illustrated) showed it to have been an elaborate and extensive Work. Its Failure caused by the Great hight of the Kiln The Gases having to traverce through a Mass of Peat 32 feet from the Hearth to the outlet, resulting in the Gases being Partly Condenced inside the Kiln in stead of in the Very elaborate Condencers. Dr Paul avoided this error, By Building 10 Kilns their aggregate Capacity not quite equal to half the one Irish Kiln, The two Gas outlets in each Kiln, one 3 feet and one 6 feet above the Fire Grates, led the Gases quickly in to the Condencers. In place of 32 feet as In the Irish Peat Co's Work.

In the Sixties From 1862 to 1868, Termed the Coal Famine, Innumerable Papers Published, and Patents taken out for Machinery to Convert Peat into Charcoal, Peat Coal, and Ellumenating Gas from Peats Giving as a precedent what was done with Peat on The Continent, Quite overlooking the Difference of Climate for Drying as compared to the United Kingdom. At that time, The principal of what is now in 1895 advocated as a new descovery termed the *Blundens Process* for the Manufacture of *Peat Coal* (See *Land and Water*, 12 January 1895) was well known 33 years since, as may be seen in the records of the British Association of that Period Where the subject was discused at length. The principal then and now advocated is to Mash (by Machenery) the raw Peat braking up the Fibers, Grass roots etc doing away with their resistance to the Contraction of the Peat when exposed for drying etc. resulting in a very supereour Peat Fewel (See farther on). The Practical objection to Machenery being used for Mashing was the Large quantity of Raw Peat to be Handled as compared with the Improved Peat Fewal manufactured.

Thus Peat Bog Contains on an Average
70 percent of Water, *30 percent Fewal*
30 percent Improved Fewal, *Peat Coal*

Tons 100 By Manual labour from Bog to Engene
Tons 100 By Manual labour from Engine to drying ground
Tons 100 For Firing steam Boiler and Mashing Machenery etc. attendance and Fewal
300 Tons of Raw Peat *operated* on *resulting* in *only 30 Tons of Peat Coal.*

If by Blunden Process now advocated the Manual labour is Minifyed, There can be no dought but the Peat Problum is solved.

Experiments on Peat Bog for Improved Peat Fewal or Coal at the Lewis Chemical Works Creed, Summer of 1866/7–8.

A soft Fibrey Part of the Bog was first selected, a strip 20 yards or ther[b]y and 2½ feet Broad was lined off, The Sod removed. A strong deal door 7 feet × 3 feet, Frames nailed to sides 3 inches high, and Two Wooden Beaters or Rammers was prepared. The Door set as a Platform beside the strip of Bog prepared to be operated on, one man standing on the Raw Peat Flung out a spaidfull on to the Platform alternate to the two Men, who with two Blows of their Beaters Mashed it up and so on till the Platform was full to top of Frames, a few claps with back of their spaids made the Mashed Peat uniform thickness with the Frame. Then a Man stood at each end of Platform (the two men mashing) quickly scored the soft Mashed Peat across the platform. Then with their spaids Flung the Peat on the surface of the Bog to dry. This was continued till the spreading ground was covered. Then the Platform removed along. In four to six days Peat so treated is fit to be Built in Dykes (Pigen hole like), and dry in a surprisingly short time as compared to Peat Cut in the usual way, and will contract in to a Hard Clean Fewal Free from dust, Hard like wood and when Chared retain its shape. Its fracture having a Metalic Lusture. The extra Cost of Mashing is more then recompensed by the quickness in Drying, The superiority and cleaness of the Fewal and lesser Bulk to be operated on by the surprising Contraction, as Compared to Peat cut in the usual Manner (as hard and clean as Wood). In this Manner what is now Claimed by Blunden's Process has been an can be atained without Expencive Machenery. An ordinary Man will in a few hours practice without removing from the platform,

Fling the peat off from his spaid fully 3 yards as even and close as new Made Brick on the Drying ground.

Experiments on Peat Gas for Illuminating Purposes at L.C. Works Creed.

A small retort 2′ 6″ long left by Dr Paul was fitted up with Condencers, and Gasometar to hold 180 Feet. Purifiers etc. Artificial Dryed Peat gave from 5½ to 6½ Thousand feet of Gas per Ton of low Illumenating Power. But great Heat. Peat artificially Dryed and saturated with Peat Tar gave Gas of from 18 to 26 Candle Power and from 8 to 9 Thousand feet per Ton. (Not practicable owing to quickness of taking fire when charging retort.) This led to a suplimentary retort 6″ pipe 3 feet long. The origenal Charged at a low Tempreture. The other kept at a red heat, receiving the Gas from the low tempreture retort giving Gas of 26 Candle Power. [Better result when lower retort was kept at blue heat.]

Gas from Peat Tar alone. A Tank was fitted up above and conected by a pipe and regulating Valve. The warm Tar gently let in to the low Retort discharging the Gas in to the higher like the Hydrolic Main at Gasworks, with the difference that the Condenced oil returned by its own Gravity in to the lower retort, now kept at a high Tempreture to be again converted in to Gas of 30 Candle Power. Retorts not opened till required to clear out the Coke.

Experiment on Peat Charcoal.

A Furnece 12 feet long 18″ broad Flat arched Roof, and on a rise of 1 in 30 was Built, Conected to the stack by a Flew, a Number of Paint (empty) Drums was procured, Their Movable lids perforated. The Drums filled with Peat Coal (Mashed Peat) was placed sideways and across in the Furnece, lids alternate. When the Furnece was heated and the Drum next the Fire bars ceased to give off Gass through the perforated lids, it was hauled out through the Furnece Door, this causing all the Drums to turn down leving space at top for a fresh drum and so on. The Drum which was removed was placed perforated lid down in a Bed of sand to cool, Emptied and refilled with Peat to be again in turn put in to the Furnece.

The advantage of this Mode of Charing was. First, the Furnece could be Conteneous kept going, Second. The Gases from the Drums at lower end saving the greatest part of the Firing. Thirdly the Charcoal more dence and Forthly. The furnece could be lenghtned to use up all the heat in drying the Peat in the drums before escaping in to the Stack. Fifthly, The Charcoal from the Prepared Peat was clean, hard and free from dust or smut.

The Drums filled with chopped Tree branches chared as above described gave equally good results. If on a large scale, stronger and larger drums would be required.

General remarks on Peat for Fewal and Distillation.

The Peat Ground took up by the L.C. Works Creed was fully $\frac{3}{4}$ of a square Mile ($3\frac{1}{2}$ miles of Tramways laid through in Branches all joining a Main Line near the Works), $\frac{1}{3}$ or therby of the Ground being hilley and unworkable.

The part of peat Ground wrought had as many as 6 different qualities of Peat. First a certain kind of Black Peat Grew in horizontal layers. If not used first year, or when dried would Crumble in to Dross.

Second a small part of the Peat Ground had a Mixture of Bog Irons. Contract and dry quick. Not sutable for the Kilns, Forming clinkers on the Firebars, and Puffing up slight explosions when Charging the Kilns. Got the name of Ammunition Peat. Burns well in an open Fireplace. Ashes Red, giving off strong sulphuret smells.

Third, Soft yellow Peat, retains its Bulk in drying, remains spongey. If mashed will contract in drying, see Page 60-61 [*i.e.* p. 209].

Fourth, Dence Black Peat Containing a High percentage of Hydrocarbon oil. When dry will sink in Water. Gives great heat when Burned in an open Fireplace. Loss in dross may be removed by Mashing when raw.

Fifth. Gray fibrey Peat, will Contract moderately in Drying, dis not Crumble. Gives good results by Distillation, also when Burnt for Fewal in an open Fireplace.

Sixth. Peat under Cotton Weed Grass has the Fibers so strong and dificult to Cut, retains its bulk in drying, not worth the Working for Fewal. Fibers like Hemp.

Peat in properly Made stacks In July and August, Kept in reserve till Next summer will Contract from $\frac{1}{3}$ to $\frac{1}{4}$ its Bulk and greatly improved for Fewal or Distillation.

Where a Large quantity of Peat is cut, say from 3000 to 4000 Tons as at the Lewis C. works, The Loss in a Wet season would be fully one Third, as compared with a dry season. This and the various qualities of Peat in the same district Is quite overlooked by Gentlemen of Literary abilitys When writing learned Essays on the Utilization of Peat.

Mashed Raw Peat left in a Trench on the Drying ground during Winter will improve the density of the Peat Coal.

Mashed Peat in a Trench slightly tramped, top clapped with Back of spaid left all winter will as it were ripen and in good Condition for slicing out with spaid to Dry in April. By the above simple apparatus all that is Claimed by Blundens Patent can be done.

D. M.

INDEXES

KALMETER'S JOURNAL

BROWN'S JOURNAL

References to specific types of woollen products manufactured by Henry and James Brown are prolific in the text and for reasons of space their names have not been included in the index. However many individual products are named in the references under 'cloths, stocks of', and 'fashion'.

NORTH BRITISH RAILWAY INQUIRY

LEWIS CHEMICAL WORKS

MEMBERSHIP

Membership of the Scottish History Society
is open to all who are interested in the history of Scotland.
For an annual subscription of £5·00
members normally receive one volume each year.
Enquiries should be addressed to
the Honorary Secretary or the Honorary Treasurer
whose addresses are given overleaf.

SCOTTISH HISTORY SOCIETY

REPORT

of the 89th Annual Meeting

The 89th Annual Meeting of the Scottish History Society was held in the Rooms of the Royal Society, George Street, Edinburgh, on Saturday, 13 December 1975, at 11.15 a.m. Professor G. W. S. Barrow, President, was in the Chair.

The Report of Council was as follows:

The Council is pleased to report that the eleventh volume of the Fourth series, *Scottish Electoral Politics: 1832–1854*, edited by Iain Brash, was issued to members early in the year. It has proved to be an interesting and popular volume.

The next two volumes to be issued to members, which are now in the hands of the printers, form the Society's memorial to Dr Annie I. Dunlop, and continue the work on the medieval Church in Scotland based on records in the Vatican Archives which she pioneered. The *Calendar of Papal Letters to Scotland* will be in two parts, the first, edited by the Right Rev. Monsignor Charles Burns of the Vatican Archives, consisting of the letters of Pope *Clement VII* of Avignon, 1378–1394, the second, edited by Mr F. McGurk, of the letters of Pope *Benedict XIII* of Avignon, 1394–1418. The first volume will also contain a memoir of Dr Dunlop by Dr I. B. Cowan, Honorary Treasurer of the Society.

The reprint programme undertaken on behalf of the Society by the Scottish Academic Press has unfortunately again suffered setbacks. The reprinted volumes, however, are now in the hands of the binders and will be available to members before the end of the year. Those members who have already indicated their intention to purchase copies of the reprints will receive them immediately on publication; other members desiring copies should order them from the Honorary Treasurer.

The continuous inflation over the past few years, especially affecting printing costs and postal charges, is making it increasingly difficult for the Society to carry out its publication programme on the present basis. The annual income from members' subscriptions, as will be seen from the accounts published with this report, does not cover the cost of publication of the volume received annually by members let alone the administrative costs of running the Society, and the Society has become almost dependent on the generosity of the Carnegie Trust and a few individual well-wishers. The Council of the Society, concerned to maintain the existence of the Society and to put it on a sounder financial basis, has regretfully decided that it must propose to the Annual Meeting that the subscription be raised to £5·00, this increase to be effective in the financial year beginning November 1976. At the same time Council is aware that it has the responsibility of keeping financial outlays as low as possible, and is investigating the possibility of using cheaper methods of producing the Society's publications. If these prove successful, the present Fourth series will be terminated with the two volumes at present in the press, and a new Fifth series will be instituted. A Fifth series cannot be so elegantly and attractively produced as the present series, but Council is determined to achieve as high a standard of quality as possible through the methods of production available within the financial means of the Society. Publication policy will remain much as at present, but will allow for more extended commentary on the documents published, without departing from the fundamental object and aims of the Society.

These changes will increase the responsibilities of the Honorary Secretary who at present combines with his administrative duties the tasks of a literary editor. Accordingly it is proposed to divide these functions in order that a literary editor may be appointed, who will have responsibility for the publications, leaving the general administration of the Society as the main responsibility of the Honorary Secretary.

Members of Council who retire in rotation at this time are Mr E. J. Cowan, Sheriff P. G. B. McNeill and Mr W. H. D. Sellar. The following will be proposed to the Annual Meeting for election to Council: Professor A. E. Anton, Mr E. J. Cowan and Mrs Enid Gauldie.

During the past year 5 members have died, 23 have resigned, and 15 removed from the list of members for non-payment of subscription. New members numbered 13. The total membership, including 233 libraries, is now 700, compared with 730 in 1974.

In presenting the Annual Report, Professor R. H. Campbell emphasised the financial position of the Society which made it necessary to raise the annual subscription and to consider more economic methods of book production; the only alternative to this was the liquidation of the Society.

The Hon. Treasurer, in presenting his report, gave the concrete figures underlying the Chairman's general statement.

Professor G. Donaldson moved the adoption of Annual Report, which was seconded and approved.

Professor A. E. Anton, Mr E. J. Cowan and Mrs Enid Gauldie were nominated as members of Council and duly elected.

The President gave an address entitled 'Landlords, Tenants and the Rent in Early Medieval Scotland'. The meeting closed with a vote of thanks to the President proposed by Mrs R. Mitchison.

ABSTRACT ACCOUNT OF CHARGE AND DISCHARGE OF THE INTROMISSIONS OF THE HONORARY TREASURER for 1 November 1974 to 31 October 1975

I. GENERAL ACCOUNT

CHARGE

I.	Cash in Bank at 1st November 1974:		
	1. Sum at credit of Savings Account with Bank of Scotland		£5,697·26
	2. Sum at credit of Current Account with Bank of Scotland		155·19
	3. Sum at credit of Savings Account with Edinburgh Savings Bank		64·53
	4. Sum at credit of Special Investment Account with Edinburgh Savings Bank		1,096·15
			£7,013·13
II.	Subscriptions received		2,006·36
III.	Past Publications sold		278·53
IV.	Interest on Savings Accounts with Bank of Scotland and Edinburgh Savings Bank		483·88
V.	Compensatory Income Tax Refund (1973–74)		51·62
VI.	Sums drawn from Bank Current Account	£4,394·69	
VII.	Sums drawn from Bank Savings Account	£2,000·00	
			£9,833·52

DISCHARGE

I. Cost of publication during year (*Scottish Electoral Politics*)		£3,474·52
Cost of printing Annual Report, Notices and Printers' Postages, etc.		107·43
		£3,581·95
II. Insurance Premiums		28·13
III. Miscellaneous Payments		134·61
IV. Sums lodged in Bank Current Account	£4,491·70	
V. Sums lodged in Bank Savings Account	£7,991·82	
VI. Funds at close of this account:		
1. Balance at credit of Savings Account with Bank of Scotland	£4,731·77	
2. Balance at credit of Current Account with Bank of Scotland	97·01	
3. Balance at credit of Savings Account with Edinburgh Savings Bank	67·09	
4. Balance at credit of Special Investment Account with Edinburgh Savings Bank	1,192·96	
		6,088·83
		£9,833·52

GLASGOW, *18 November 1975*. I have examined the General Account of the Honorary Treasurer of the Scottish History Society for the year from 1 November 1974 to 31 October 1975, and I find the same to be correctly stated and sufficiently vouched.

I. M. M. MACPHAIL
Auditor

SCOTTISH HISTORY SOCIETY

LIST OF MEMBERS

1977-1978

ABBOT, D. M., 4/10 Orchard Brae Avenue, Edinburgh EH4 2HW
ADAM, Professor R. J., Westoun, Kennedy Gardens, St Andrews
ADAMS, I. H., PH.D., 58 Blackett Place, Edinburgh EH9
ADAMSON, Duncan, 39 Roberts Crescent, Dumfries, CD4 27RS
ADAMSON, Miss Margot R., 100 Handside Lane, Welwyn Garden City, Herts.
AGNEW, Sir Crispin, of Lochnaw, Bt., c/o Regimental Headquarters, Royal Highland Fusiliers, 518 Sauchiehall Street, Glasgow G3
AIKMAN, Miss Christian W. H., Talisker, 2 Brighton Place, Peterculter, Aberdeen AB1 0UN
ALDERSON, J. J., Havelock, Victoria, 3465, Australia
ALEXANDER, Joseph, Trust, per J. A. Carnegie & Smith, solicitors, Bank of Scotland Buildings, Kirriemuir, Angus.
ALLENTUCK, Professor Marcia, B.A., PH.D., 5 West 86 Street, Apt. 12B, New York, N.Y. 10024, USA
ANDERSON, J. Douglas, F.S.A. SCOT., 16 Grantley Gardens, Glasgow G41 3PZ
ANDERSON, Mrs Marjorie O., West View Cottage, Lade Braes Lane, St Andrews KY 16
ANDREW, H., 39 Hawkhead Road, Paisley
ANGUS, G., 73 Findlay Gardens, Edinburgh EH7
ANGUS, Rev. J. A. K., T.D., M.A., The Manse, 90 Albert Road, Gourock, Renfrewshire
ANNAND, A. McK., T.D., F.S.A., SCOT., Somerton, High Street, Findon, Worthing, West Sussex BN14 0TA
ANNAND, James K., 174 Craigleith Road, Edinburgh EH4
ANTON, Professor A. E., 41 Braid Farm Road, Edinburgh EH10 6LE
ARMET, Miss Catherine M., Mount Stuart, Rothesay, Isle of Bute
ARMSTRONG, Campbell, 66 North Kilmeny Crescent, Wishaw, Lanarkshire ML2 8RS
ARMSTRONG, Murdo, Royal Bank House, Muir of Ord, Ross-shire
ASH, Miss Marinell, M.A., PH.D., B.B.C., Queen Street, Edinburgh
ASPLIN, P. W., Strathcraig, Loganswell, Newton Mearns, Glasgow
AULD, Mrs Joan, Carngeal, Almondbank, Perth

BACSICH, Mrs Anna B., 11 Ashton Road, Glasgow G12
BAIN, Miss Sheila M., M.A., M.E.D., Dept of Geography, University of Aberdeen AB9 2UB
BAIRD, Miss Mary Myrtle, Scottish Record Office, H.M. General Register House, Edinburgh EH1 3YY
BANKS, Noel, Wolverton, Stratford-on-Avon, Warwickshire
BANNERMAN, John W. M., PH.D, Arrochy Beg, Balmaha, Stirlingshire

BARNES, Professor Thomas G., D.PHIL., Department of History, University of California, Berkeley, California, 94720, USA

BARR, Mrs A. R., Bonahaven, Colintraive, Argyll

BARROW, Professor G. W. S., Department of Modern History, The University of St Andrews, Fife KY16 9AI

BARROWS, Mrs Eunice, 207 Mary Avenue, Missoula, Montana, 59301 USA

BASDEN, E. B., 7 Leyden Park, Bonnyrigg, Midlothian EH19 2DG

BAXTER, John, 65 Canterbury Road, Redcar, Yorks.

BEBBINGTON, D. W., PH.D., Department of History, University of Stirling, Stirling FK9 4LA

BECKET, Miss Lindsay D., 2 St Michaels Court, Keere Street, Lewes, Sussex

BENNETT, George P., 42 Balnagown Drive, Glenrothes, Fife KY6 2SJ

BENNETT, Miss Josephine M., B.L., 91 Victoria Road, Dunoon, Argyll

BERNARD, K. N., B.A., F.S.A. SCOT., 21 Machrie Drive, Clyde Arran, Helensburgh, Dunbartonshire

BIGWOOD, Mrs A. R., 38 Primrose Bank Road, Edinburgh EH5 3JF

BIRD, A. G., 49 Woldcarr Road, Anlaby Road, Hull, Yorks HU3 6TP

BOGIE, Rev. A. P., M.A., The Manse, Forgan, Newport-on-Tay. Fife DD6 8RB

BONNAR, Maurice K., 1 Dubbs Road, Port Glasgow

BOYACK, James E., DIP. T.P., 25 Barnton Park Gardens, Edinburgh EH4 6HL

BRASH, J. I., M.A. (OXON), Department of History, University of Western Australia, Nedlands, W.A., 6009

BRISTOL, Major Nicholas M. V., Breacachadh Castle, Isle of Coll, Coll

BROUN LINDSAY, Lady, Colstoun, Haddington, East Lothian

BROWN, Jennifer M., M.A., PH.D., Scottish History Department, The University, Glasgow G12 8QG

BROWN, Miss M. F., M.A., 9 Redford Loan, Colinton, Edinburgh EH13

BRUCE, Fraser F., M.A., LL.B., 18 Delnie Road, Inverness

BRUCE, Iain, 39 Comely Bank Road, Edinburgh EH4

BRYCE, Arthur, F.L.A., F.S.A. SCOT, 17 Pinedale Terrace, Scone, Perth PH2 6PH

BRYSON, William, 16 Jubilee Street, Mornington, Dunedin, New Zealand

BUCHANAN, John, 67 Great King Street, Edinburgh EH3 6RP

BUCHANAN, Professor W. Watson, M.D., F.R.C.P., 20 Rosslea Drive, Giffnock, Glasgow

BUCKROYD, Mrs Julia, 60 Highlands Court, Highland Road, Gipsy Hill, London, SE19

BUIST, Frank F., Faireyknowe, by Arbroath, Angus

BULLIVANT, Mrs Margaret S., Brockhampton, Bringsty, Worcester

BULLOCH, Rev. James, D.D., Manse of Stobo, Peebles

BURNS, Right Rev. Monsignor Charles, Archivio Segreto, Citta de Vaticano, Roma, Italy
BURNS, David M., M.A., W.S., 7 Heriot Row, Edinburgh EH3 6HU
BURNS, R. R. J., M.A., LL.B., 4 Spylaw Avenue, Edinburgh EH13 0LR
BURRELL, Professor Sydney A., A.B., PH.D., Department of History, Boston University, Bay State Road, Boston, Mass., 02215, USA

CADELL, Patrick, B.A., 11A Tipperlinn Road, Edinburgh EH10 5ET
CAIRD, Professor J. B., D. DE L'UNIV., Department of Geography, The University, Dundee DD1
CAIRNS, Mrs Trevor, B.A., 4 Ashmore Terrace, Sunderland, Co. Durham SR2 7DE
CALDER, Dr Angus, 6 Buckingham Terrace, Edinburgh EH4 3AB
CAMERON, Alexander D., 14 Esplanade Terrace, Edinburgh EH15 2BS
CAMERON, The Hon. Lord, 28 Moray Place, Edinburgh EH3
CAMPBELL, Colin, P.O. Box 8, Belmont 78, Massachusetts, USA
CAMPBELL, J. L., of Canna, D.LITT., LL.D., Isle of Canna, Inverness-shire
CAMPBELL, Peter H., Levensholme, Tyneview Road, Haltwhistle, Northumberland
CAMPBELL, Professor R. H., Department of History, University of Stirling, Stirling
CAMPBELL-PRESTON, Lt.-Col., Ardchattan Priory, Connel, Argyll
CANAVAN, Vincent J., LL.B., 2 Borlum Road, Inverness
CANT, R. G., 2 Kinburn Place, St Andrews KY16
CARMICHAEL, Major G. B., Three Ways, Cold Ash, Newbury, Berks.
CARMICHAEL, P. O., Arthurstone, Meigle, Perthshire
CARNEGIE, David F., L.B.S.M., 44 Murrayfield Road, Edinburgh EH12 6ET
CAROON, Robert G., B.A., B.D., 910 N. Third Street, Milwaukee, Wisc., 53203, USA
CASPERS, Miss Jane E. de M., B.A., M.A., 13 Napier Road, Edinburgh EH10
CHAMBERS, J. W., B.S.C., M.B., CH.B., F.R.C.P.(GLASG.), 14 Woodburn Road, Glasgow G43 2TN
CHECKLAND, Professor S. G., PH.D., Department of Economic History, The University, Glasgow G12 8QG
CHEYNE, Rev. Professor A. C., B.LITT., B.D., 11 Tantallon Place, Edinburgh EH9
CHRISTIE, William, M.A., 306 Blackness Road, Dundee DD2 1SB
CLARK, Rev. Ian D. L., PH.D., St Catherine's College, Cambridge CB2 1RL
CLAVERING, R. J., Lucarne House, 56 Farnley Road, Menston, Ilkley, Yorks.
CLAYTON, Stuart A., 3 Clifton Square, Corby, Northants

CLOW, Robert, G. M., John Smith & Son (Glasgow) Ltd., 57-61 St Vincent Street, Glasgow G2

COHEN, Mrs M. C., 8 Norfolk Road, London, NW8

COLLINS, Denis, F., M.A., LL.B., Stirling House, Craigiebarn Road, Dundee DD4 7PL

COLLIS, Ms Lin, M.A., 104 Jeanfield Road, Perth

COSH, Miss Mary, M.A., 63 Theberton Street, London N1

COVENTRY, Charles S., M.A., A.L.A., 4 Rose Terrace, Perth

COWAN, Edward J., M.A., Department of Scottish History, William Robertson Building, 50 George Square, Edinburgh EH8 9JY

COWAN, Ian B., PH.D., 119 Balshagray Avenue, Glasgow G11 7EG (*Hon. Treasurer*)

COWE, F. M., 10 Ravensdowne, Berwick-upon-Tweed

CRAWFORD, Iain A., M.A., The Dower House, Thriplow, Nr. Royston, Hertfordshire

CRAWFORD, Thomas, M.A., 61 Argyll Place, Aberdeen

CREGEEN, E. R., Eaglesview, Auchterarder, Perthshire

CRORIE, William D., B.S.C., 34 Dumyat Drive, Falkirk, Stirlingshire

CROSBIE, George, M.A., East Crookboat, Sandilands, by Lanark, Lanarkshire

CROSS, Mrs Margaret B., 13 Grange Road, Edinburgh EH9 1UQ

CUMMINGS, Andrew J. G., B.A., Department of History, University of Strathclyde, McCance Building, 16 Richmond Street, Glasgow G1

DAICHES, Professor David, Philipstoun House, by Linlithgow, West Lothian EH19 7NB

DARRAGH, James, M.A., 103 Deakin Leas, Tonbridge, Kent

DAVIDSON, Nimmo C. M., M.A., B.MUS, 72 Auldhouse Road, Glasgow G43 1UR

DAVIS, E. D., Craigie College of Education, Beech Grove, Ayr KA8 0SR

DE BEER, E. S., 31 Brompton Square, London SW3

DEVINE, T. M., B.A., PH.D., Department of History, McCance Building, University of Strathclyde, Glasgow G1

DIACK, William G., 20 Howes View, Bucksburn, Aberdeen

DICKSON, D., 17 Laurel Avenue, Lenzie, Dunbartonshire G66 4RX

DI FOLCO, John, M.A., B.PHIL., 151 South Street, St Andrews, Fife

DILWORTH, Rev. A. Mark, Fort Augustus Abbey, Fort Augustus, Inverness

DIXON, George A., 13 Thirlestone Road, Edinburgh EH9

DOBSON, L. D. S., 13 Queen Street, Carnoustie, Angus DD7 7AA

DOCHERTY, Rev. Henry, PH.L., 8 Crookston Grove, Glasgow G52

DONALDSON, Professor Gordon, D.LITT., Preston Tower Nursery Cottage, Prestonpans, East Lothian, EH32 9EN

DONALDSON, Rear Admiral Vernon D'Arcy, 36 Tregunter Road, London SW10

DONNELLY, R., 8 Newtonlea Avenue, Newton Mearns, Glasgow

DOUGLAS, Dr Elma P., 4 Dowanhill Street, Glasgow G11 5HB
DOUGLAS, Gordon G., 3390 Norman Drive, Reno, Nevada, 89509, USA
DOUGLAS, James H., 1 Canmore Grove, Dunfermline KY12 1JT
DRAFFEN, George S., of Newington, M.B.E., Meadowside, Balmullo, Leuchars, Fife KY16 0AW
DRALLE, Professor Lewis A., M.A., PH.D., Department of History, Wichita State University, Kansas 67508, USA
DRUMMOND-MURRAY, P., Old Hadlow House, Hadlow Down, nr. Uckfield, Sussex
DUNBAR, John G., F.S.A., Royal Commission, Ancient & Historical Monuments (Scotland), 52–54 Melville Street, Edinburgh EH3 7HF
DUNCAN, Archibald, 37 Buckingham Terrace, Edinburgh EH4 3AP
DUNCAN, Professor Archibald A. M., Department of Scottish History, The University, Glasgow G12 8QG (*President*)
DUNDAS-BEKKER, Mrs A., Arniston House, Gorebridge, Midlothian
DUNLOP, Rev. A. Ian, 11 Bellevue Place, Edinburgh EH7 4BS
DUNLOP, Professor D. M., D.LITT, 423 West 120th Street, New York, N.Y. 10027, USA
DURBAC, Mrs Isabel J., 87 Comiston Drive, Edinburgh EH10
DURIE, Alastair J., M.A., PH.D., Department of Economic History, University of Aberdeen, Aberdeen
DURKAN, J., PH.D., 37 Earlsburn Road, Lenzie

ELLIOT, Mrs Margaret R., B.A., 8 Easter Belmont Road, Edinburgh EH12 6EX
EWAN, Alan D., M.A., 12 View Drive, Dudley, West Midlands
EWING, Mrs Elsie, 6 Rullion Road, Penicuik, Midlothian EH26 8HT
EWING, Mrs Winifred, M.P., LL.B., 52 Queen's Drive, Glasgow G42 8BP

FARQUHARSON, R. 20 Monaro Crescent, Red Hill, ACT 2603, Australia
FENTON, Alexander, M.A., 132 Blackford Avenue, Edinburgh EH9 3HH
FERGUSON, William, PH.D., Scottish History Department, William Robertson Building, 50 George Square, Edinburgh EH8 9JY
FINDLAY, Donald R., 52 Morningside Road, Edinburgh EH10
FINDLAY, William, B.A., 36 Firpark Road, Bishopbriggs, Glasgow
FINLAYSON, G., Department of History, The University, Glasgow G12 8QG
FISHER, Ian, B.A., Royal Commission, Ancient & Historical Monuments (Scotland), 52–54 Melville Street, Edinburgh EH3 7HF
FLATT, Roy Francis, 6 Comrie Street, Crieff, Perthshire PH7 4AX
FLECK, John M. M., M.A., Ard-Coile, Conon Bridge, Ross-shire N7 8AE
FLEMING, A. M. H., Glenfintaig House, Spean Bridge, Inverness-shire, PH34 4DX
FLEMING, Mrs M. J. P., M.B., CH.B., 17 Graham Park Road, Gosforth, Newcastle-upon-Tyne

FORD, Neil R., 105 Carnoustie Crescent, Greenhills, East Kilbride G75 8TF

FOSTER, Mrs Linda, B.A., Hilton View, Pattiesmuir, nr. Dunfermline, Fife

FOTHRINGHAM, H. Steuart, of Grantully, F.S.A.SCOT., Grantully Castle, Aberfeldy, Perthshire PH15 2EG

FRASER, Mrs Agnes P., D.A., F.S.A. SCOT., 76 Moira Terrace, Edinburgh EH7

FRASER, Lady Antonia, 33 Launceston Place, London W8 5RN

FRASER, Barclay S., Viewforth, Glebe Road, Cramond, Edinburgh

FRASER, The Hon. Lord, 30 Cleaver Square, London SE11 4EA

FULTON, Henry L., PH.D., Department of English, Central Michigan University, Mount Pleasant, Michigan 48859, USA

FYFE, Ronald, 74 Mile End Avenue, Aberdeen

GALBRAITH, The Hon. T. G. D., M.P., 2 Cowley Street, London SW1

GAULD, Miss Mary B., 29 Beechgrove Terrace, Aberdeen AB2 4DR

GAULDIE, Mrs Enid, B.PHIL., Waterside, Invergowrie, by Dundee

GIBSON, Dr J. A., M.D., D.R.C.O.G., M.R.C.G.P., Foremount House, Kilbarchan, Renfrewshire

GIBSON, John G., 28 Cramond Gardens, Edinburgh EH4 6PU

GIBSON, Mrs Rosemary, M.A., 158 Brunton Gardens, Montgomery Street, Edinburgh EH7 5ER

GILBERT, John M., M.A., PH.D., 182 Beech Avenue, Longlee, Galashiels TD1 2LG

GILFILLAN, J. B. S., Edenkerry, Helensburgh, Dunbartonshire G84 7HQ

GILL, W. M., M.A., Woodburn, Cairnryan, Stranraer, Wigtownshire

GILLANDERS, Farquhar, M.A., The University, Glasgow G12 8QG

GILMORE, John T., B.A., Sydney Sussex College, Cambridge

GLADSTONE, John, Capenoch, Penpont, Dumfriesshire

GLEN, F. J., Flat 1, St Margaret's Hospital, Crossgate, Durham City

GORRIE, D. C. E., M.A., 54 Garscube Terrace, Edinburgh EH12

GOULDESBROUGH, Peter, LL.B., Scottish Record Office, H.M. General Register House, Edinburgh EH1 3YY

GOURLAY, Miss Teresa, M.A., 4 Thorburn Road, Edinburgh EH13

GRAHAM, Miss Barbara, M.A., F.S.S.A., 42 Annanhill Avenue, Kilmarnock, Ayrshire KA1 2LQ

GRAHAM, Sir Norman W., Suilven, Kings Road, Longniddry, East Lothian

GRAHAM, Thomas, M.A., 21A Rosebery Street, Aberdeen AB2 4LN

GRANGE, R. W. D., Aberdour School, Burgh Heath, nr. Tadworth, Surrey

GRANT, I. D., 94 Polwarth Gardens, Edinburgh EH11 1LJ

GRANT, Ian R., 72 Dundas Street, Edinburgh

GRANT, Miss Margaret W., 3 Ben Bhraggie Drive, Golspie, Sutherland

GRANT-PETERKIN, K., B.A., Invererne, Forres, Moray

GRIEVE, Miss Hilda E. P., B.E.M., B.A., 153 New London Road, Chelmsford, Essex CM2 0AA
GROVES, Mrs Jill, 77 Marford Crescent, Sale, Cheshire
GROVES, William N., 5 Staikhill, Lanark ML11 7PW
GUILD, Ivor R., 16 Charlotte Square, Edinburgh EH2 4YS
GUNN, Colin, M.B., CH.B., 12 Abbots Walk, Kirkcaldy

HAIG, Mrs Eve, 41 Great King Street, Edinburgh EH3 6QR
HAIG, Miss Lilian S., 30 Hazel Avenue, Kirkcaldy, Fife
HALDANE, A. R. B., C.B.E., W.S., Foswell, Auchterarder, Perthshire
HALL, Sir John B., Bt., M.A., Inver House, Lochinver, Lairg, Sutherland IV27 4LT
HALL, John N. S., 27 Carseloch Road, Alloway, Ayr
HALLIDAY, J., 10 Argyle Street, Maryfield, Dundee
HALLIDAY, Rev. Canon R. T., B.D., Holy Cross Rectory, 18 Barnton Gardens, Edinburgh EH4 6AF
HAMILTON, D. N. H., PH.D., F.R.C.S., 21 Partick Hill Court, Partickhill Avenue, Glasgow G11 5AA
HAMILTON, Matthew, Damside House, 19 Stanely Crescent, Paisley
HAMPTON, Gordon B. I., 809 Tak Shing House, 20 Des Voeux Road Central, Hong Kong
HANHAM, Professor H. J., PH.D., School of Humanities and Social Science, Massachusetts Institute of Technology, Cambridge, Mass., 02139, USA
HANNAH, Alexander, Roebucks, Hollybank Road, Hookheath, Woking, Surrey
HARDIE, Rev. R. K., Manse of Stenhouse and Carron, Stenhousemuir, nr. Larbert, Stirlingshire FK5 4BU
HARDING, Alan, M.A., B.LITT., 3 Tantallon Place, Edinburgh EH9 1NY
HARGREAVES, Professor John D., 146 Hamilton Place, Aberdeen
HAWES, Timothy L. M., 8 Keswick Road, Cringleford, Norwich NR4 6UG
HAWORTH, John C., PH.D., 519 Witherspoon Drive, Springfield, Illinois, 62704, USA
HAWS, Charles H., B.A., Department of History, Old Dominion University, Norfolk, Virginia 23508, USA
HAY, Professor Denys, 31 Fountainhall Road, Edinburgh EH9
HAY, Frederick G., M.A., Department of Political Economy, The University, Glasgow, G12 8QG
HAY, George, F.S.A., 29 Moray Place, Edinburgh EH3 6BX
HAY, Col. R. A., New Club, 86 Princes Street, Edinburgh EH2 2BB
HAYES, David, Landmark, Carrbridge, Inverness-shire
HEDDLE, Miss Joan, 4 Cliff Court, Military Road, Sussex, TN36
HENDERSON, Mrs M. I. O. Gore-Browne, 41 Cluny Gardens, Edinburgh EH10 6BL

HENDERSON, W. R., Cedar Grove, Dirleton, North Berwick, East Lothian

HENDERSON-HOWAT, Mrs A. M. D., 7 Lansdowne Crescent, Edinburgh EH12

HERD, Ian L., 29 Monument Road, Ayr

HESKETH, Lady, Towcester, Northamptonshire

HILDEBRAND, Dr Reinhard, Anatomisches Institut, Vesaliuswet 2-4, D4400 Münster, West Germany

HILTON, Miss Margaret, B.A., The Senior House, Malvern Girls' College, Great Malvern, Worcs.

HOGG, James C. T., M.A., A.L.A., 5 Cleghorn Street, Dundee

HOPE, Col. Archibald J. G., Luffness, Aberlady, East Lothian

HORN, Miss B. L. H., 5 Rothesay Terrace, Edinburgh EH3 7RY

HOUSTON, Professor George, Department of Political Economy, The University, Glasgow G12 8QG

HOWATSON, William, M.A., Cairn Park, Templand, Lockerbie, Dumfriesshire

HOWELL, Roger, Jr., M.A., PH.D., Department of History, Bowdoin College, Brunswick, Maine 04011, USA

HUIE, A. W., 15 Louisville Avenue, Aberdeen

HUME, John R., B.SC., 28 Partickhill Road, Glasgow G11 5BP

HUNTER, Mrs Jean, M.A., Stromcrag, 2 Mary Street, Dunoon, Argyll PA23 7ED

HUNTER, R. L., F.S.A., 74 Trinity Road, Edinburgh EH5

HUNTER, R. L. C., LL.B., Department of Jurisprudence, University of Dundee, Dundee DD1

HUNTER SMITH, Norval S., M.A., Institute for General Linguistics, Spuïstraat 210, Amsterdam, Holland

HUTTON, B. G., 9 Wilton Road, Edinburgh EH16 5NX

IIJIMA, Keiji, B.LITT., 4–34–8 Yayoi-cho, Nakano-Ku, Tokio, Japan

IMRIE, John, LL.D., 41 Bonaly Crescent, Edinburgh EH13 0EP

INNES, Malcolm, of Edingight, M.A., LL.B., Court of the Lord Lyon, H.M. New Register House, Edinburgh EH1 3YT

IREDELL, Godfrey W., LL.M., PH.D., D.P.A., F.S.A. SCOT., Woodlands, Braithwaite, Keswick, Cumbria CA12 5TW

JAMIESON, Morley, 57 West Holmes Gardens, Musselburgh, Midlothian

JOHN, Stanley, DIPL. RTC., 34 Killermont Place, Kilwinning, Ayrshire KA13 6PZ

JOHNSON, Mrs Christine, 5 Johnsburn Road, Balerno, Midlothian

JOHNSTON, Ivor S., Rhu Arden, 1 Upper Sutherland Crescent, Helensburgh, Dunbartonshire

KANE, Patrick, A.L.A., 83 Carvale Avenue, Salsburgh, Shotts ML7 4NF
KAYES, Brian, 18 Broomley Drive, Giffnock, Glasgow G46 6PD
KEILLAR, Ian J., 80 Duncan Drive, Elgin, Moray
KENNEDY, A., Craigmullen, Dundrennan, Kirkcudbright DG6 4QF
KIDD, Matthew P., Coorie Doon, Queen Victoria Street, Airdrie ML6 0DL
KILPATRICK, P. J. W., Pythouse, Tisbury, Salisbury, Wilts SP3 6PB
KINLOCH, Sir John, Aldie Cottage, Fossoway, nr. Kinross, Kinross-shire
KIRK, David C., 4 Bridstone Place, London W2
KIRK, James, PH.D., Woodlea, Dunmore, by Falkirk
KIRKPATRICK, Miss Alice, The Library, Kings College, Old Aberdeen AB9 2UB
KIRKPATRICK, H. S., F.S.A. SCOT., 28 Betley Hall Gardens, Betley, Crewe CW3 9BB, Cheshire

LAIDLAW, James G., 1 Gloucester Walk, London W8 4HZ
LAMBIE, Brian, Gairland, Biggar, Lanarkshire ML12 6DN
LAWRIE, John J., 51 Colcokes Road, Banstead, Surrey
LAWSON, William A., 3 Mansionhouse Road, Paisley
LEE, Professor Maurice, Jr., Douglass College, Rutgers University, New Brunswick, New Jersey, 08903 USA
LEGGE, Professor M. D. B.LITT., 191A Woodstock Road, Oxford OX2 7AB
LENMAN, Bruce P., M.A., M.LITT., Cromalt, Lade Braes, St Andrews KY16 9ET
LENNIE, John C., 119 Fordbridge Road, Ashford, Middlesex, TW15 3RZ
LESLIE, The Hon. J. W., East Kintrockat, Brechin, Angus
LILBURN, Alistair J., B.S.C., Newlyn, Aboyne, Aberdeenshire AB3 5HE
LILBURN, Gavin C., c/o National Liberal Club, Whitehall Place, London SW1
LOCKETT, G. D., M.B.E., Clonterbrook House, Swettenham, Congleton, Cheshire
LOCKHART, Douglas G., Department of Geography, University College of Swansea, Singleton Park, Swansea, Glam. SA2 8PP
LOCKHART, S. F. MacDonald, Newholm, Dunsyre, Carnwath, Lanarkshire M11 8NQ
LOGUE, Kenneth J., 4 Oxford Street, Edinburgh EH8 9PJ
LOLE, F. P., Seaton Cote, Branthwaite Lane, Seaton, Workington, Cumberland
LORIMER, Hew, R.S.A., Kellie Castle, Pittenweem, Fife
LOW, Donald A., PH.D., Department of English Studies, University of Stirling, Stirling FK9 4LA
LYTHE, Professor S. G. E., 45 Aytoun Road, Glasgow G41

MACALLISTER, R. B., 34 Thomas Telford Road, Langholm, Dumfriesshire
McALLISTER, R. L., 6 Oglivie Place, Bridge of Allan, Stirlingshire
MACARTHUR, D., 8 Dempster Terrace, St Andrews KY16
McARTHUR, James N., M.A., 7 Westerlea Court, Bridge of Allan, Stirlingshire
McAULAY, Alexander C., 308 Glenacre Road, Cumbernauld, Glasgow G67 2MZ
MACAULAY, James M., M.A., PH.D., 6 Hamilton Drive, Glasgow G12 8DR
McCAFFREY, J. F., PH.D., 12 Balmoral Drive, Cambuslang, Glasgow
McCOSH, Bryce K., of Huntfield, Quothquan, Biggar, Lanarkshire
McCRAW, Ian, 27 Pitcairn Road, Downfield, Dundee DD3 9EE
McCULLOCH, Miss M. M., 13 Brunstane Bank, Edinburgh EH15 2NS
MACDONALD, Miss C. A., Gruinard, Auchendoon Road, Newton Stewart, Wigtownshire DG8 6HO
MACDONALD, D., 10 Pearce Avenue, Corstorphine, Edinburgh EH12
MACDONALD, Hector, M.A., PH.D., c/o National Library of Scotland, George IV Bridge, Edinburgh EH1 1EW
MACDONALD, J. M., Bruach, Sidnish, Locheport, North Uist
MACDONALD, Rev. R., S.T.L., Reul nu Mara, Brandon Street, Dunoon PA23 8BU
MACDONALD, Ranald C., Post Office, Barcaldine, Connel, Argyll
MACFARLANE, L. J., F.S.A., 113 High Street, Old Aberdeen
MACFARQUHAR, Roderick, 8 Glencairn Crescent, Edinburgh EH12
McFAULDS, John, 2F Milton Street, Airdrie ML6 6JN
McINNES, Alan I., 13 North Gardiner Street, Glasgow G11
McINTOSH, Alexander, 57 Haworth Road, Bradford, North Yorkshire BD9 6LH
MACINTOSH, Farquhar, M.A., 212 Colinton Road, Edinburgh EH14 1BP
MACINTYRE, J. Archibald, B.A., M.A., Department of Sociology, University of Guelph, Guelph, Ontario, Canada
MACINTYRE, Robert D., M.B., CH.B., J.P., 8 Gladstone Place, Stirling
MacINTYRE, Stuart, M.A., 57 Wills Street, Kew, Victoria, Australia, 3101
MACIVER, I. F., M.A., c/o National Library of Scotland, George IV Bridge, Edinburgh EH1 1EW
MACKAY, Rev. Hugh, M.A., F.S.A. SCOT., The Manse, Duns, Berwickshire
MACKAY, Miss Inez W., 25A Inverleith Terrace, Edinburgh EH3 5NU
MACKAY, James S., Barcaldine Lodge, Connel, Argyll
MACKAY, Miss Margaret L., 3 Braid Mount, Edinburgh EH10
MACKAY, Rev. P. H. R., M.A., Clola, 1 Dirleton Road, North Berwick
MACKAY, William, 4 St Barnabas Road, Cambridge
MACKAY, Wiliam A., M.A., B.SC., Chemin des Hutins 5, 1247 Anieres, Geneva, Switzerland

MACKECHNIE, Miss Catherine B., 59 Polwarth Street, Glasgow G12
MACKECHNIE, Donald, Schoolhouse, Bridge of Douglas, Inveraray, Argyll
MACKENZIE, Mrs P. C., The Cottage, Upper Clatford, Andover, Hants.
MACKIE, Professor J. D., 67 Dowanside Road, Glasgow G12
McKNIGHT, G., A.R.I.C.S., 167 Harburn Drive, West Calder, West Lothian
MACLACHLAN, Gardiner S., B.A., F.S.A. SCOT., 25 Montgomery Avenue, Beith, Ayshire KA15 1EL
MACLACHLAN, H. S., 1 Blackhill View, Law, Lanarkshire
McLAUCHLAN, Miss Elise R. M., B.L., 55 Spottiswoode Road, Edinburgh EH9 1DA
MACLEAN, Dr J., Van Neckstraat 102, 's-Gravenhage 1, Netherlands
MACLEAN, Mrs L. M., of Dochgarroch, Hazelbrae House, Glen Urquhart, Inverness IV3 6TJ
McLELLAN, Miss Maureen A., M.A., 32 Royal Circus, Edinburgh EH3
MACLEOD, D. R., M.A., Achtercairn Schoolhouse, Gairloch, Ross-shire
MACLEOD, Innes F., M.A., Department of Extra-mural Studies, 57/59 Oakfield Avenue, Glasgow G12 8LW
MACLEOD, Col. James H. Calder, 80 Whittinghame Court, Glasgow G12
McMAHON, Geo. I. R., M.A., B.LITT., Homerton College, Cambridge
McMILLAN, N. W., LL.B., 160 West George Street, Glasgow G2 2LA
McNAUGHT, James, Kilneiss, Moniaive, Thornhill, Dumfriesshire
McNEILL, Hugh M., 29 Ennismore Mews, London SE7 1AP
McNEILL, Sheriff Peter G. B., 185 Nithsdale Road, Glasgow G41
MACPHAIL, I. M. M., PH.DR., Rockbank, Barloan Crescent, Dumbarton
McPHERSON, A., F.S.V.A., Exors. of W. H. Berry, Canada House, 3 Chipstow Street, Manchester M1 5FU
MACPHERSON, Captain J. Harvey, F.S.A. SCOT., Dunmore, Newtonmore, Inverness-shire
MACQUEEN, Professor John, School of Scottish Studies, University of Edinburgh, 27 George Square, Edinburgh EH8 9LD
McROBERTS, Right Rev. Monsignor David, S.T.L., F.S.A., 16 Drummond Place, Edinburgh
MACHIN, G. I. T., D.PHIL., Department of Modern History, The University, Dundee DD1 4HN
MACK, Donald W., 88 Brownside Road, Cambuslang, Glasgow
MAGRUDER, Thomas G., Jr., 331 North Henry Street, Williamsburg, Virginia 23185, USA
MAKEY, W. H., M.A., PH.D., 3/2 Chessels Court, Edinburgh EH8 8AD
MANNING, Mrs Doreen Caraher, B.A., Gowanlea, Willoughby Street, Muthil, by Crieff, Perthshire PH5 2AE
MARSHALL, Rev. James S., M.A., 4 Claremont Park, Edinburgh EH6 7PH

MARSHALL, Miss Rosalind K., PH.D., 11 St Clair Terrace, Edinburgh EH10 5NW
MARWICK, W. H., 5 Northfield Crescent, Edinburgh EH8 7PU
MATTHEW, Mrs Irene W., Whinniehill Cottage, Allander Toll, Milngavie, Glasgow G62 6EW
MAXWELL, Stuart, F.S.A. SCOTT., 23 Dick Place, Edinburgh EH9
MEEK, Donald E., Department of Celtic, University of Glasgow G12
MEIKLEHAM, Miss H. L., M.A., 70 Glenluce Terrace, East Kilbride, Glasgow G74 7DT
MENZIES, George M., 34 Brighton Place, Edinburgh EH15 1LT
MICHAEL, James, O.B.E., Achtemrack, Drumnadrochit, Inverness-shire
MILLER, E. J., 4 Victoria Crescent Road, Glasgow G12
MILLER, Jonathan, Wellcraig, Tayport, Fife
MILNE, Miss Doreen J., PH.D., Department of History, King's College, Old Aberdeen AB9 2UB
MINTO, B. L. J., C.A., 25 Strathkinnes High Road, St Andrews, Fife KY16
MICHELL, Brian, 5 Park View, Brechin, Angus
MITCHELL, Miss Rosemary, M.A., 24 Alexandra Place, Oban, Argyll
MITCHISON, Mrs R., Great Yew, Ormiston, East Lothian EH35 5NJ
MONCRIEFFE, Sir Iain, PH.D., F.S.A., House of Moncreiffe, Bridge of Earn, Perthshire
MOORE, Hugh P., 1906 Montezuma Way, West Coving, California, 91791, USA
MOORE, R. L., 11 Ribble Avenue, Rainhill, Prescott, Lancs. L35 0NJ
MORPETH, R. S., 11 Albert Terrace, Edinburgh EH10
MORRIS, F. G., 45 Potton Road, Everton, Sandy, Beds SG19 2LE
MORRISON, Charles, Innis Righ, Peebles EH45 9HR
MORRISON, Miss Linda H., M.A., D.M.S., 44 Woodlands Crescent, Turriff, Aberdeenshire
MUI, Hoh-cheung, PH.D., Department of History, Memorial University, St John's, Newfoundland, Canada
MUNN, Charles W., B.A., PH.D., 26 East Greenlees Avenue, Cambuslang G72 8TZ
MUNRO, D. J., M.A., 7 Midfield Drive, Barnehurst, Bexley Heath, Kent
MUNRO, Mrs R. W., 15A Mansionhouse Road, Edinburgh EH9 1TZ
MUNRO, R. W., 15A Mansionhouse Road, Edinburgh EH9 1TZ
MURCHISON, Very Rev. Dr T. M., 10 Mount Stuart Street, Glasgow G14 3YL
MURDOCH, Mrs S. M., Aird House, Badachro, Gairloch, Ross-shire
MURRAY, A. L., PH.D., LL.B., 33 Inverleith Gardens, Edinburgh EH3
MURRAY, David, Maclay, Murray & Spens, 169 West George Street, Glasgow G2 2LA
MURRAY, Murdoch D., M.R.C.V.S., 3 Gardiner Grove, Edingurgh EH4 3RT

NAPIER, Sandy, 3 Moir Street, Alloa, Clackmannanshire

NAUGHTON, Miss J. M., M.A., 9 Summerside Street, Edinburgh EH6
NEIL, J. K., The Viewlands, Blakeshall, nr. Kidderminster, Worcs.
NEILLY, Miss Margaret, R.G.N., 9 Woodmuir Road, Whitburn, West Lothian
NICHOLSON, C. B. Harman, Galleria Passarella 1, 20122-Milan, Italy
NICHOLSON, R. G., Rockhill Castle, High Craigmore, Isle of Bute
NICOL, Miss Mary P. M.A., 15 Falcon Road West, Edinburgh EH10
NICOLL, Mrs I. M., Westcroft, Wardlaw Gardens, St Andrews KY16
NIMMO, Mrs A. E., 9 Succoth Gardens, Edinburgh EH12
NOBLE, John, Ardkinglas, Cairndow, Argyll
NOTMAN, R. C., B.L., W.S., c/o Morton, Fraser and Milligan, W.S., 15-19 York Place, Edinburgh EH1 3EL
NUTTER, Bryan, 21 Taywood Close, Poulton-Le-Fylde, nr. Blackpool FY6 7EY

OLIVER, Col. W. H., M.B.E., Blain, Nether Blainslie, Galashiels TD1 2PR, Selkirkshire

PAGE, R. A., 47 Pittenweem Road, Anstruther, Fife KY10 3DT
PALMER, Kenneth W., 4 Cumin Place, Edinburgh EH9 2JX
PARKER, Major H. F., Torlochan, Gruline, Isle of Mull, Argyll
PATTERSON, Roland W. 34 Thistle Street, Carnoustie, Angus
PATTULLO, David, Fairhaven, Elie, Fife
PATTULLO, Miss Nan, 29 Ormidale Terrace, Edinburgh EH12
PHILLIPSON, N. T., History Department, University of Edinburgh, William Robertson Building, 50 George Square, Edinburgh EH8 9JY
PRAIN, Sheriff A. M., Castellar, Crieff, Perthshire
PREBBLE, John, F.R.S.L., Shaw Coign, Alcocks Lane, Burgh Heath, Tadworth, Surrey

RAE, Miss Isobel, Dunlugas Cottage, Nairn
RAE, Thomas L., PH.D., National Library of Scotland, George IV Bridge, Edinburgh EH1 1EW (*Honorary Publication Secretary*)
RAMSAY, Alan D. M., Bolland of Galashiels, Selkirkshire
REID, Professor W. Standford, Department of History, University of Guelph, Guelph, Ontario, Canada
RIDDELL, Miss Margaret, Longfaugh, Ford, Midlothian
RITCHIE, Alexander, 19 Langside Drive, Kilbarchan, Renfrewshire
RITCHIE, James S., M.A., 42 Dudley Gardens, Edinburgh EH6 4PS
ROBERTSON, A. Irvine, T.D., LL.B., The Old Manse, Park Avenue, Stirling
ROBERTSON, F. W., PH.D., 17 Sinclair Terrace, Wick, Caithness
ROBERTSON, James J., LL.B., Faculty of Law, University of Dundee, Dundee DD1
ROBERTSON, Miss Kathleen, M.A., 120 Albert Road, Gourock, Renfrewshire

ROBERTSON, Lewis, C.B.E., The Blair, Blairlogie, Stirling FK9 5PX
ROBERTSON, The Hon. Lord, 49 Moray Place, Edinburgh EH3 6DT
RODGER, George N., 9 The Cross, Forfar, Angus DD8 1BX
RODGER, Mrs Margaret M., Hazelwood, Glebelands, Rothesay, Isle of Bute PA20 9HN
ROSS, Rev. Anthony, O.P., S.T.L., 24 George Square, Edinburgh EH8 9LD
ROSS, Douglas H., Killorn, Milngavie, Glasgow
ROSS, Ian S., Department of English, University of British Columbia, Vancouver V6T 1W5, B.C., Canada
ROWAN, Miss Elizabeth I. S., 35 Gray Street, Prestwick KA9 1LX
RUSSELL, D. F. O., Rothes, Markinch, Fife KY7 6PW
RUSSELL, Miss Florence M., Spring Grove, 95 Victoria Road, Dunoon, Argyll PA23 7AD

SANDERSON, Miss Elizabeth C., 28 Highfield Crescent, Linlithgow, West Lothian
SANDERSON, Miss Margaret H. B., PH.D., 28 Highfield Crescent, Linlithgow, West Lothian
SCARLETT, James D., 9 Bellevue Terrace, Edinburgh EH7 4DT
SCOTLAND, James, M.A., LL.B, M.ED., 67 Forest Road, Aberdeen
SCOTT, David, 22 Blomfield Road, London, W9 1AD
SCOTT, J. G., M.A., 10 Abbotsford Court, Colinton Road, Edinburgh EH10 5EH
SCOTT, P. H., 40 House o' Hill Road, Blackhall, Edinburgh EH4 2AN
SCOTT, R. Lyon, Braeside, Loanhead, Midlothian
SCOTT, Thomas H., M.A., B.L., 1 Thimblehall Place, Dunfermline
SCOTT, W. W., 26 Braid Hills Road, Edinburgh EH10 6HY
SEFTON, Rev. H. R., PH.D., Department of Church History, King's College, Aberdeen AB9 2UB
SELLAR, W. D. H., 2 Bellevue Terrace, Edinburgh EH7
SEMPLE, Walter G., 47 Newark Drive, Glasgow G41
SERVICE, Commander Douglas, of Torsonce, 16 Redington Road, Hampstead, London NW3 7RG
SHARP, Brian, 12 Shelley Drive, Bothwell, Glasgow G71 8TA
SHARP, Buchanan, B.A., M.A., College V, University of California, Santa Cruz, California, USA
SHAW, Dr Frances J., 211 Morningside Road, Edinburgh EH10 4QT
SHAW, Rev. Duncan, PH.D., 4 Sydney Terrace, Edinburgh EH7
SHEAD, N. F., 16 Burnside Gardens, Clarkston, Glasgow
SHEARER, J. G. S., M.A., 36 Snowdon Place, Stirling
SHEPHERD, James P., M.A., 14 East Fettes Avenue, Edinburgh EH4 1AN
SHORT, Mrs Anges, B.A., M.LITT., 20 The Chanonry, Old Aberdeen AB2 1RQ
SIMPSON, Eric J., 1 Pinewood Drive, Dalgety Bay, Dunfermline, Fife
SIMPSON, Grant G., PH.D., F.S.A., Department of History, University of Aberdeen, Taylor Building, King's College, Old Aberdeen AB9 2UB

SIMPSON, John M., Scottish History Department, William Robertson Building, 50 George Square, Edinburgh EH8 9JY

SINCLAIR, Alexander, M.A., DIP.M.S., A.M.B.I.M., 16 Kensington Drive, Bearsden, Glasgow G61 2HG

SINCLAIR, John N., Hamarsland, 12 Lovers Loan, Lerwick, Shetland ZE1 OBA

SKINNER, Basil C., 10 Randolph Cliff, Edinburgh EK3 7UA

SLADE, H. Gordon, T.D., A.R.I.B.A., 15 Southbourne Gardens, London SE12

SLAVEN, Anthony, Department of Economic History, Adam Smith Building, University of Glasgow, Glasgow G12

SLIMMINGS, Sir William K. M., C.B.E., D.LITT., C.A., 62 The Avenue, Worcester Park, Surrey

SMAIL, James E., 2 Bright's Crescent, Edinburgh EH9 2DA

SMITH, Annette, PH.D., Kingarth, Lade Braes, St Andrews KY16 9ET

SMITH, David B., LL.B., 30 Great King Street, Edinburgh EH3

SMITH, Harold, M.A., 13 Newhailes Crescent, Musselburgh, Midlothian

SMITH, J. A., B.ED., 108 Queen Victoria Drive, Glasgow G14 9BL

SMITH, J. A. B., M.A., B.SC., 38 Poplar Walk, London SE24 OBU

SMOUT, Professor T. C., PH.D., 19 South Gillsland Road, Edinburgh E10 (*Chairman of Council*)

SMYTHE, Thomas, 4 Whorterbank, Lochee, Dundee

SOUTHESK, The Rt. Hon. The Earl of, K.C.V.O., Kinnaird Castle, Brechin, Angus

STARKEY, A. M., PH.D., History Department, Adelphi University, Garden City, N.Y. 11530, USA

STENHOUSE, B. A., 6/14 Orchard Brae, Edinburgh EH4 2HP

STEVENSON, David, B.A., 15 Binghill Park, Milltimber, Aberdeenshire AB1 OEE (*Honorary Secretary*)

STEWART, H. C., Netherton, Wellside Road, Falkirk, Stirlingshire

STEWART, John R., DIP.TEX., 70 Weir Road, Kibworth Beauchamp, Leics. LE8 OLP

STEWART, Robert G., 12 Nutt Road, Auburn, New Hampshire, 03032 USA

STIRLING, Matthew, 20 Westbourne Terrace, London W2

STIRRAT, Hugh, B.SC., 8 Stronsay Drive, King's Gate, Aberdeen

STORER, Derek, B.SC., 57 Beach Road, Troon, Ayrshire

STRACHAN, M. F., M.B.E., 7 Napier Road, Edinburgh EH10

STRAWHORN, John, PH.D., 2 East Park Avenue, Mauchline, Ayrshire

STUART, Lt. Cdr. C. McD., 12 Cotmandene, Dorking, Surrey RH4 2BL

STUART, Peter Maxwell, Traquair House, Innerleithen, Peeblesshire EH44 6PW

SUNTER, J. R. M., M.A., PH.D., Department of History, University of Guelph, Guelph, Ontario, Canada

SUTHERLAND, The Countess of, Uppat House, Brora, Sutherland
SWAINSTON, Mrs A. Y. Imrie, 8 Sheldon Avenue, London N6

TAYLOR, David, F.S.A. SCOT., 39 Ashley Drive, Edinburgh EH11 1RP
TAYLOR, David B., M.A., F.S.A. SCOT., Delvine, Longforgan, by Dundee
TAYLOR, W. PH.D., 25 Bingham Terrace, Dundee
THOMPSON, F. G., 17 Urquhart Gardens, Stornoway, Isle of Lewis
THOMS, David, Strathview, Trinity Road, Brechin, Angus
THOMSON, A. G., PH.D., 5 Alison's Close, St Andrews, Fife KY16 9EQ
THOMSON, A. McLay, F.R.H.S., 94 Baldwin Avenue, Glasgow G13 2QU
THOMSON, J. A., Summerhill House, Annan, Dumfriesshire
THOMSON, J. A. F., D.PHIL., History Department, The University, Glasgow G12 8QG
THOMSON, James M., 27 Kilrymont Road, St Andrews, Fife KY16 8DE
THORNBER, Ian, Ardtornish, Morvern, Oban, Argyll PA34 5UZ
TODD, J. M., Redbourn House, Main Street, St Bees, Cumberland
TORRANCE, Donald R., B.SC., 76 Findhorn Place, Edinburgh EH9 2NW
TREVOR-ROPER, Professor H. R., Chiefswood, Melrose
TROUP, J. A., St Abbs, 34 Hillside Road, Stromness, Orkney
TURNER, Professor A. C., College of Letters and Sciences, University of California, Riverside, California 92502, USA
TURNER, Miss Anne E., M.A., 16 Kersland Street, Glasgow G12

URQUHART, Kenneth T., ygr., of Urquhart, 4713 Orleans Blvd, Jefferson, La., 70121, USA

VEITCH, Rev. Thomas, M.A., F.S.A. SCOT., St Paul's and St George's Rectory, 53 Albany Street, Edinburgh EH1

WALKER, Bruce, B.A., 149 Strathearn Road, West Ferry, Dundee DD5 1BR
WALKER, Professor David M., Q.C., PH.D., LL.D., 1 Beaumont Gate, Glasgow G12
WALLACE, J. C., M.A., 9 Spottiswoode Street, Edinburgh EH9 1EP
WALLS, Andrew F., M.A., B.LITT., Department of Religious Studies, King's College, Old Aberdeen AB9 2UB
WALTON, Mrs P. M. Eaves, 55 Manor Place, Edinburgh EH3
WARD, Miss Anne, 1A South Hamilton Road, North Berwick, East Lothian EH39 4NJ
WARD, Rev. David F., Chaplaincy for University Catholics, 172 Perth Road, Dundee
WATSON, Miss Elspeth G. Boog, Pitsligo House, Pitsligo Road, Edinburgh EH10 4RY
WATSON, Miss Janet, 138 Chamberlain Road, Glasgow G13
WATSON, T. A., M.A., 8 Melville Terrace, Anstruther, Fife

WATT, Professor Donald E. R., Department of Medieval History, St Salvator's College, St Andrews KY16

WEBSTER, A. Bruce, F.S.A., 5 The Terrace, St Stephens, Canterbury, Kent

WEDGWOOD, Dame C. V., 22 St Ann's Terrace, London NW8 6PJ

WEIR, David Bruce, Q.C., M.A., LL.B., 9 Russell Place, Edinburgh EH3 3HQ

WEIR, Thomas E., U.S.N.R., B.D., PH.D., Correctional Facility, Camp Lejeune, N.C. 28542, USA

WHITEFORD, Rev. D. H., Q.H.C., B.D., PH.D., Gullane Manse, Gullane, East Lothian

WHYTE, Donald, 4 Carmel Road, Kirkliston, West Lothian

WILLIAMS, J. W. C., 17 Cliftonville Court, Burnt Ash Hill, London SE12 0AN

WILLIAMSON, J. C., 21 Nearmouth Crescent, West Calder, West Lothian EH55 8AF

WILLIAMSON, John, New Grunnasound, Bridge End, Shetland

WILLOCK, Professor I. D., Department of Jurisprudence, University of Dundee, Dundee DD1

WILLS, Mrs Peter, Allan Gowan, 109 Henderson Street, Bridge of Allan, Stirlingshire

WILSON, Miss Florence Eva, 164 Forest Avenue, Aberdeen AB1 6UN

WILSON, Gordon, 2 Strathmore Road, Hamilton, Lanarkshire ML3 6AQ

WILSON, Miss Isabel J. T., 2 Segton Avenue, Kilwinning, Ayrshire KA16 6LQ

WILSON-FRASER, Hugh, 28 Akers Avenue, Locharbriggs, Dumfries

WISKER, R. F., 17 Merridale Lane, Wolverhampton, WV3 9RD

WITHRINGTON, D. J., M.ED., Centre for Scottish Studies, University of Aberdeen, Old Aberdeen AB9 2UB.

WOOLASTON, Graeme, 10 Sandrock Road, London SE13 7TR

WYLIE, Lawrence A., RFD1, Box 3, Bishop, California 93514, USA

YOUNG, Mrs E. M., M.A., F.R.G.S., Beechwoods, Kittishaws Road, Dalry, Ayrshire KA24 4LL

YOUNG, Kenneth G., LL.B., W.S., Dunearn, Auchterarder, Perthshire

YOUNG, Miss Margaret D., 1 Craiglockhart Gardens, Edinburgh EH14 1ND

YOUNG, Mrs Margaret D., 73 Kingslynn Drive, Glasgow G44 4JB

YOUNG, R. M., Rustlings, 389 Cross Lane, Congleton, Cheshire CW12 3JX

YOUNGSON, Professor A. J., D.LITT., Research School of Social Science, Australian National University, PO Box 4, Canberra ACT 2600, Australia

Aberdeen College of Education
Aberdeen Public Library
Aberdeen University Library
Adelaide University Barr Smith Library, Australia
Adelphi University Swirbul Library, Long Island, NY, USA
Alabama University Library, Ala., USA
Alberta University Library, Edmonton, Canada
Arbroath Public Library, Montrose
Argyll and Bute Library, Dunoon
Auckland University Library, New Zealand
Ayr Carnegie Public Library
Ayr, Craigie College of Education

Baillie's Institution Free Library, Glasgow
Belfast Library and Society for Promoting Knowledge (Linenhall Library)
Bibliothèque Nationale, Paris, France
Birmingham Central Libraries
Birmingham University Library
Blackwell, B. H., Ltd., Oxford
Boston Athenaeum, Mass., USA
Boston Public Library, Mass., USA
Boston University Libraries, Mass., USA
Bowdoin College Library, Brunswick, Maine, USA
Bristol University Library
British Columbia University Library, Vancouver, Canada
British Library, Lending Division, Boston Spa

Calgary University Library, Canada
California University at Berkeley Library, USA
California University at Davis Library, USA
California University at Los Angeles Library, USA
California University at Riverside Library, USA
California University at San Diego, USA
Cambridge University Library
Cape Breton College Library, Sydney, Canada
Capetown University J. W. Jagger Library, South Africa
Cardiff Free Library
Chicago University Library, Ill., USA
Cincinnati University General Library, Ohio, USA
Cleveland Public Library, Ohio, USA
Coatbridge Carnegie Public Library
Columbia University Library, New York, NY, USA

Copenhagen Royal Library, Denmark
Cornell University Library, Ithaca, NY, USA

Dalhousie University Library, Halifax, Canada
Dartmouth College Library, Hanover, NH, USA
Delaware University Memorial Library, Newark, USA
Denny High School
Duke University Library, Durham, NC, USA
Dumbarton Public Library
Dumfries County Library
Dundee College of Education
Dundee Public Library
Dundee University Library
Dunfermline Public Library
Durham University Library

Ealing Central Library
East Anglia University Library, Norwich
East Lothian County Library, Haddington
Edinburgh City District Council
Edinburgh, Hope Trust
Edinburgh, Moray House College of Education
Edinburgh New Club
Edinburgh Public Library
Edinburgh University, Fraser Chair of Scottish History
Edinburgh University Library
Edinburgh University, Scottish Studies Library
Enoch Pratt Free Library, George Peabody Department, Baltimore, Md., USA
Episcopal Church of Scotland Theological Library, Edinburgh
Exeter University Library

Falkirk, Callendar Park College of Education
Falkirk Public Library
Flinders University of South Australia, Bedford Park
Folger Shakespeare Library, Washington, DC, USA
Forfar Public Library
Fort Wayne and Allen County Public Library, Ind., USA
Free Church of Scotland Library, Edinburgh

Glasgow Art Gallery and Museum
Glasgow, Jordanhill College of Education
Glasgow University Library
Glasgow University, Scottish History Class Library
Glasgow University, Scottish History Department
Glencoe, 1745 Association and National Military History Society

Gothenburg University Library, Sweden
Grangemouth Victoria Public Library
Guelph University Library, Canada

Hamilton College Library, Cambridge, Mass., USA
Harvard College Library, Cambridge, Mass., USA
Houston University Libraries, Tex., USA
Hull University Library
Huntington Library and Art Gallery, San Marino, Calif., USA

Idaho Springs Public Library, Idaho, USA
Illinois University Library, Urbana, USA
Indiana University Library, Bloomington, USA
Inverness Divisional Library
Iowa State University Libraries, Iowa, USA

Kilmarnock Public Library
Kirkcudbrightshire County Library, Castle Douglas
Kirkintilloch Patrick Memorial Library

Lambeth Palace Library, London
Lancaster University Library
Leeds Reference Library
Leeds University Brotherton Library
Leicester University Library
Library of Congress, Washington, DC, USA
Liverpool University Library
London Coporation Guildhall Library
London Library
London University, Institute of Historical Research Library
London University Library
London University, Queen Mary College Library
Los Angeles Public Library, Calif., USA
Louvain Université Catholique, Bibliothèque Centrale, Belgium
Loyola University E. M. Cudahy Memorial Library, Chicago, Ill., USA

McGill University Library, Montreal, Canada
McMaster University Mills Memorial Library, Hamilton, Canada
Manchester Public Library
Manchester University, John Rylands Library
Maryland University McKeldin Library, College Park, USA
Melbourne University Baillieu Library, Australia
Miami University Alumni Library, Oxford, Ohio, USA
Michigan State University Library, East Lansing, USA
Michigan University General Library, Ann Arbor, USA
Minnesota University General Library, Minneapolis, USA

Missouri University General Library, Columbia, USA
Mitchell Library, Glasgow
Montreat Historical Foundation of Presbyterian Reformed Churches, NC, USA
Motherwell Public Libraries

Nashville University Joint Libraries, Tenn., USA
National Library of Australia, Canberra
National Library of Canada, Ottawa
National Library of Ireland, Dublin
National Library of Scotland, Edinburgh
National Library of Scotland, Lending Division
National Library of Wales, Aberystwyth
National Museum of Antiquities of Scotland, Edinburgh
National Trust for Scotland, Edinburgh
Nebraska University Library, Lincoln, USA
Netherlands Royal Library, The Hague
Newberry Library, Chicago, Ill., USA
Newcastle-upon-Tyne Public Library
Newcastle-upon-Tyne University Library
New England University Library, Armidale, Australia
Newfoundland Memorial University Library, St John's, Canada
New South Wales Library, Sydney, Australia
New York Public Library, NY, USA
New York State Library, Albany, USA
New York State University at Buffalo Lockwood Memorial Library, USA
New York University Elmer Holmes Bobst Library, NY, USA
North East Scotland Library Services, Aberdeen
Northwestern University Library, Evanston, Ill., USA
Notre Dame University Library, Ind., USA
Nottingham County Library

Ohio State University Library, Columbus, USA
Old Dominion University Hughes Library, Norfolk, USA
Oregon University Library, Eugene, USA
Orkney County Library, Kirkwall
Oxford University, All Souls College Library
Oxford University, Balliol College Library
Oxford University Bodleian Library
Oxford University, Worcester College Library

Paisley College of Technology
Pennsylvania Historical Society, Philadelphia, USA
Pennsylvania State University Patee Library, University Park, USA
Pennsylvania University Library, Philadelphia, USA
Perth and Kinross County Library

Perth Sandeman Public Library
Princeton Theological Seminary Library, NJ, USA
Princeton University Library, NJ, USA
Public Record Office, London

Queen's University Library, Belfast

Reading University Library
Renfrew District Libraries, Paisley
Rochester University Library, NY, USA
Royal College of Physicians Library, Edinburgh
Royal Scottish Geographical Society, Edinburgh
Rutgers University Library, New Brunswick, NJ, USA

St Andrews Hay Fleming Library
St Andrews University Library
St Andrews University, Scottish History Class Library
St Benedict's Abbey, Fort Augustus
St Francis Xavier University Library, Antigonish, Canada
St Peter's College, Cardross
Saltire Society, Edinburgh
Sancta Maria Abbey, Nunraw, Haddington
Scottish Catholic Archives, Edinburgh
Scottish Genealogy Society, Edinburgh
Scottish Record Office, Edinburgh
Scottish Reformation Society, Edinburgh
Sheffield City Libraries
Sheffield University Library
Signet Library, Edinburgh
Society of Antiquaries, London
Society of Australian Genealogists, Sydney, NSW, Australia
Society of Genealogists, London
Southern California University Library, Los Angeles, Calif., USA
Speculative Society, Edinburgh
Stanford University Library, Calif., USA
Stechart McMillan Inc., Stuttgart, West Germany
Stewart Society, Edinburgh
Stirling District Library
Stirling University Library
Stockholm Royal Library, Sweden
Strathclyde Regional Archives, Glasgow
Strathclyde University Andersonian Library, Glasgow
Sydney University Fisher Library, Australia

Texas University Library, Austin, USA
Toronto Reference Library, Canada

Toronto University Library, Canada
Trinity College Library, Dublin

Uppsala Royal University Library, Sweden
Utrecht Historische Genoostschap, Netherlands

Vaticana Biblioteca Apostolica, Citta del Vaticano, Italy
Victoria State Library, Melbourne, Australia
Victoria University of Wellington, New Zealand
Virginia State Library, Richmond, USA

Washington University Libraries, St Louis, Mo., USA
Washington University Libraries, Seattle, USA
Western Australia University Reid Library, Nedlands, Australia
Western Washington State College Wilson Library, Bellingham, USA
West Highland Museum, Fort William
Wick Carnegie Public Library
William and Mary College Library, Williamsburg, Va., USA
Wisconsin University General Library, Madison, USA

Yale University Library, New Haven, Conn., USA

Zetland County Library, Lerwick

Copies of the Society's publications are presented to the British Library, London, and to the Carnegie Trust, Edinburgh.